The Picture History of Painting

The Picture History of Painting

H. W. Janson & Dora Jane Janson

THE PICTURE

FROM CAVE PAINTING

HISTORY OF

Painting

TO MODERN TIMES

HARRY N. ABRAMS, INC. / *PUBLISHERS, NEW YORK*

Editor, MILTON S. FOX • Layout & Design by HOWARD J. MORRIS

Table of Contents

How Painting Began

PEOPLE ALL DREAM, whether they want to or not. Even animals dream. A cat's ears and tail sometimes twitch in his sleep, while dogs whine and growl and paw the air, just as if they were having a fight or chasing a squirrel. Even

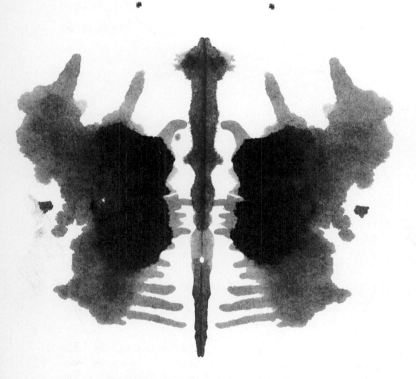

1. INK BLOT ON FOLDED PAPER. *With a bit of effort, it is not too difficult to find two galloping animals here.*

when they are awake, animals "see things," so that a cat's fur will rise on his back, for no apparent reason, as he peers into a dark closet. And we, too, have goose pimples when we feel frightened.

That is imagination at work. People are not the only animals who have imagination, but we are the only ones who can tell each other about it. If we tell each other in words, we have made a story out of it, and if we take a pencil and draw it, we have made a picture. To imagine means to "make an image" or a picture in our minds.

There are many different ways for our imaginations to get started. Thus it may happen, at times when we are sick in bed with nothing to do, that a crack in the ceiling will suddenly begin to look like an animal or a tree after we have kept our eye on it for some time. Our imagination fills in the lines that aren't there. Even an ink blot on folded paper (figure 1) will make us think of a lot of other things, although it was made entirely by accident. Psychologists know this and have made up ink blot tests to find out what is on our minds; for each of us, depending on the sort of person we are, will see different pictures in the same blot.

The Magic Pictures of the Cavemen

IN THE OLD STONE AGE, some 20,000 years ago, when the first pictures we know of were made, people lived in caves, and their biggest worry was how to find enough to eat. They had not yet learned how to keep cattle, and they did not know about farming, so they depended mainly on hunting for their food supply. When the hunting had not been good, they had to go hungry. There were, of course, all sorts of birds and fish and small animals they could catch, but these were not enough to live on, so they always hoped to kill something big, like a deer or a buffalo, which would yield enough meat to last them for some time. They wanted very badly to kill these animals, but they were afraid of them, too, for they only had the simplest of weapons as yet. In fact, they knew nothing about metal, so that whatever tools they had were made of wood, bone, or stone.

And they had to hunt on foot because they had not yet learned how to ride horses.

No wonder, then, that the cavemen's minds were always full of the idea of hunting large animals for food, and of how dangerous this was. And because they thought so much about these things, it is not surprising to find that almost all of their paintings are of these animals, which always look very powerful and lifelike.

How did the cavemen learn to make such skillful pictures? We don't really know for sure. But since the pictures are done on the sides of caves, which are rough and bumpy, it is possible that the idea of making pictures came from these bumps, just as the ink blot suggests ideas to us. Some hungry caveman, staring at the wall of his cave, might have imagined that a particular bump looked like an animal and perhaps drew an outline around it with a burned stick from the fire. He could then complete the picture by filling in the parts that were not there, and finally he learned how to make such a drawing all by himself, without the help of the bump on the wall of the cave.

Figures 2 and 4 are modern copies after cave paintings. Figure 5 shows you a cave wall as it really looks, and you will notice that the animals are all scrambled together, without any kind of order. Once you get them sorted out, you can recognize each one easily. Why, then, did the cavemen spoil their pictures by doing one on top of another? It is because they did *not* want them for decorations. Even if the pictures were not such a jumble, we could tell this from the fact that all the caves that have pictures in them are very dark and difficult to get into.

If the cavemen artists had done their animal paintings merely for pleasure, they would have put them near the entrance of the cave, where

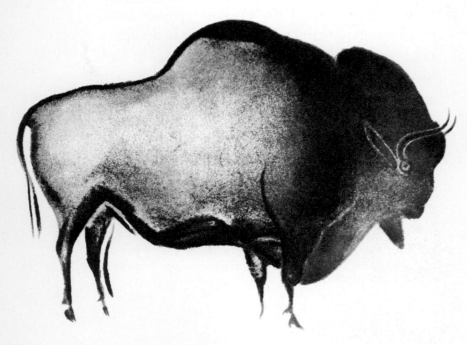

2.   OLD STONE AGE CAVE PAINTING / *Standing Buffalo* / About 20,000 B.C. Font-de-Gaume, France. *See comment above. The smoothly curved outlines, the huge body and head as against the small, tapering legs, make the animal appear even more powerful and menacing than it must have been in reality.*

3. OLD STONE AGE CAVE PAINTING / *Wounded Bison* / About 20,000 B.C. Altamira, Spain. *Here we see one of the most extraordinary achievements of prehistoric art. The dying animal has collapsed on the ground, its legs no longer able to carry the weight of the body. Yet even in this helpless state the head is lowered in defense against the spears of the hunters that threaten it from the lower left hand corner. Only the keenest observation could yield such an image.*

everybody could look at them. As it is, they are so well hidden that they have been discovered only recently and by chance. The cave in figure 5 was, in fact, found in 1940 by some boys who had gone out hiking with their dog. Suddenly the dog was gone, and in looking for him they found the hole, overgrown with brambles and weeds, through which he had fallen into the cave.

But what were the pictures for, then? They must have been a kind of hunting magic, because some of the animals have spears or arrows sticking into them (see figure 6). The cavemen must

4. OLD STONE AGE CAVE PAINTING / *Wild Boar* / About 20,000 B.C. Altamira, Spain. *The ease with which the Stone Age artists were able to depict motion is one of the most astonishing things about them. This boar is the very image of speed and energy as it bounds forward in attack, or flight.*

9

5, 6.   OLD STONE AGE CAVE PAINTING / *General View of Cave and Detail* / About 20,000 B.C. Lascaux, France. *The animals here are different from those in Font-de-Gaume and Altamira: stags, wild horses, and cattle. (The fierce black beast below could be the ancestor of the fighting bulls of today.) Except for a few that seem to have been done as a group, the images overlap without any kind of order. There are also great differences in scale (the largest figures are life-size).*

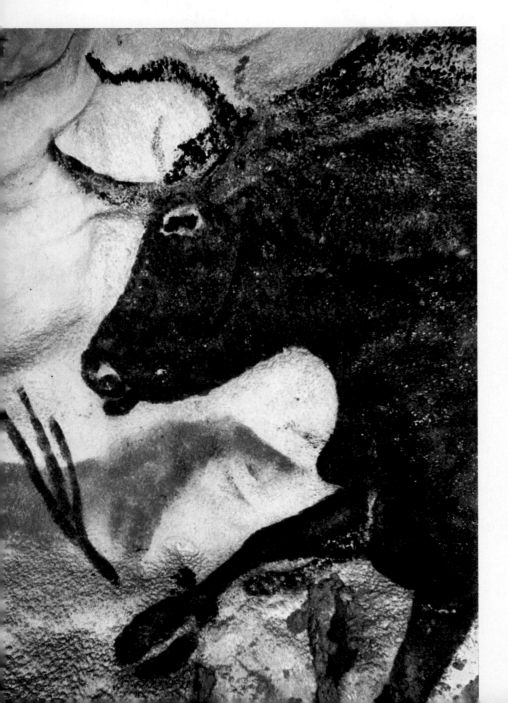

have thought that if they made a painting that looked real, and then "killed" it, it was almost like killing the animal itself. Perhaps they threw stones or jabbed the picture with their spears, too. This made them feel stronger and surer, so that when they finally went out to hunt their prey, they had a better chance of success because they were no longer afraid. Once they had "killed" the picture, they did not care about it any more. One cannot kill a real animal twice, and so they felt that one cannot kill a painted animal twice, either. The next time they got ready to hunt, they had to make a new picture to "kill" first.

It is remarkable that the cavemen took so much trouble with their animal paintings. After all, they were going to use them only once. Perhaps they felt that the magic would work best if the animal looked as much like the real thing as possible. And they were probably right, since they used the pictures as targets, to learn exactly where to hit the animal in order to bring it down.

In any case, it took a good deal of skill to make such convincing pictures. There must have been some cavemen who were better at this than the rest—who had special talent for art. After a while they were probably allowed to stay home and practice making pictures, while all the others had to go out hunting. Even 20,000 years ago, then, the painter was a special kind of person, although we might say that he was mainly supposed to be a magician.

Today we no longer believe in that kind of magic. We know better than to get mixed up between living things and the pictures of these things. But even now our feelings sometimes get confused, no matter what our reason tells us. For instance, it still happens that after a sudden quarrel people will tear up the photograph of someone they used to love; they know well enough that they cannot actually hurt anybody by doing so, yet it gives them great emotional satisfaction. We need hardly be surprised, therefore, that the men of the Old Stone Age, who understood very much less than we do about the difference between thinking and feeling, could get pictures confused with real things.

Art is always as much concerned with the way

7. BUSHMAN PAINTING / *Two Bull Elands* / Before 1900 A.D. Ceiling of a cave at Glengyle, Cape Colony, South Africa. *Until not long ago the Bushmen, living relics of the Stone Age, did vividly realistic pictures similar to those in the caves of France and Spain. They even knew about foreshortening.*

people feel about things as it is with the way things really are. Usually, both knowing and feeling go to make up a picture, and so paintings are different from one another, depending on whether the artist was more interested in what he saw or knew, or in what he felt; also on *how much* he saw, and knew, and felt.

8. ABORIGINAL PAINTING ON TREE BARK / *A Spirit Man Spearing Kangaroos* / Contemporary Western Arnhem Land, North Australia. *The drawings of the North Australian natives are another modern survival of Stone Age art. Their magic purpose is strikingly evident: not only are they done on pieces of bark, so they could actually be taken along on the hunt, but they are "X-ray" pictures showing some of the bones and inner organs of particular importance to the hunter.*

Pictures For the Dead: Egypt

THE CAVE PICTURES tell us a good deal about life in the Stone Age, and also about the way our imagination works. We say *our* imagination, because the minds of the cavemen were not really so very different from our own, otherwise we would not understand their pictures as well as we do. The difference between us and the cavemen is not in the kind of minds we have. It is in the things we think about and feel about. Perhaps pictures will also help us to understand how men managed to leave the life of the Stone Age behind and how, over many thousands of years, they gradually changed into the kind of people we are today.

When we speak of these changes we call them *history*. There are many ways of looking at history. Perhaps the simplest is to ask ourselves about the main differences between us and the men of the Stone Age. Even though the cavemen had far greater physical strength than we do, their life was very much more dangerous than ours— and much less interesting. The big animals they hunted were really their masters, because the people depended on them so completely. When the animals moved away, they had to move, too, so they never built houses for themselves, only rough shelters. And if they could find no animals to hunt, they starved. In the Stone Age, men worked together only in hunting (and the painters helped,

9. EGYPTIAN WALL PAINTING / *Men, Boats, and Animals* / About 3500 B.C. Hieraconpolis, Upper Egypt. *What strikes us when we compare this picture with those of the cavemen is the flat, pattern-like effect. There is no shading any more, and the figures have been simplified to the point where they look like a kind of shorthand. They are, however, carefully planned to fill the entire surface without crowding or overlapping. This sense of order is a new, important achievement.*

10. EGYPTIAN TOMB PAINTING / *Harvest Scenes* / About 1400 B.C. Thebes, Upper Egypt. *Here the sense of order has congealed into a strict set of rules which the Egyptian painter did not dare to break for almost three thousand years. Characteristically enough, the measuring of the fields (at the top) and the exact recording of the yield (in the center) were just as important to the Egyptians as the actual cutting of the grain (bottom right).*

too, with their magic) but today we cooperate in a thousand complicated ways; we depend on each other much more than the cavemen did.

Now, this modern way of living could come about only because we are very much more orderly than the people of the Stone Age. We think ahead. We *plan* things, while the lives of the cavemen were just as disorderly as their paintings. How did people discover the need for order? Just as soon as they found out that there were ways of controlling their supply of food instead of letting the food supply control them. First they learned how to tame and keep some of the animals they had hunted before. They became herdsmen who moved about with their sheep, or goats, or cattle,

or camels, always looking for grazing lands.

Other people found a different and even better way to control their food supply. They tamed not only animals but plants, too, collecting the seeds and growing their own crops. In order to do this, they needed a warm climate and a good source of water. That is why the first farmers settled along the banks of the big rivers, such as the river Nile, in Egypt. And we shall now take a better look at the ancient Egyptians, because the history of Europe and America really begins with them. When they started planting their grain, they also planted the seeds of a way of life which has grown into our own way of life today.

Figure 9 shows you a part of the oldest paint-

ing in Egypt. It was made on the wall of a temple or tomb in a place called Hieraconpolis, on the banks of the Nile, almost 6000 years ago. There are some lively animals in it, and people fighting with them and with each other. The big white shapes are boats. At this time, then, the Egyptians still did a lot of hunting, but they no longer depended on it as the cavemen had. They knew how to make and use all sorts of tools, for they built solid buildings of brick and stone, with smooth

walls, and boats for sailing up and down the river. There must have been many separate tribes or states along the valley that made war on each other. Notice the two men in the lower right-hand corner: the one with the white, dotted body is beating the one with the black body, who belongs to another tribe.

If we compare this picture with the cave paintings, we shall find that the figures in it are not nearly so real-looking. There is no shading such as we see in the buffalo (figure 2). They seem flat, as if they were glued to the wall, and the artist has left out many details. He uses a kind of shorthand, the way some modern comic strips do, so that a circle with a dot stands for a face, a crooked line for an arm, and so on.

As a matter of fact, the Hieraconpolis painting was probably meant to tell a story, somewhat like a comic strip. At the time it was made, the Egyptians had just invented the earliest kind of writing, which was done with pictures and is called hieroglyphics. The painter now was also a writer. When he had to tell a story he did it with these simple figures, which were actually "letters" or "signs" that stood for things or words. Because the figures were used over and over again, they came to look less and less real as time went on. We say they became "conventional" or "stylized"—and at last they turned into the letters of our own alphabet, which are no longer pictures at all.

There is something else we notice about the Hieraconpolis painting. We cannot tell whether or not the figures in it are supposed to be connected in some way, because there is no "setting," no indication of landscape or even of the ground they stand on. But there is no messy overlapping, either, and the figures are spread evenly over the whole surface. These animals, then, were not made to be "killed" for hunting magic. But the

Egyptian painting is connected with another, more complicated kind of magic; and in order to understand that we must know something of Egyptian ideas about religion, and especially about life and death.

When the Egyptians settled down to farming, order and planning became much more important to them than ever before. They had to know when to plant and harvest their crops. So they began to observe the regular movements of the sun, the moon, and the stars, and invented a calendar almost as good as our own. They also kept written records. But the Egyptians found that their harvest depended on a great many things besides the times of year. If the weather was bad, or if they did things the wrong way, they would not have enough food for the winter.

It was hard for them to understand why this sometimes happened, while at other times everything turned out just right. The only explanation they could think of was that the sun, the moon, the clouds, the water, the animals, the plants, and even the earth itself, were all inhabited by powerful spirits that could be either helpful or harmful,

depending on whether they liked you or not. The more important among these "nature spirits" came to be worshiped as gods. The Egyptians thought of them as great rulers like their own kings, except that they were wiser and lived forever.

"Forever" was a very important idea with the Egyptians. They believed that men, too, had a vital spirit, or soul, inside them, and that when a person died his soul would leave his body and keep on living separately. But they also thought that in this "afterlife" the soul still needed a body to come back to. Because of this, they went to great trouble to preserve the bodies of the dead— they made mummies of them by drying them and wrapping them up, and then put them in strong tombs made of stone, so nobody would disturb them. Their kings, the Pharaohs, and other important and wealthy people even had statues of themselves placed in their tombs, as "replacements" if something should happen to the real body.

They also believed that the spirit of the dead needed the same material things as a living person, so they furnished their tombs like a regular

13. EGYPTIAN WALL PAINTING / "The Daughters of Ikhnaton," from Tell El-Amarna / About 1360 B.C. Ashmolean Museum, Oxford. *Ikhnaton was the most extraordinary of all the Pharaohs. He tried to make his people worship a single supreme being instead of the many different gods of the traditional religion. During his reign the strict rules of art, too, were relaxed to some extent; in this picture, the King's daughters behave more like playful little girls than like royal princesses.*

14. EGYPTIAN PAINTING / *Limestone Flake with Sketch of Two Bulls Fighting* / 1500-1100 B.C. Metropolitan Museum of Art, New York. *Flat bits of limestone were the cheapest surface the Egyptian artist had for sketches and practice drawings. Many show a freedom never permitted otherwise.*

household, except that everything was made to last forever. Of course, even the richest man could not take all the things he owned with him into the tomb, such as his land, his animals, and his servants. Instead, he had pictures of them made on the walls, where his spirit would find them.

Figure 10 shows you such a wall painting, or "mural," from a tomb in Thebes, done about 2000 years after the one from Hieraconpolis. It was painted almost exactly 1400 years before the birth of Christ, during a period of Egyptian history known as the Empire, when the power of the Pharaohs reached far beyond the Nile valley proper into the neighboring regions to the East

and South. At the top of the mural, the dead man's servants are measuring a wheatfield with a rope. At the bottom, they are cutting the wheat with sickles, while the dead man himself sits under a canopy which protects him from the sun. In the center, there are his chariot and some servants measuring a pile of grain. This harvest scene strikes us as very orderly and carefully drawn. The figures no longer look as if they were floating—they have their feet firmly on the ground, even if the ground is only a thin, straight line. We can also tell right away what they are doing.

Still, the picture is not very lifelike. For one thing, the figures are put together in a strange way: their heads, arms, and legs are shown from the side, while the bodies and the eyes are seen from in front. Now, the artist must have known that we don't see people that way in real life, where we never get a very good view of anything in one glance, because most things are round rather than flat, and we can see only one side of them at a time. We don't really mind this, for if we want to know what is around the corner, we just walk up to it and then take another look; or if we see somebody's back and want to know what his face is like, we wait until he turns around. But we can't walk through a picture, and the figures in it cannot turn around. So the Egyptian painter made up for this by inventing a special kind of human figure where all the important parts of the

15. EGYPTIAN PAPYRUS / *The Sky Goddess Nut* / About 1000 B.C. Department of Antiquities, Cairo. *The great curving body of the goddess represents the star-covered firmament, supported by the god of the air. The reclining figure is the god of the earth. Symbolic pictures such as this are the most rigidly formal and rule-ridden in all of Egyptian art. The images of the gods here are interspersed with hieroglyphic writing, and there is only a difference of degree between the two.*

16. EGYPTIAN TOMB PAINTING / *"Girl Dancers and Musicians," from Thebes, Upper Egypt* / About 1400 B.C. British Museum, London. *There were few pleasures the well-to-do Egyptian was willing to forego in the hereafter. Evidently the painter, too, liked doing these girls; he has captured them so well that we can almost hear the piercing music as we watch them wriggle. Egyptian art as a whole is so solemn that it tends to make us forget how fully the Egyptian enjoyed life.*

body show up equally well in one view. He also knew that in real life a harvest is a complicated business, with many people doing different things one after the other. We would have to watch them for quite some time if we wanted to understand what they are doing. How could the same story be told in a picture, where there is no space and no movement?

The Egyptian artist realized that a lifelike painting, of the kind the cavemen had done, was not what he wanted, because it would let him show the harvest only the way it looked at one particular moment, and not the whole story of the harvest. And since he was working to please the spirit of a dead man, the story had to be complete; otherwise the spirit might miss something. So our painter has made everything much clearer and more orderly than it ever is in real life. His figures are spread out on the wall, and they overlap only when several of them are doing the same thing; some are extra large, to show that they are more important than the rest. And if he wants to tell us that something is far away, such as the trees in the top strip, he puts it above, not behind, the foreground figures.

Our painter, then, does not show us what he actually *sees,* but what he *knows.* He follows a strict set of rules, which we call the Egyptian "style"—the Egyptian painter's way of doing things. These rules may strike us as a bit peculiar at first, but after a while we come to feel that they are really very wise and well thought out. Sometimes, too, the rules could be broken. Look at the horse in our picture: its dappled color, its prancing movement make it seem much gayer and livelier than the rest. Now, horses were unknown in Egypt when the rules for painting were set up, so our painter did not apply his rules as strictly as usual in this case. And that is why the horse looks so much less "frozen" than the other figures.

17. EGYPTIAN PAPYRUS / *Lion and Antelope Playing Draughts* / About 1000 B.C. British Museum, London. *Whether or not the Egyptians had a "sense of humor," they certainly did not lack a sense of fun, although it is uncommon in their art. The two animals here probably illustrate a fable.*

Pictures For the Living: Crete

IF WE SAILED NORTH and a little to the west from the mouth of the Nile on the Mediterranean Sea, we would come to a long, rocky island called Crete, and then to the southern tip of Greece. There, between 2500 and 1000 B.C., we would have found an astonishing nation of sailors quite unlike the Egyptians. While the riches of Egypt came mainly out of the Nile valley, the Cretans were bold traders and pirates who made up for the poor soil of their homeland by bringing in food and many other important things from all the countries round about.

We have not yet learned very well how to read their kind of writing, so that we do not know a great deal about them. But from the ruins of their palaces, and from the pictures they did, we can guess that they were perhaps the richest and most adventurous of the early Western nations.

The wild boar hunt in figure 21 is a Cretan painting from the walls of the Palace of Tiryns, in southern Greece, done about 1200 B.C. Unfortunately, only a part of it has come down to us, so we can no longer see the hunter whose hand, on the right, sticks a spear into the animal. But what

18. CRETAN WALL PAINTING / *"Toreador," from the Palace at Knossos / About 1500 B.C. Museum, Candia, Crete. A youth (in the center) and two girls are playing a dangerous game: they seize the horns of a charging bull and somersault over his back. This was no mere sport but a ritual test, a way of worshiping the bull as a sacred animal. Echoes of it appear in the Greek legend of the Minotaur, and in the bullfights of today, while its origins may well go back to the Stone Age (see figures 5, 6).*

is still there—the racing hounds and the ferocious, galloping boar—reminds us more of the cave paintings, with their vigorous, real-looking animals, than it does of the "frozen" Egyptian style. Yet the Cretan painter must have learned something from the Egyptians, for his picture, despite its rapid movement, is an orderly scene, not just a wild tangle of animals. And like the Egyptians, too, he makes his forms cling to the wall, and follows definite rules—the three dogs are all done from the same pattern, except for their spots. There is no hunting magic here, but there is no service of the dead, either. For the Cretans, hunting was a sport, and the picture was done not from fear but for pleasure. It tells us of the thrill of the chase, and of the enjoyment of nature that we find in all of Cretan art. The gay and graceful shapes, the clear colors, must have made it a splendid decoration for the palace wall.

19. CRETAN WALL PAINTING / "Cat and Pheasant," from the Palace at Hagia Triada / 1700-1580 B.C. Museum, Candia, Crete. *This little drama of a cat silently stalking its prey shows how vividly Cretan art could record the actual behavior of animals. The sprays of foliage, in contrast, are flat and patterned.*

20. CRETAN POTTERY / "The Octopus Vase," from Gournia / About 1500 B.C. Museum, Candia, Crete. *As a nation of sailors, the Cretans loved the sea and its creatures. On this vase the strands of seaweed and the waving arms of the octopus are drawn with such freedom of movement that they seem to be floating in the water.*

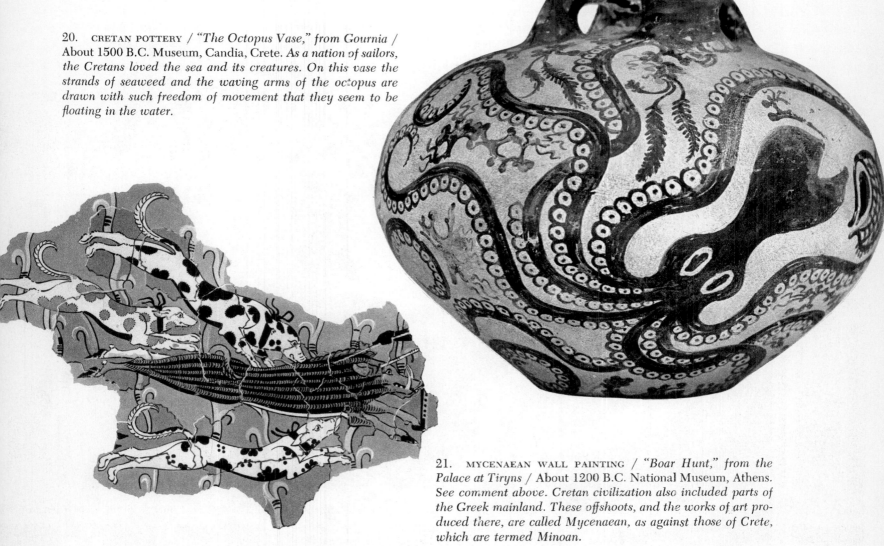

21. MYCENAEAN WALL PAINTING / "Boar Hunt," from the Palace at Tiryns / About 1200 B.C. National Museum, Athens. *See comment above. Cretan civilization also included parts of the Greek mainland. These offshoots, and the works of art produced there, are called Mycenaean, as against those of Crete, which are termed Minoan.*

Greek and Roman Painting

the Cretans, and this helped them to build up a great civilization of their own—greater, in some ways, than any the world has seen since. They soon settled and formed separate states, each named after its main city. Athens, in the region we call Attica, became the most important of these city-states, and it was there, between the eighth and the third centuries B.C., that the Greeks produced their keenest thinkers and their finest artists.

When we talk about the masterpieces of Greek art, we usually think of temples and statues, and not of paintings. That is because quite a few of the famous temples and statues are still there, while the paintings that used to be on the walls of the temples and houses have all been destroyed. We can read about these pictures in an-

THE CRETANS WERE CONQUERED, and their palaces destroyed, by warlike tribes that came into Greece from the north around 1100 B.C. These Greek tribes also learned a great deal from

22. GREEK VASE PAINTING / *Hercules Feasting Among the Gods on Olympus (detail)* / About 510 B.C. Staatliche Antikensammlungen, Munich. *The hero, wine cup in hand, is enjoying a well-earned rest in the abode of the gods, after a life filled with strenuous labors. His sword and shield are suspended among the vines behind him, to show that his fighting days are over. The subject is very well suited to the purpose of the vase on which it appears, a large two-handled vessel for wine.*

23, 24. GREEK VASE PAINTING / *Funerary Vase (below right) and Detail with Mourning Scene (above), from Attica / Eighth century B.C. Metropolitan Museum of Art, New York. Huge vessels like this one served as grave monuments. They are open at the bottom, so that offerings could be poured through them into the ground. The pictures which decorate them, however, do not refer to the hereafter but show the funeral itself, "geometric" in style but with great expressive power.*

25. GREEK VASE PAINTING / *Hercules Strangling the Lion of Nemea / About 500 B.C. Metropolitan Museum of Art, New York. This scene, like that in figure 22, done in the Archaic style, still has some of the rigid qualities of Egyptian painting but strives for ever-greater freedom of action.*

21

26. GREEK VASE PAINTING / *A Music Lesson* / About 510 B.C. Staatliche Antikensammlungen, Munich. *Shortly before 500 B.C., Greek vase painters began to switch from black figures to black backgrounds, so that the bodies showed the natural reddish color of the clay. The figures stood out more boldly, and details could be filled in with greater ease by painting instead of scratching lines into the clay. Artists now began to sign their work; this vase is by Phintias.*

cient writings, and we know that the Greeks were just as proud of their great painters as they were of their architects and sculptors. Fortunately, however, we have lots of Greek painted pottery (or "vases," as we call them, although they were made to hold wine or oil or water, rather than flowers). These vase paintings are often very beautiful, but of course they are much simpler than the large pictures were. From them we can get at least an idea of what the lost wall paintings must have been like.

In figures 23 and 24 you see a very early vase, from the eighth century B.C. Most of the forms

27. GREEK VASE PAINTING / *Lapith Killing a Centaur* / 490-480 B.C. Staatliche Antikensammlungen, Munich. *The advantages of the "red-figured" technique are evident here; the elaborate detail of the armor and the boldly foreshortened centaur's body would be impossible in a "black-figured" vase.*

are made up of triangles and squares, and everything is fitted into such a tight pattern that it takes us a while to realize that this is a scene of mourning: in the middle, the dead man is stretched out on a simple bed, and there are long lines of people on both sides, wringing their hands or tearing their hair in sorrow. How different this is from the Egyptian paintings, where nobody ever betrays his emotions! Here at last we find a picture of people not only *doing* things but *feeling* things. This shows us that the Greeks, from the very start, were much more interested in the living than in the dead. To them, life was a glorious adventure, and the dead were only shadows whom nobody had to fear.

The vase in figure 25 was made about 500 B.C., in a style called Archaic to distinguish it from the earlier, Geometric style. It is painted in black and dark red against the natural clay color of the vase. The lines inside the figures are made by scratching away the paint with a needle. This illustration shows us the hero Hercules wrestling with a lion. The Greeks believed that Hercules became a god instead of a shadow after he died, because of his heroic deeds on earth (see figure 22). Their gods behaved very much like a family of human beings—they quarreled among themselves, fell in love, or played jokes, and when they liked somebody especially they would adopt him as one of their own. The two figures on our vase are a bit stiff in the joints, because the Archaic artist was still using pretty much the same rules as the Egyptian painters. But they are also full of energy and spirit, and that is exactly what the Egyptian painters had left out of their pictures.

In the hundred years that followed, the Greeks concentrated more than ever before on facing the problems of this world instead of the next. They completely discarded all the age-old painting rules which the Egyptians had so carefully worked out and which had stuck in everybody's mind for thousands of years. Look at figure 33, a pottery disk done about 460 to 450 B.C. in what we call the

28.   ALEXANDROS OF ATHENS / *"The Knuckle-Bone Players,"* *from Herculaneum* / First century B.C. National Museum, Naples. *This small picture on a marble panel is a faithful copy after a Classic Greek original four hundred years older, which must have looked rather like the vase painting in figure 29.*

29.   GREEK VASE PAINTING / *Bridal Scene* / About 420 B.C. National Museum, Athens. *The fluid ease of this group of young women makes a strong contrast with the Archaic red-figured vase in figure 26, done less than a century earlier. Here is an example of the Classic style of Greek art at its best.*

30, 31. ETRUSCAN TOMB PAINTING / *Fishing Scene* / About 520 B.C. Tarquinia, Italy. *The Etruscans were the ancient inhabitants of Central Italy until they were conquered and absorbed by the Romans. Their religion included a strong belief in afterlife, somewhat like that of the Egyptians, and their art, too, was greatly concerned with the needs and comforts of the dead. The pictures on the walls of Etruscan tombs, however, are as lively and energetic as Cretan or Greek paintings.*

32. EGYPTIAN TOMB PAINTING / *Festival Preparations* / About 1400 B.C. Thebes, Upper Egypt. *Since the Egyptian painter had no interest in rendering deep space, he did not vary the scale of things according to their distance from the beholder. Size to him had an absolute meaning—it indicated degrees of importance. The two servant girls in our picture are very much smaller than their mistress, not because the artist thought of them as children but because they belong to a different class.*

33.   GREEK PAINTED DISK / *Goddess Offering a Ribbon to a Youth* / About 460-450 B.C.
Metropolitan Museum of Art, New York. *These figures no longer look flat; the Greek painter
has discovered how to foreshorten the forms of the body, so that they seem round and natural.*

34. ROMAN WALL PAINTING / *"Lady Musician and Young Girl," from a villa at Boscoreale* / First century B.C. Metropolitan Museum of Art, New York. *Here we find not only foreshortening but skillful modeling in light and shade, to make the figures look as solid and real as statues. The flat red background helps to emphasize their three-dimensional quality.*

35. EGYPTO-ROMAN / *Portrait Panel, from the Faiyum, Lower Egypt* / Second century A.D. Metropolitan Museum of Art, New York. *Even though this panel was attached to a mummy, in accordance with age-old Egyptian funeral custom, its style is purely Roman.*

36. ETRUSCAN TOMB PAINTING / *Musicians* / About 480 B.C. Tarquinia, Italy. *The style of this picture gives us a fairly good notion of what the lost Archaic wall paintings of the Greeks must have been like. The Etruscans had great admiration for the artistic genius of Greece, and imported Greek works of art in large numbers; many of the finest Greek vases (such as that in figure 27) have been found inside Etruscan tombs.*

37. ETRUSCAN TOMB PAINTING / *A Pair of Dancers* / 480-470 B.C. Tarquinia, Italy. *The Etruscans' ideas about the hereafter appear to have included punishment by fierce demons, corresponding to the later notion of Hell, and a "paradise" of eternal bliss. Their visions of the latter state, however, were rather raucous by modern standards, as suggested by this gay couple who are dancing, wine jug in hand, with a sensuous abandon oddly reminiscent of "jitterbugging" or "rug-cutting."*

38, 39.   ROMAN WALL PAINTING / *Frieze* / About 30 B.C. Villa of the Mysteries, Pompeii. *The subject of this composition of almost life-size figures can be defined only in general terms: it has to do with the mysteries of the cult of Bacchus. While the breath of Classical Greek art can be felt strongly here, especially in the magnificent fleeing woman (see below), this is not a copy but an original creation of the time of the Emperor Augustus, when the glory of Rome was at its height.*

Classic style. The painter has used several colors on a white ground, almost as if he were working on a piece of paper, and the picture does indeed look much more "modern" than those we have seen before. The lines are no longer scratched in but drawn with a brush, so that they flow more gracefully and smoothly.

But the most remarkable thing about these lines is that they somehow make the figures look round and natural, rather than flat. If you compare the disk with the Archaic vase, you will see why: in the Hercules, we still find the old combination of front and side views, but the young man in the later picture is drawn the way he would actually look from where we stand, so that we see much more of his left side than of his right. The right shoulder, for instance, is strongly foreshortened—it looks much smaller than the other. But exactly because of this we get the impression that it is farther away from us, and this makes us feel that the entire figure reaches back into space instead of sticking to the surface of the picture.

Figure 29 shows a slightly later example of the Classic style. It is even more freely drawn, and the forms have even greater roundness. It comes from a vase that was a wedding present and shows

40.   ROMAN WALL PAINTING / *Architectural View, from the bedroom of a villa at Boscoreale* / First century B.C. Metropolitan Museum of Art, New York. *By means of such elaborately foreshortened vistas of buildings or gardens, Roman painters "opened" walls and made small rooms seem larger.*

41.   ROMAN WALL PAINTING / *"Actor and Mask," from Herculaneum* / About 30 A.D. National Museum, Naples. *The brushwork is freer and more sketchy here, and there is a greater sense of light and air than in the frieze on the opposite page. Yet the finely balanced design is equally Classical in spirit.*

42.   ROMAN WALL PAINTING / *"View of a Garden," from the Villa of Livia, wife of Augustus, at Primaporta* / About 20 B.C. National Museum, Rome. *The astonishing range of Roman painting becomes evident when we realize that this sumptuous and painstakingly faithful view of a garden was done about the same time as the frieze in the Villa of the Mysteries. The artist's sensuous pleasure in the beauty of flowers, fruit, and foliage was not to be equaled until 1400 years later (see figure 98).*

43. ROMAN WALL PAINTING / *"Peaches and Glass Jug," from Pompeii / About 50 A.D. National Museum, Naples. Still lifes such as this, usually creating the illusion of a niche, were another way for the Roman painter to "break through" the solid surface of the wall.*

the crowning of the bride—a part of the wedding festivities—and the bringing of presents. Here the artist has sketched his figures directly on the red clay body of the vase, and then filled the spaces in between with black. These graceful young women, standing or sitting with such ease and assurance, make us feel completely at home. We must not think, however, that they were meant to be portraits. The Classic Greek artist was not yet interested in particular people, with all their personal imperfections; he preferred to make all his figures as beautiful as he could—he idealized them.

Only in later times, when Greek art had spread to all the countries around the Mediterranean Sea, do we find real portraits, such as the very fine one in figure 47. It comes from Egypt, about the third

44, 45. ROMAN MOSAIC / *"The Battle of Issus" (details), from Pompeii / About 100 B.C. National Museum, Naples. Mosaic, an ancient method of making designs out of small cubes of colored marble set into plaster, was brought to such technical perfection by the Romans that they could use it to copy paintings. The Battle of Issus reproduces a famous Greek picture of about 315 B.C.; below we see the defeated Persians under Darius (Alexander the Great and the Greeks are off to the left).*

46. ROMAN PAINTING / *Male Portrait on Gold-Backed Glass /
Third Century A.D. Archeological Museum. Arezzo. This tiny
picture (the original is slightly smaller than our reproduction)
has the intimacy of a personal keepsake. Such portrait miniatures became popular again in the sixteenth century.*

century A.D., but its style and technique are
Greek. The picture is done on a wooden panel,
and the colors are not mixed with water, as in all
the paintings we have seen so far, but with hot
wax. This makes a thicker, creamier kind of paint,
which allows the artist to model his forms by
blending light and dark shades of color right on
the panel.

The man who painted our portrait has done a
wonderful job of modeling; that is one reason
why his work looks so solid and real. But our
painter also had a special feeling for all the little
things that make this boy's face different from
anybody else's: the stubby nose, the square jaw,
the small, curved mouth, and the dark, shiny eyes.
Of course the picture has style, too—otherwise
we could not tell it from a snapshot—but we find
it difficult to say just what this style is, since everything seems so fresh and natural to us. If we did
not know that our picture was done 1700 years
ago, we might well think that it was painted only
yesterday.

The technique of painting with wax could be
used not only on wooden panels but also on the
walls of houses. However, the favorite way to do
mural paintings in ancient times was by another
method called "fresco," which means that the
artist worked with water colors on the freshly applied, moist plaster. The Romans were particularly good at this, as we know from the many
murals that have been dug up among the ruins of
their towns.

In the fifth century B.C., Rome was a small
city-state like Athens, but the Romans had a
much greater talent for government and politics
than the Greeks. Their state grew more powerful
as time went on, until it became a mighty empire
that stretched all the way from England to Egypt
and from Spain to Southern Russia. Although they

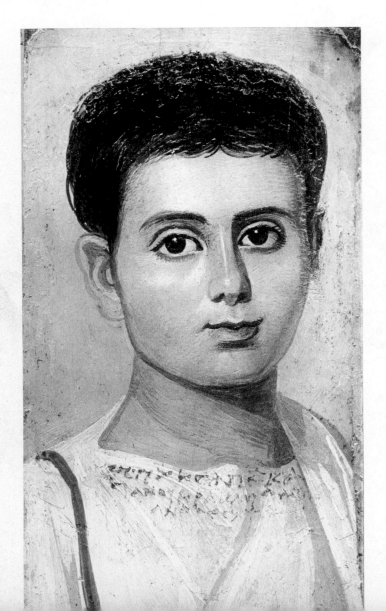

47. EGYPTO-ROMAN / *Portrait of a Boy, from the Faiyum,
Lower Egypt.* Third century A.D. Metropolitan Museum of
Art, New York. *See comment above. The term "Egypto-
Roman" does not refer to the style of the work but only to the
fact that it was done while Egypt was under Roman rule.*

48. ROMAN MOSAIC / *A Ship in Distress* / About 450 A.D. S. Giovanni Evangelista, Ravenna. *The craftsman who laid the floor of which this is a piece, no longer knew the sophisticated technique of the "mosaic-paintings" of Pompeii. His radically simple, flat design grows out of the nature of his materials.*

49. ROMAN MOSAIC / *Cat and Chicken; Ducks and Still Life of Birds, Fish, and Sea Shells, from Pompeii* / About 50 B.C. National Museum, Naples. *Here the realism of paintings like the still life in figure 43 is translated as successfully as* The Battle of Issus *renders the dramatic force of its Greek original.*

had conquered the Greeks as early as the second century B.C., the Romans always had a great respect for Greek art, so that many of their own painters (as well as their sculptors and architects) were influenced by the Greeks.

If we put these Roman pictures together with some of the Greek vases, they help to give us a better notion of the lost masterpieces of Greek wall painting. In figure 34 you see such a Roman mural, from a house in the small town of Boscoreale, near Naples. It was done less than a hundred years before the birth of Christ and is so large that the figures in it are just about life-size. Yet it will remind you of those in figure 29, which in reality are only a few inches tall.

50. ROMAN MOSAIC / *Girl Athlete (detail of a pavement)* / About 400 A.D. Piazza Armerina, Sicily. *This oddly modern-looking maiden was recently found in a villa that must have been one of the last outposts of the pagan way of life after Christianity had become the official religion of the Roman state.*

51. ROMAN MOSAIC / "Gladiators" (detail), from the pavement of a Villa at Torrenuova / About 300 A.D. Borghese Gallery, Rome. The bloody and cruel combat of gladiators was a favorite "spectator sport" in Imperial Rome. Our mosaic must have been made for a man who owned a stable of these brutish professional fighters and was proud enough of their victories to have them pictured. Such scenes are a far cry indeed from the athletic contests of the Greeks (compare figure 33).

The Roman lady still has something of the idealized beauty that we find in the Greek picture, even though she is not nearly as graceful. At the same time, she seems more real, and not only because of the careful shading. Her face, with its strong nose, looks as if it might be a portrait, and the little girl behind the chair could be her daughter. The Roman painters often combined the real and the ideal in this fashion. It is hard to say how much they took from the Greeks and how much they invented, but they are important to us because through their work the Greek style of painting was kept alive so that it could be handed on to the artists of the Christian era.

52. ROMAN MOSAIC / Tiger Killing a Bull / Fourth century A.D. Palazzo dei Conservatori, Rome. The most demanding technique the Romans developed for translating paintings into more durable materials was sectional mosaic, which consists of cutout pieces of marble fitted together like a jigsaw puzzle.

The Middle Ages

WHEN WE THINK of the many countries and the different kinds of people that came under their rule, we cannot help wondering how the Romans ever succeeded in holding their Empire together. It must have been a difficult task. Fortunately, the Romans were too wise to rely on military force alone. After they had conquered a country, they made the people into "Romans" of a sort by teaching them Roman ways and even allowing them to become Roman citizens, with rights and duties fixed by law. There was one thing, however, that the Romans failed to do: they did not give the people within the Empire a common religious faith. The official Roman religion was similar to that of the Greeks,

but the Romans never insisted that everybody had to accept it. All they required was a formal sacrifice every year to the emperor, who was to them a kind of hero-god, like the Greek Hercules. For the rest, the Greek gods, the Egyptian gods, and all the other local gods were allowed to compete with each other; and since there were so many of them, nobody really knew *what* to believe in.

Such confusion was all very well as long as the Empire was stable and peaceful, but when things began to go badly people felt a great need for the comfort and assurance that comes from a strong faith. It was then that they turned to the followers of Jesus Christ, the group most zealous in offering such a faith to the rest of the world. By the time

53. EARLY CHRISTIAN WALL PAINTING / *The Good Shepherd, the Story of Jonah, and Praying Figures* / 200–250 A.D. Ceiling of the Catacomb of Saints Peter and Marcellinus, Rome. *The design forms a cross, the basic symbol of the new faith. To Early Christians, the miraculous rescue of Jonah held the promise that they, too, would rise from their graves through the power and mercy of the Lord. The image of the Good Shepherd who gives his life for his sheep, stands for Christ.*

the Empire was about to collapse, Christianity had won out over all the other religions, and the Christian Church was well established.

Jesus of Nazareth was born among the Jews, who had long believed in a single God while their neighbors worshiped many different gods. God, as the Jews thought of him, was all-powerful; he had created the entire universe and ruled over everything. All men were his children, but he had a special concern for the Jews, his chosen people, to whom he had made known his will in the form of laws or commandments. These laws, written down in the Old Testament, told men exactly how they must act toward the Lord and toward each other in order to lead good lives. This was a great and new concept: that God is just, and that the only way to please him is by obeying his commandments.

Jesus, too, accepted the laws of the Old Testament. But he said that to observe these laws was less important than to love God, because God was filled with kindness and mercy for all men, even those who broke his laws. Jesus also believed that we must be as kind and forgiving to other people as God is to us. His own life, and his death on the cross, as told in the Gospels of the New Testament, give us a perfect example of what he meant by this. To his followers, Jesus was the Son of God, the Saviour whose coming had been predicted in the Old Testament. They believed that those who placed their trust in Christ would rise after death and live forever in Paradise; and that God offered this hope not only to the Jews but to all races and nations, to rich and poor alike.

54. EARLY CHRISTIAN WALL PAINTING / *Madonna and Child* / Third century A.D. From the Catacomb of Priscilla, Rome. *Here, as in figure 53, the style of the picture still reminds us quite strongly of earlier Roman murals, even though the poses tend to become "frozen" and forms lose their roundness.*

55. EARLY CHRISTIAN PANEL / *Madonna and Child* / Fifth or sixth century A.D. S. Francesca Romana, Rome. *This image is painted in the same hot-wax technique as the portrait of a boy in figure 47, but the ideal of beauty represented here is already far removed from Classical art. Compare the Byzantine Madonna in figure 67.*

This last part of their faith explains why the followers of Jesus were so eager to spread their message everywhere. Soon after his death, they went to different parts of the Roman Empire. There they taught the new religion and formed the earliest Christian congregations, or Churches. The most important Church was in Rome; and there, too, we find the first pictures by Christian artists. They were painted on the walls of long underground passages called catacombs, where the Early Christians buried their dead. Figure 53 shows you the remains of a ceiling decoration from such a catacomb, done about two centuries after the death of Christ. Its style is borrowed from Roman painting, but the figures in it look a bit stiff, and seem to cling to the white background. Obviously, our artist was not much interested in modeling or foreshortening.

We can tell from this that the Early Christians even then had a new and different outlook on life.

Their thoughts were centered on the Saviour and on the life hereafter, rather than on their own strength or on the glories of this earth. Thus the beauty and power of the human body, so important in Greek and Roman art, no longer held much meaning for them; instead, they wanted pictures that would show the power and glory of Christ, and tell of his mission on earth.

Now, the Early Christian painter could not do this directly. He could only hint at it by using symbols—that is, figures or signs that stand for something which we cannot see. The picture in the middle of the ceiling is such a symbol; it shows a shepherd and his flock, but it stands for Christ, the Good Shepherd of men's souls. Since everything depends on Christ, the other scenes are arranged around this center like the spokes of a wheel. They form a big cross, the simplest and most general symbol of the new faith. The standing figures represent the members of the Church,

56. BYZANTINE MOSAIC / *Emperor Justinian and Attendants* / About 547 A.D. S. Vitale, Ravenna. *See also color plate, figure 68. Under Justinian the Byzantine Empire reached the height of its political power, and Byzantine artists produced their finest work. Mosaics such as this differ from Roman ones (compare figures 49, 50) not only in style but also in technique and material; composed of little cubes of glass, rather than marble, their rainbow-bright color dazzles the beholder.*

57. ROMAN MINIATURE / *Illustration from the "Vatican Vergil"* / *Fifth or sixth century A.D. Vatican Library, Rome. This scene, separated from the text by a heavy frame, looks like a window cut into the page of the book. Its style still recalls Roman wall paintings of an earlier day (see figure 42).*

58. EARLY CHRISTIAN MINIATURE / *Illustration from the "Vienna Genesis" / Early sixth century A.D. National Library, Vienna. The pages of this manuscript are deep purple, and the lettering silver (now turned black). Here the figures are no longer inside a "window"; the page itself now serves as sky.*

with their hands raised in prayer, pleading for help from above. In the four half-circles our artist tells the story of Jonah, from the Old Testament. Jonah had gone on a boat against the wishes of God, so the sailors threw him into the sea and a whale swallowed him. You see this in the scene on the left (the whale is shown as a kind of sea monster). On the right, the whale is letting him out again, because Jonah had prayed to God while inside the big fish. At the bottom, he is back on dry land, meditating upon the mercy of God.

To the Early Christians this story meant that they, too, would rise from the dead through the power of God, just as Jonah had risen from the whale. And they needed to be reassured, for they were having quite a hard time themselves. Still, more and more people joined them as time went on, so that in the fourth century even the emperors were Christians. Not long after this, Christianity became the official religion of the Roman Empire, and Christian art, too, began to take on a more official look. But by this time the western part of the Empire was falling to pieces, and the capital had been moved to Byzantium, in eastern Greece. The official Christian style of painting is called Byzantine after that city, whose modern name is Istanbul.

This style of painting lived on, without any important changes, for a very long time. The Byzan-

tine *Madonna* in figure 67—that is, the Virgin Mary with her son, the Infant Christ—probably dates from around 1200, but it would be much the same if it had been painted a few centuries earlier or later. It is done on a wooden panel, like the portrait of the boy in figure 47, and the subject may remind you of the lady with the little girl in figure 34; but these comparisons only show us how different it is from Roman or even Early Christian painting. The Byzantine artist did not think of the Madonna as anything like an ordinary, human mother. To him she was the Queen of Heaven, far removed from everyday life and beautiful beyond any man's imagination. And he has painted her the way he *felt* about her: not as a woman of flesh and blood but an ideal figure bathed in the golden light of heaven.

If we now look at the Early Christian *Madonna* in figure 54, we can see that it stands about halfway between the Roman lady and the Byzantine *Madonna*. It is much more human than the later picture, but the dark, staring eyes and the stiffness of the body tell us that we are looking at something sacred and symbolic. Subjects like this were repeated over and over again, and each time they became a little less natural as one painter copied from another (compare figure 55), until at last they reached the frozen, superhuman majesty of the Byzantine style.

The Earlier Middle Ages in the West

MEANWHILE, WESTERN EUROPE had been invaded by warlike tribes from the north and east. They conquered the Roman armies and made independent local kingdoms of the various provinces of the Empire, mixing with the people whom they found there. The nations of western Europe as we know them today—the English, the

59. IRISH MANUSCRIPT / *Page from the Book of Durrow* / About 700 A.D. Trinity College Library, Dublin. *The monk who decorated this page borrowed his interlacing bands and fighting animals from the art of his pagan ancestors. The tiny cross is the only Christian element here.*

60. IRISH MANUSCRIPT / *Crucifixion, from a Gospel Book* / About 750-60 A.D. Stiftsbibliothek, St. Gall, Switzerland. 61. CAROLINGIAN MANUSCRIPT / *St. Matthew, from the Gospel book of Charlemagne* / About 800, A.D. Schatzkammer, Kunsthistoriches Museum, Vienna. 62. CAROLINGIAN MANUSCRIPT / *St. Mark from the Gospel Book of Ebbo of Reims* / 816-35 A.D. Municipal Library, Epernay, France. *During the "Roman revival" under Charlemagne, Northern artists quickly learned how to master the images of Early Christian art. The Christ in figure 60 is still a mere knot of interlacing bands, while the St. Matthew could almost be mistaken for a Roman author. The St. Mark clearly derives from such models, but here every line has the energy of the interlacing bands of figure 60.*

French, and the rest—all got their start in this melting pot. But first the tribes had to be taught about Roman civilization and about Christianity. They were now the heirs of everything that had been achieved by the older nations, and there was a great deal they had to learn.

During this troubled time, the Church was the only stable institution left in western Europe. The task of spreading both faith and education fell to the monks—devoted religious men who lived together under strict discipline in special communities. The monks, however, were not only priests and teachers. From the fifth to the twelfth centuries—that is, for most of the period we know as the Middle Ages—they were also the leading artists and craftsmen.

In those days almost every monastery had a workshop for making copies of the Bible and other books. This was done by hand, since printing had not yet been invented. The monks did not even know about paper; they wrote on vellum, a material made from the skin of calves, which was much more expensive but also a great deal tougher. Medieval manuscripts, produced so laboriously, were meant to last for a long time, and many of them are still in fine shape. The writing shops also included painters whose job it was to illuminate—to "brighten up"—the manuscripts with pictures and ornament. These miniatures (from "minium," a red pigment) were done with marvelous care. For many centuries they were the most important kind of medieval painting, and the best of them can stand comparison with any mural or panel picture.

It is not surprising that the monks took manuscript painting so seriously. After all, their faith was based on the Bible, which to many people is still simply "the Book." Since it contained the word of God, every copy of it was sacred, and to illuminate it, to make it as beautiful as possible, was a way of worshiping God. Perhaps this idea will help us understand the manuscript page in figure 59, from the *Book of Durrow*, which was done by Irish monks in the eighth century. The words that go with this picture are those of the Gospels—the life of Christ written by the four

63. CAROLINGIAN MANUSCRIPT / *Illustration to Psalm 44, from the Utrecht Psalter* / About 832. University Library, Utrecht. *The frantic movement in this pen drawing shows a style closely related to that of figure 62. The angels grouped around the bed in the upper center illustrate verse 23: "Awake, why sleepest thou, O Lord?" On the left, the faithful crouch before the Temple, "for . . . our belly cleaveth unto the earth." At the gate, they are killed "as sheep for the slaughter."*

64. SICILIAN MOSAIC / *Christ in Majesty* / About 1148. Cathedral, Cefalù, Sicily. *Southern Italy and Sicily had belonged to the Eastern Roman Empire, and Byzantine influence persisted even under the Normans, who established a kingdom there in the eleventh century. This awesome Christ, gazing upon us with almost hypnotic intensity, is equal to the finest works of Byzantine art in Greece itself. Note that one page of the book he is holding bears an inscription in Greek, the other in Latin.*

Evangelists, Matthew, Mark, Luke, and John—but our artist has not tried to illustrate the sacred story. Instead, he has "brightened it up" with a wonderful piece of ornament. These interlaced bands and weird, bandlike animals do not come from Early Christian art; they are borrowed from the native art of the tribes that had just settled in western Europe. And yet, the picture has a Christian meaning. You will notice that it is made up of a circle with a small cross in the center, and a wide frame around it. This is our artist's way of showing the contrast between two different worlds: the frame, with its fighting monsters, stands for the cruel, dark world of the pagans, the unbelievers; while the circle is a symbol of the world under Christ.

Let us now turn to figure 61, a miniature painted around 800 A.D., at the time of Charlemagne, the first medieval emperor, who ruled over France, Germany, and most of Italy. Charlemagne not only revived the idea of the Roman Empire in the West; he also wanted his people to learn everything they could about Roman civilization and about Early Christian art (because

igris uocata ppt uoluate fuga. ita H no
minant pse greci. ce medi sagitta. Sit enī
bestia uariis distincta maclis. uirtute oc uelo

65. ENGLISH ROMANESQUE MANUSCRIPT / *Tiger and Cub,
from a Bestiary* / About 1185. *The Pierpont Morgan Library,
New York. The medieval interest in animals was moral rather
than scientific. Here the tiger licks her own image in the mirror,
mistaking it for her cub, which is being carried off.*

that, too, came from Rome). In the pictures of
Charlemagne's own Gospel Book, there are no
interlacing bands and tangled-up animals. Instead, we find the four Evangelists, carefully copied from Early Christian manuscripts. The one
you see in figure 61 is Saint Matthew. Everything
about him—the powerful body, the bold head, and
especially the use of shading and foreshortening
—reminds us of Roman art. We might well mis-
take him for an ordinary author if it weren't for
the halo, the large disk behind his head, which is
a symbol to tell us that he is filled with the spirit
of God. (The Byzantine Madonna and Child in
figure 67 have halos, too.)

But the Roman spirit of Charlemagne's time
did not last. His empire was split up among his
heirs, and in art, too, the native ornamental style
of interlacing bands and animal forms came back
after a few years. However, the painters also remembered what they had learned under Charlemagne—how to draw human figures and tell stories
with pictures (see figures 62, 63). So they began
to combine the two styles into one. The result was
a great new style, the so-called Romanesque,
which flowered in the eleventh and twelfth centuries. Despite its name, it is not at all Roman in
spirit, although many of its forms are of Roman
origin.

Figure 69 shows you a fine early example of
Romanesque painting. It is the first page of the
Gospel of Luke, from a manuscript illuminated in
a French monastery soon after the year 1000 A.D.
Look at the marvelous way the ornament, the text,
and the illustrations are woven together here!
There is so much to see that we hardly know
where to start. The wide frame reminds us of the
one from the *Book of Durrow,* but the interlacing
bands have sprouted leaves and flowers, and the
animals are less fierce and easier to recognize. The
large shape in the middle of the page is the initial
letter "Q," again outlined with plant and animal
forms. It frames a scene from the Gospel: the
angel Gabriel announcing the birth of Saint John
the Baptist to Zacharias. In the tail of the "Q" we
see another sacred story, the birth of Christ.

These pictures show us that the Romanesque
painter was well acquainted with Byzantine art

66. ANGLO-NORMAN EMBROIDERY / *The Bayeux Tapestry (detail)* / About 1080. *Town Hall, Bayeux, France. The entire
work, ordered for Bayeux Cathedral, is a linen strip 230 feet long depicting the Norman conquest of England in 1066. The
lively narrative style and the agitated gestures of the figures show the influence of the Utrecht Psalter style (compare figure 63),
which could be felt on both sides of the Channel until the twelfth century.*

67. BYZANTINE SCHOOL / *Madonna and Child Enthroned* / About 1200. National Gallery of Art, Washington, D.C. (Mellon Collection.) *The frozen, superhuman majesty of this image rests on a tradition that began more than seven hundred years earlier (compare figures 54, 55).*

68. BYZANTINE MOSAIC / *Emperor Justinian and Attendants (detail of figure 56)* / About 547 A.D. S. Vitale Ravenna. *The Emperor shares with the Madonna in figure 67 not only the halo but the shimmering gold background, intended to represent the splendor of heavenly space. The intense stare of the large, dark eyes stresses the life of the spirit, rather than of the body, which is hidden away behind flat, pattern-like garments.*

69. ROMANESQUE MANUSCRIPT / *Initial Page of the Gospel of St. Luke* / French, about 1000 A.D. The Pierpont Morgan Library, New York. *Here is a splendid example of the medieval illuminator's genius for weaving together ornament, text, and illustration into one harmonious whole. Inside the large letter "Q," Gabriel announces the birth of St. John to Zacharias; the tail frames the birth of Christ.*

70. ROMANESQUE MANUSCRIPT / *The Death of the Virgin* / German, about 1010 A.D. Staatsbibliothek, Munich. *This miniature has all the expressive force and the monumental design of a wall painting. In the upper part, the soul of the Virgin, carried by two angels, is received by the Lord.*

and respected its authority. When he designed the ornament of the frame, he simply invented his patterns as he went along, but for the sacred stories of the Bible he did not trust his own imagination. They had to be illustrated "correctly"—that is, the way they had been done by earlier artists—otherwise people might not recognize them. But if our artist has used Byzantine pictures as his models, he has not copied them very exactly. While his figures have a good deal in common with the Byzantine *Madonna* in figure 67, they are much more forceful and expressive. In fact, they seem to be full of the same kind of energy and excitement as the plant and animal forms of the frame. This also explains why the design of the whole page hangs together so well, despite its many different elements.

The story telling power of the Romanesque style can be seen even better in another picture (figure 71), a mural of the twelfth century from St. Savin in France. The subject here is the story of the Tower of Babel, from the Old Testament.

This tower was to be a real skyscraper. The people who built it wanted to reach all the way up to heaven, to show that they were just as powerful as God. But they never finished it, for God suddenly made each of them speak a different language, so they could no longer communicate with each other. In our picture, the men on the right, led by the giant Nimrod, are carrying stone blocks for the masons on the tower. On the left you see God warning them to stop. The artist has put all this into a long, narrow strip that may remind you of the "strip pictures" of ancient Egypt (figure 10). But how intensely and dramatically the Romanesque painter tells his story! In the Egyptian painting, all the figures seem to be standing still. Here, every line is in motion; people are beckoning to each other, straining under the load of the stones, arguing with God. We know right away that this is a great test of strength between ambitious men and their Creator, and we share the excitement the artist must have felt when he painted the picture.

71. ROMANESQUE WALL PAINTING / *The Building of the Tower of Babel* / Twelfth century. Saint-Savin-sur-Gartempe, France. *See comment above. The walls and vaults of Romanesque churches provided ample space for murals such as this, but only a small number of examples have survived to the present day. The forms here, bounded by solid dark outlines, have greater weight, and the figures are more densely crowded together, than before (compare figures 63, 66).*

The Rise of the Towns: Gothic Art

73. GOTHIC MINIATURE / *Page from the Psalter of St. Louis* About 1260. Bibliothèque Nationale, Paris. *The slender, swaying figures are characteristic of Gothic art. So is the shading, which gives the forms roundness, though as yet very limited. The architecture, too, is now rendered more exactly.*

DURING THE EARLIER MIDDLE AGES, the towns left over from the time of the Roman Empire were almost deserted, and those that had been newly founded remained small and quite unimportant. Most of the people lived in the open country, where they farmed the land belonging to the monasteries or the nobles. But from the twelfth century on, the towns began to grow

again. More and more people left the countryside to become "burghers," free town-dwellers no longer bound to the land owning overlords. This brought about a great change in medieval life. The burghers were skilled craftsmen and enterprising traders, so that the towns soon became the centers of wealth, and of art and learning as well. Also, city life made people more independent and practical-minded. It opened them up to new ideas, and gave them a greater interest in the world around them.

Out of this new spirit came a new style in art called the Gothic. It started in France about 1150 A.D. and spread from there to all the other countries of the Western world. The miniature in figure

72. NICHOLAS OF VERDUN / *The Crossing of the Red Sea* 1181. Enamel plaque from the altar at Klosterneuburg Abbey, Austria. *This splendid work stands on the threshold of the Gothic style. Romanesque expressiveness is here combined with a new interest in modeling, and the figures seem far more natural than before.*

74, from a prayerbook dated 1295 A.D., will show you how very different Gothic painting is from Romanesque. It was done by a burgher, a professional manuscript painter in the city of Paris, rather than by a monk. The subject is the famous Biblical story of David's victory over Goliath, but our artist has treated it as if it had happened in his own lifetime. The giant Goliath, in the center, and King Saul, on the left, are wearing the armor of medieval knights. What really surprises us, however, is the new interest in shading, which gives all the forms a softer, more natural look. While our picture as a whole has little depth, there is enough modeling here to lift the figures away from the flat pattern of the background, and the way their feet overlap the frame shows us that they are meant to be *in front of* the page, not just *on* it.

Another kind of painting that flourished in Gothic times was done on small pieces of colored glass, which were cut to shape and then fitted together with lead frames into large stained glass windows, as in figure 79. This difficult and limited technique makes modeling almost impossible. But perhaps we should not think of stained glass windows as pictures at all; they are really transparent screens whose beauty depends on the marvelously rich and brilliant color patterns. These windows were an essential part of Gothic architecture. In France, England, and Germany they reached such great size that the churches began to look like glass houses, and there was little space left for murals.

Italy alone was an exception to this rule. There the churches kept their solid walls, and mural painting continued to be a great art for many centuries. But the Italians were different from the nations to the north in other ways as well.

74. MASTER HONORE (?) / *David and Goliath, from "The Prayer Book of Philippe the Fair"* / 1295. Bibliothèque Nationale, Paris. *See comment on the left. The shading here is so vigorous that the figures look as if they were carved in relief. Note the well-observed leaves of oak and maple trees.*

75. GOTHIC WALL PAINTING / *Madonna and Child Enthroned* About 1260. Cathedral, Gurk, Austria. *This impressive mural is done in a peculiarly German style that combines Gothic influence from France with sharp-edged, angular drapery patterns derived from Byzantine art (compare figure 64).*

77. CIMABUE / *Crucifix* / About 1285-90. S. Croce, Florence. *Although he was supposed to have been the teacher of Giotto, Cimabue's art is actually closer to Duccio. In this Christ we see not only a new concern with the weight and bulk of the body but a very moving expression of suffering.*

76. DUCCIO / *Christ Entering Jerusalem* / 1308-11. Museum of the Cathedral, Siena. *Duccio, like Giotto, wanted to lead Italian art back to more natural forms, but he went about it another way: he "unfroze" the Byzantine style of painting, so that it became more lively and realistic.*

78. GIOTTO / *Christ Entering Jerusalem* / 1305-1306. Arena Chapel, Padua. *This mural forms an interesting contrast with figure 76. While Duccio strives to bring the story to life by elaborating upon the setting and the incidental detail, Giotto's approach is radically simple and direct.*

79. STAINED GLASS WINDOW / *The Virgin with Apostles (detail)* About 1150. Cathedral, Le Mans. *The style of these figures, on the threshold of the Gothic era, still has the expressive energy of Romanesque painting (compare figure 71), intensified by glowing color.*

80. GIOTTO / *Lamentation over Christ* / About 1305-06. Arena Chapel, Padua. *See also figure 78. To his con-*
temporaries, Giotto's pictures seemed as real as nature herself; here was an art that had broken through the
barrier of the Byzantine tradition, an art of solid, tangible figures expressing grave and powerful emotions.

81.   GIOTTO / *Madonna and Child Enthroned* / About 1310. Uffizi Gallery, Florence. *The revolutionary boldness of Giotto, his majestic sense of volume, is particularly striking if we compare this panel with its Byzantine ancestry (see figure 67).*

82. SIMONE MARTINI / *Christ Carrying the Cross* / About 1340. The Louvre, Paris.
Simone had learned from Duccio how to stage a scene like this; the colorful crowd pour-
ing out of the city gate recalls the older master's Christ Entering Jerusalem *(figure 76).*

83. BOHEMIAN MASTER / *The
Crucifixion* / About 1360. Formerly
State Museums, Berlin. *Like Southern France, Bohemia in the mid-
fourteenth century became a gateway of Italian influence. The
International atmosphere of Prague
produced the finest painters of Central Europe.*

84.   ENGLISH MASTER / *The "Wilton Diptych" / About 1415. National Gallery, London. The style of this charming work is so international that some scholars still regard it as French. It shows Richard II being presented to the Virgin by his patron saints. The King's face is not an individual likeness (he died in 1399).*

AT RIGHT:

85.   PAUL OF LIMBURG AND BROTHERS / *February, from the "Very Rich Book of Hours" of the Duke of Berry / About 1415. Condé Museum, Chantilly, France. In contrast to the refined elegance of its courtly scenes (such as that reproduced above), the International Style also fostered sharp-eyed observation of nature and everyday life.*

86. GENTILE DA FABRIANO / *The Adoration of the Magi* / 1423. Uffizi Gallery, Florence. *Even though the figures here have greater weight and solidity, this Italian masterpiece of the International Style betrays its kinship with the Northern examples on the two preceding pages (compare the Madonna of The "Wilton Diptych").*

87. AMBROGIO LORENZETTI / *Presentation of the Infant Christ in the Temple* / 1342. Uffizi Gallery, Florence. *The monumental figures of this painter from Siena betray the influence of Giotto, while the setting shows a bold new interest in deep space. The interior of the temple is no longer a mere frame or backdrop; it has become a real "container" for the figures, which are now clearly indoors (notice how they are overlapped by the two columns in the foreground).*

They had never quite forgotten that they were the heirs of the Romans and Early Christians, and they knew much more about city life. Italy had wealthy and powerful medieval towns earlier than any other country, so that we meet a particularly bold and modern spirit among Italian Gothic painters. The greatest of them all was Giotto, born in the city of Florence in 1266. He is the first painter in history who is as much admired today as he was during his own lifetime. Since a good many of his works have come down to us, we can find out for ourselves why he became so famous. Looking at his *Lamentation over Christ* (figure 80), which is one of a series of murals in a private chapel in Padua, we feel right away that it must be a large picture, rather than a miniature. This

has little to do with the actual size—it's the bigness of the shapes that makes the painting seem so large. There is no fussy detail in these strong and simple figures. Their weight and roundness almost makes them look like great rocks. We call such figures monumental, because they remind us of a stone monument, firmly set in place for all time.

Yet Giotto's people are full of human feeling. We share their sorrow over the death of Christ, whether we look at the weeping angels in the sky or at the mourners below. Through their gestures, and the expressions on their faces, they speak to us so clearly and simply that we ourselves become part of the scene. There is something else, too, that makes *The Lamentation* such a powerful

88. AMBROGIO LORENZETTI / *A Tuscan Town* / About 1340. Picture Gallery, Siena. *Here is another daring thrust into unknown territory—a bird's-eye view of a hilltop town by the sea. (It is not a detail from a larger painting but a complete work in its own right.) If Ambrogio's picture, with the ground tilted upward so steeply as to leave no room for the sky, suggests a kind of relief map rather than a true landscape, it still contains the seeds of the full-fledged landscapes of the future.*

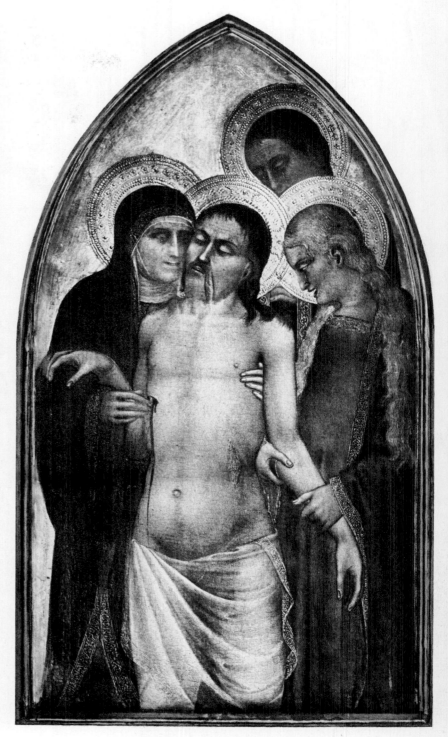

89. TOMMASO DA MODENA / *A Saint of the Dominican Order* / 1352. Chapter House, S. Niccolò, Treviso, Italy. *Tommaso combines the influence of Giotto with the detailed realism of Northern Gothic art. He has left us the oldest known picture of eyeglasses (invented a few decades earlier).*

90. GIOVANNI DA MILANO / *Lamentation over Christ* / 1365. Academy, Florence. *This image of the Christ of the Passion, dead yet with a semblance of life since he is shown standing, is less dramatic than Giotto's* Lamentation; *yet it has an intimacy of feeling that touches us even more deeply.*

work of art: its composition—by which we mean the way the figures and other forms are arranged inside the frame. When we look at story telling pictures like the Romanesque mural or the Gothic miniature, our eye travels from one detail to the next. In *The Lamentation*, on the other hand, the large, simple forms and the strong grouping of

the figures allow us to see the entire scene at one glance. Giotto has composed it the way a great stage director would put on a dramatic play in the theater. Even the scenery makes us think of a stage set; it leaves just enough room for the bulky figures, but the background looks flat. If we follow the foreshortened right arm of the Saint John,

91. FRANCESCO TRAINI / *The Three Living and the Three Dead, detail from the fresco "The Triumph of Death"* / *About 1350. Camposanto, Pisa. The startling realism of this scene reminds us that the Middle Ages were not only a time of faith but a time of pestilence, when whole towns could be depopulated by the plague, as in Tuscany in 1348. Traini probably drew on personal memories in depicting the terror of men and animals at the sight and smell of rotting flesh.*

in the center, we can measure the actual depth of the "stage."

Before Giotto, Italian painting had been closely tied to the Byzantine style. If you compare his work with the Byzantine *Madonna* in figure 67, you will understand why he came to be remembered as the man who led Italian art back to natural forms. The painters of Siena, a town not far from Florence, had a similar aim but went about it another way (see figures 76, 78). They "unfroze" the Byzantine style, so that it became more lively and realistic. Among the best was

Simone Martini, who painted the small wooden panel of *Christ Carrying the Cross* (figure 82). The picture is done in tempera, a technique used for both miniatures and panels (the colors are mixed with egg yolk and water, making a thin, smooth paint that dries to a tough enamel-like film). The fine detail and the brilliant colors give this kind of painting a jewel-like quality very different from fresco. Some of Simone's figures still remind us of Byzantine art, while others show the influence of Giotto in their bulk and expressiveness. Giotto's sense of drama is missing, to be sure,

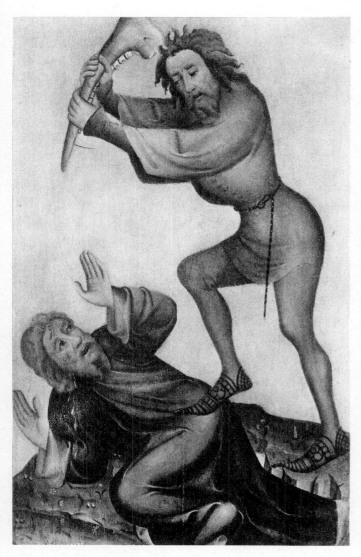

92. MASTER BERTRAM / *Cain Slaying Abel, from the St. Peter's Altar* / 1379. Kunsthalle, Hamburg. *This North German artist was influenced by Bohemian painting (compare figure 83), which in turn owed a good deal to such Italians as Tommaso da Modena. Bertram may have visited Italy in the 1390's.*

93. THE MASTER OF HEILIGENKREUZ / *The Annunciation* / About 1400. Kunsthistorisches Museum, Vienna. *Once regarded as French, this charming example of the International Style is now considered Austrian. The stone being put in place by the two tiny angels symbolizes the Coming of Christ.*

94. GOTHIC MINIATURE / *A Hawking Party, from "Queen Mary's Psalter"* / About 1320. British Museum, London. *Everyday scenes such as this delicately tinted drawing appear on the margins of Gothic manuscripts long before they are permitted to enter into sacred subjects. Compare the Romanesque hunting scenes in figure 69.*

but Simone has a wonderful eye for the little touches that bring the scene to life, such as the costumes, or the pushing and pulling of people in a crowd. Notice how he has struggled to give depth to his painting: he shows us not only the people pouring out of the city, but the city itself. The foreshortened view is a bit awkward still, but at least the picture space is no longer limited to a narrow foreground stage.

Simone Martini also became an important link between Italy and Northern Europe. He spent some years in the south of France, where he came to know French Gothic art while the French learned about the new Italian style from him (compare figure 98). By the end of the fourteenth century, exchanges of this kind had become so frequent that there was no longer much of a difference between the Italian and the Northern

95. MELCHIOR BROEDERLAM / *Presentation in the Temple and Flight into Egypt* / About 1395. Municipal Museum, Dijon. *The left half recalls the* Presentation *of 1342 by Ambrogio Lorenzetti (figure 87). Like many other artists then working for French patrons, Broederlam was a Fleming.*

96. THE MASTER OF THE PAREMENT DE NARBONNE / *The Crucifixion, with Portraits of Charles V of France and His Queen (silk hanging)* / About 1370. The Louvre, Paris. *Slender, graceful figures, subtle modeling, and softly curving drapery distinguish this masterpiece of the School of Paris.*

97. GOTHIC MINIATURE / *Hares, from "The Hunting Book of Gaston Phébus"* / About 1400. Bibliothèque Nationale, Paris. *Such lovingly observed animals are characteristic of the International Style; so is the inconsistent scale. Decorative effect still seems more important to this artist than spatial depth.*

painters. They all worked in a style which we often call "International Gothic" in order to stress their similarity of outlook.

Let us look at some pictures from this period, which lasted until about 1420. The panel in figure 95 was painted in the 1390's by Melchior Broederlam for the Duke of Burgundy. It is one of a pair of wings to fit an altar shrine (this explains its odd shape). On the left side, which shows the Christ Child being presented to the High Priest in the Temple, we see how much Broederlam has learned from the Italians about architectural space in painting (see figure 87). His temple looks a bit unreal, as if it were a sort of cage built around the figures, yet it has a good deal of depth. There is Italian influence, too, in the heavy-set figures. The soft, flowing folds of the costumes, on the other hand, remind us of the *David and*

Goliath miniature. Such ample garments were popular among the artists of that time, since they made the figures look bulkier. On the right we see the Holy Family—Mary, Joseph, and the Infant Christ—fleeing into Egypt. The softly shaded rocky slopes, the trees and flowers done with such loving care, show us how important landscape painting had become by now. For Broederlam, every detail of the natural world was worth looking at—plants, animals, and people; his charming donkey is certainly painted from life, and the Joseph makes us think of a rough, simple farmer.

The same interest in nature and the everyday world is found in the *Very Rich Book of Hours*, painted around 1415 by Paul of Limburg and his two brothers for the Duke of Berry, one of the great noblemen of France. Figure 85 shows the calendar for the month of February and the min-

98. FOLLOWER OF SIMONE MARTINI / *Scenes of Country Life (detail)* / About 1345. Palace of the Popes, Avignon. *For most of the fourteenth century Avignon, rather than Rome, was the official residence of the Popes, and thus became a gateway for Italian influences in France. In these frescoes the handling of space is very much bolder than in the work of Northern painters; the trees here serve the same depth-creating purposes as the columns in Lorenzetti's* Presentation *(figure 87).*

99. PISANELLO / *Pen Sketch of Monkeys* / About 1430-40. The Louvre, Paris. *These vivid sketches from life were probably done at a private zoo. Exotic animals had become a fashionable collector's item at the time of the International Style, especially among the princes of Northern Italy.*

iature that goes with it, telling us about country life in midwinter. And what a complete and delightful picture it is! We can almost feel the cold in the still, clear air as we watch the birds scratching for feed in the barnyard, the farmhands warming themselves at the fire, or the peasant driving

his donkey toward the village among the snowy hills in the distance.

The Birth of Christ (figure 100) was done in 1423, as part of the great altar in figure 86, by Gentile da Fabriano, an Italian who must have known the work of such Northern painters as Broederlam and the Limburg brothers. The soft shading, the loopy folds of drapery, the carefully studied animals and plants—all these are familiar to us by now; what really interests us about this panel is the lighting. In the pictures we have seen so far, we could never tell what time of day it was, or what kind of light the artist had in mind. Here for the first time we have a real night scene, and we know exactly where the light is coming from. Its main source is the Christ Child himself. He had been called "the light of the world," but until now nobody had painted this divine light as if it were a warm little campfire. Only in the years around 1400 did artists begin to realize that light is something separate from form and color and perhaps even more important, since the way we see things depends on how the light strikes them. You will read more about this discovery in our next chapter.

100. GENTILE DA FABRIANO / *The Birth of Christ* / 1423. Uffizi Gallery, Florence. *See comment above. The panel forms part of the base (or "predella") of the large altar in figure 86. Gentile had a strong influence on Pisanello. He, too, must have had the habit of sketching animals directly from life; the ox and ass in our picture show far keener observation than the human figures, whose softly flowing draperies still recall the style of the* Parement de Narbonne (figure 96).

Explorers and Discoverers

IT IS ALWAYS HARD to find out exactly when something new began. The calendar may tell us that March 21 is the first day of spring, but if we are asked about the *real* start of the new season we find we cannot pin it down as neatly as that. It is just as hard for us to say when the modern age began. We do know, however, that the Middle Ages came to an end between the fourteenth and the sixteenth centuries —in some places this happened much sooner than in others—and that the Western world entered a new era called the Renaissance. Gothic art, with its growing interest in nature and its more human approach to religious subjects, has shown us that people's outlook on life was beginning to change even earlier.

From about 1420 on, this curiosity about animals, plants, and people became a tremendous

101. HUBERT OR JAN VAN EYCK / *"The Baptism of Christ," from a Book of Hours* / About 1416-20. Museo Civico, Turin. *This landscape shows us a piece of the real world, as if a window had been cut into the page, not a toy-size world as in the February miniature by Paul of Limburg (compare figure 85). Such imaginary windows do not fit very well on a manuscript page, so the Van Eycks soon switched to panel pictures instead.*

urge to explore the whole world and everything in it. People were less and less willing to take things on faith; they wanted to ask their own questions and look for themselves. Bold seafarers set out for unknown lands and came back with reports that helped to fill in the blank spots on the map. Columbus, who discovered America in 1492, was one of these. Other men explored the field of mechanics and invented important new techniques, such as printing (about 1450) which made books so cheap that many more people could afford them than before. And the artists, too, turned into explorers. Simply by taking a fresh look at things, they discovered that the world around them was full of beauties and wonders that no one had been aware of until then. In fact, they often knew more about the workings of nature than the scientists of their day, because they had learned how to use their eyes, while the scientists still relied on medieval "book learning."

102. *Detail of Figure 108. Into this scene of Hell, which has the awful reality of a nightmare, the Van Eycks have poured all the violent action they seem to avoid everywhere else. Their realistic way of painting makes even such an "unnatural" subject, with its demons and damned, believable.*

103. JAN VAN EYCK / *Man in the Red Turban (Self-Portrait?)* 1433. National Gallery, London. *In medieval art there had been no real portraits. Now people wanted likenesses they could recognize, and painters learned how to record the things that make one person look different from another.*

Late Gothic Art

WHILE BOTH THE ITALIAN and the Northern painters broke away from the International Style at the same time, they did not do it in the same way. That is the reason we use different names for their work. Italian fifteenth-century art is called "Early Renaissance"; that of the Northern countries "Late Gothic"—even though the two styles have a good many things in common. Late Gothic painting had its start in the wealthy towns of Flanders (or Belgium, as we call it today). Let us look at the earliest of these great masters, the brothers Hubert and Jan van Eyck. One or the other of the two probably did the miniature of the Baptism of Christ (figure 101). It was painted only a year or two after the *Very Rich Book of Hours* (figure 85), and yet what a difference there is if we compare the two! The Limburg brothers were more interested in all the charming details they had collected than in the scene as a whole; their picture makes us think not of a real landscape but of a toy model where everything is just as small as they have painted it.

104. JAN VAN EYCK / *The Madonna Enthroned with the Chancellor Nicholas Rolin* / About 1434. The Louvre, Paris. *The man who ordered this painting no longer seems to need a Saint to introduce him to the Madonna (see figure 84). As large as she, he confronts her in her heavenly throne room.*

105. ROBERT CAMPIN / *Portrait of a Lady* / About 1425-30. National Gallery, London. *This master was another great explorer of the natural world at the time of the Van Eycks. He is, however, less interested in light and color than in making his forms look as solid and rounded as possible.*

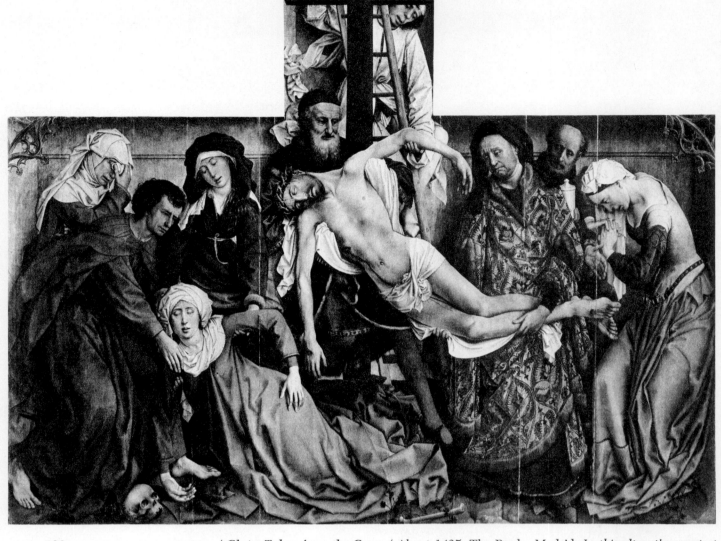

106. ROGER VAN DER WEYDEN / *Christ Taken from the Cross* / About 1435. The Prado, Madrid. *In this altar, the greatest of his youthful works, Roger shows how much he owes to the art of Robert Campin. The figures are placed not in a landscape, as we might expect, but in a shallow boxlike shrine, as carved and painted statues are. Yet their mournful faces and gestures speak to us so powerfully that we cannot help feeling ourselves part of the scene.*

In *The Baptism of Christ,* on the contrary, we are shown a piece of the real world, as if a window had been cut into the page. If we could wander about in this landscape, we would find everything to be life-size, not toy-size.

And why are we so convinced of this? Because the van Eycks had made a great discovery: what we see in real life depends on how the light is picked up by the things we are looking at, and also on the air that is between these things and ourselves. Some surfaces, such as rocks or trees, swallow up most of the light that hits them, while others make it bounce back, like a mirror. In our

107. *Detail of Figure 109. One of the two men in the mirror is the artist (his signature reads, in Latin, "Jan van Eyck was here"). He has acted as a witness, and the picture thus becomes a sort of marriage certificate.*

108. HUBERT OR JAN VAN EYCK / *The Crucifixion and The Last Judgment* / About 1420. Metropolitan Museum of Art, New York. *These panels are painted in a complicated new technique the Van Eycks had helped to develop, combining oil paint and tempera. It produces softer shades and a richer blending of tones than does tempera alone. Notice how the colors get paler in the distance until we can no longer tell where earth leaves off and sky begins.*

109.   JAN VAN EYCK / *Giovanni Arnolfini and His Bride* / 1434. National Gallery, London. *This strangely solemn couple is exchanging marriage vows before two witnesses who are reflected in the mirror (see figure 107). The scene is full of symbols disguised as everyday objects: the "sacred matrimonial bed" behind the bride, the wooden shoes (which the groom has discarded because he is standing on "holy ground"), and the "faithful" dog.*

110. ROBERT CAMPIN / *Madonna and Child* / About 1425. National Gallery, London. *Never before had the Queen of Heaven been shown in a setting as humble and homelike as this. Even her halo has become part of the everyday world; it is a round fire screen placed—as if by chance—behind her head.*

111. ROGER VAN DER WEYDEN / *Christ Appearing to His Mother* / About 1440. Metropolitan Museum of Art, New York. *The Virgin Mary has been reading her prayer book; suddenly, she feels the presence of her Son, who has risen from the grave, and turns her grief-stricken face toward him while he raises his hands as if to reassure her. Here Roger van der Weyden shows that his main concern is not the world around us but the world of human feeling within us.*

112. HUGO VAN DER GOES / *The Birth of Christ* / About 1476. Uffizi Gallery, Florence. *The altar of which this is the center panel was done in Bruges for Tommaso Portinari, a Florentine businessman, by the boldest and most dramatic Flemish master of the time. Not since Roger van der Weyden's* Christ Taken from the Cross *(figure 106) have we met such expressive power. Note especially the wonderful group of shepherds staring in breathless, wide-eyed adoration at the newborn child.*

113. JEROME BOSCH / *Portion of Central Panel of "The Garden of Worldly Delights," (detail of figure 127) / About 1500.*
The Prado, Madrid. *The theme of this altar is the vice of lust. Bosch here shows man's life on earth as an unending repetition of the Original Sin of Adam and Eve, which has doomed us all to be the prisoners of our carnal desires.*

114. JEROME BOSCH / *Portion of Right Wing of "The Garden of Worldly Delights," (detail of figure 127) / About 1500.*
The Prado, Madrid. *Bosch's Hell is a vast, nightmarish landscape. The burning town is the infernal counterpart of the City
of God, while the phantastic instruments of torture serve the punishment not only of lust but of every other vice as well.*

picture, the calm water of the river acts in this way—it reflects not only the light of the sky but the trees and the castle along the bank. Earlier artists had not bothered with mirror images. The van Eycks, on the other hand, looked upon them as an important test of the painter's power: if you could show the difference between a reflection and the real thing in your pictures, then you had learned all there was to know about light.

What the van Eycks found out about air was equally new and important. We all know that in foggy weather the air sometimes gets so "thick" that we can see only a few feet ahead. But the air is never completely clear. It always acts like a hazy screen between us and the things we are looking at; the farther away these things are, the dimmer and greyer they seem. The van Eycks were the first painters to understand this clearly. In *The Baptism of Christ*, every form is both "air-conditioned" and "light-conditioned," so that all the details fall into place just as they do in nature. What holds the scene together, then, is a new kind of order based on the behavior of light and air. It is a very strict order, which works only if the artist sticks to it in every detail. If he makes any exceptions, for the sake of story telling, or symbolic meaning, or decoration, his picture will no longer look like a window into the natural world. The van Eycks knew this, too; they have put Christ and Saint John in the best spot they could find, but the figures are still so small that we hardly notice them in the wide and wonderful landscape.

Imaginary windows don't fit very well on a manuscript page, because the letters and the ornament keep telling us that the page is something flat and white, and that we must not *try* to look through it. No wonder the van Eycks soon

AT LEFT:

115. SOUTHERN FRENCH MASTER / *The Avignon Pietà* / About 1470. The Louvre, Paris. *"Pietà" is the Italian word for "pity," but it has also come to mean the image of the dead Christ in the lap of His mother. Such pictures are intended to make us share the Virgin's grief by reminding us of the happier days when the Madonna held the Infant Christ on her lap. Although this work is entirely Late Gothic in feeling, it has a monumentality more Italian than Flemish.*

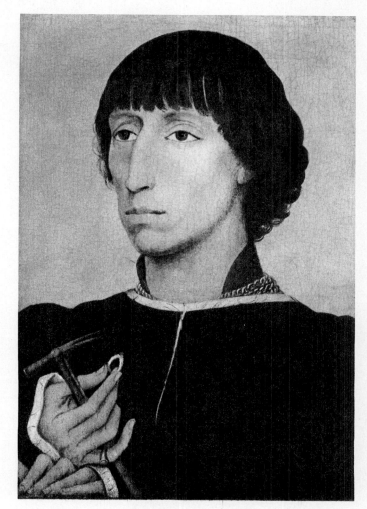

116. ROGER VAN DER WEYDEN / *Francesco d'Este* / About 1455. Metropolitan Museum of Art, New York. *Unlike Jan van Eyck, Roger stresses the main outlines of the face, instead of exact detail. His portraits have a more striking "personality" but tell us less about the way the sitter actually looked.*

117. PETRUS CHRISTUS / *Portrait of a Young Girl* / About 1465-70. Formerly State Museums Berlin. *This delicate, graceful picture shows a happy union of influences from both Jan van Eyck (with whom Petrus Christus had worked in the early 1440's) and Roger van der Weyden.*

81

switched to panel pictures, where they could "paint away" the entire surface inside the frame. You will see how successful they were in this if you turn to the two pictures of figure 108. These are painted in a complicated new technique the van Eycks had helped to develop, using one or more coats of very thin oil paint on top of tempera. The oil paint would let the colors underneath shine through, producing softer shades and a richer blending of tones. The tall and narrow shape of our panels indicates that they are the wings of a small altar; perhaps they flanked a larger center panel which has been lost.

The left-hand wing shows the Crucifixion. We seem to be looking down at it, as if we were watching it from a helicopter. This was the only way the van Eycks could tell the story of the Crucifixion clearly but without breaking the rules that made a window out of the picture. If they had put us down on the ground, they would have had to make the figures in the foreground so large that our view would have been cut off.

118. DIRC BOUTS / *The Prophet Elijah in the Wilderness* / About 1465. Altar panel in St. Peter's, Louvain. *Bouts, the gentlest and most poetic of the early Flemish painters, here shows Elijah being awakened by an angel who bids him to eat of the heaven-sent food that will sustain him "for forty days."*

119. CONRAD WITZ / *Christ Walking on the Water* / 1444. Musée d'Art et d'Histoire, Geneva. *The most remarkable part of this altar panel by a Flemish-trained Swiss painter is the background, a faithful "portrait" of the Lake of Geneva. Such a realistic setting makes Christ's miracle, too, seem very real.*

tails of the costumes, the landscape—as to the human figures. But this does not mean that they were any less religious than the painters of the Middle Ages. If you could ask them, they would probably say that God had created not only man but the rest of the natural world as well; why then should a pebble or a blade of grass be less worthy of our respect than man himself?

While the story of the Crucifixion could be told in terms of the natural world, the subject of the right-hand wing had to be made up entirely from the artist's imagination. It is the Last Judgment: at the end of time, so the prophecy goes, all the dead will rise from their graves to have their deeds judged by God. We can see them coming out of the ground and the ocean in the middle of the picture. Above them is the Lord, surrounded by the blessed souls who are being admitted to everlasting life in Paradise. Down below, the sinners who have been condemned to living death in Hell are being tortured by devilish monsters (figure 102). Into this Hell, which has the awful reality of a nightmare, the van Eycks have poured all the violent action, all the expressiveness they seem to avoid everywhere else. Here we see that the new painting rules can be applied even to a subject as "unnatural" as this; far from

120. "MASTER OF AIX" / *Jeremiah* / About 1450. Royal Museums of Fine Arts, Brussels. *Here we have another portrait imposed on a Biblical subject: this Jeremiah bears the features of King René of Anjou, who ruled in southern France at the time our picture was painted (for an altar in the town of Aix).*

121. UNKNOWN MASTER / *Coeur Reading the Inscription on the Magic Well, miniature from "The Heart Seized with Love"* / About 1460. National Library, Vienna. *This splendid manuscript was once owned by King René. Poet and painter, he composed the text and may also have done the illustrations.*

Here you can see even better than before how completely the van Eycks have mastered the light and air of the natural world. Notice how the colors get paler in the distance until we can no longer tell where the earth leaves off and the sky begins. Perhaps it will have struck you that despite the milling crowds there is hardly any drama or action in the picture. The van Eycks have paid just as much attention to all the things that are *not* part of the story—the rocks on the ground, the de-

stifling the artist's imagination, they only help him to make these fantastic demons more believable, and the pains of the damned more heart-rending, than ever before.

In medieval painting there had been no real portraits, because nobody had thought it worthwhile to record the things that make one person look different from another. Now, in the fifteenth century, people wanted portraits they could recognize, such as the *Man in the Red Turban* (figure 103), which was done by Jan van Eyck in 1433. The sitter may very well be the artist himself (there is a slight strain about the eyes, as if the man were gazing into a mirror). Here again we marvel at the rich play of light and shade, which gives us the "feel" of every surface, from the stubble of beard on the chin to the crinkly fabric of the turban. Yet we learn very little about the character of this man; his face is as calm as the landscape in *The Baptism of Christ*.

The picture in figure 111 dates from about 1440. It is the work of another great Flemish master, Roger van der Weyden, who had been strongly influenced by the van Eycks. Roger's main concern, however, was not the world around us but the world within us—he was the great explorer of human feelings in religious art. Our panel shows Christ appearing to His mother after He had risen from the grave. The Virgin Mary has been reading her prayerbook; suddenly, she feels the presence of her son and turns her grief-stricken face toward him, while he raises his hands as if to reassure her. There is an air of deep

122. THE MASTER OF MOULINS / *A Young Princess* / About 1490. Collection Robert Lehman, New York. *This important French artist was strongly influenced by Hugo van der Goes (see figure 112). The hint of sadness in the little girl's face might be an echo of the style of Roger van der Weyden.*

123. JEAN FOUQUET / *Etienne Chevalier and St. Stephen* / About 1450. Formerly State Museums, Berlin. *Fouquet, like so many French painters, was much impressed with Italian art. The architecture in this picture is Italian, and the figures, too, have an Italian strength and simplicity.*

124. MICHAEL PACHER / *The Four Latin Fathers (Jerome, Augustine, Gregory, and Ambrose) / About 1483.* Pinakothek, Munich. *This master from the Austrian Tirol was both a painter and a wood carver; his figures here actually look like statues in richly decorated niches. Their sharp-edged, spiky forms are characteristically Late Gothic, but Pacher's mastery of perspective foreshortening betrays the influence of North Italian painting (compare Mantegna, figure 146).*

sadness and suffering about these two figures that immediately touches our heart, because their feelings seem as real to us as the painted architecture or the fine, airy landscape in the background. The setting may strike you at first as rather too elaborate, but if you study it more closely you will find that almost every detail has a meaning related to the main figures: the stone carvings on the arched portal tell us about other events in the life of the Virgin, and in the distance we see Christ leaving His tomb while the soldiers on guard are asleep. This is perhaps the most astonishing thing about Late Gothic painting—how the natural world is

125. HANS MEMLING / *Portrait of an Italian / About 1485.* Royal Museum of Fine Arts, Antwerp. *Memling, working in Bruges, must have known not only Italians but Italian pictures, too. From them he learned how to place this sitter against an open landscape and to give him the kind of self-assurance we usually miss in Flemish portraits.*

126. GEERTGEN TOT SINT JANS / *The Birth of Christ* / About 1490. National Gallery, London. *This wonderfully gentle night-time scene, by a fellow countryman of Jerome Bosch, recalls the "discovery of light" at the time of the International Gothic Style around 1400 (compare figure 100).*

made to contain the world of the spirit in such a way that the two actually become one.

It was Roger who made the new Flemish style known all over Northern Europe. Among the countless artists from neighboring countries who felt his influence there was a Frenchman whose name has been forgotten; we know only a single work by his hand, but that picture is one of the most famous in all of Late Gothic painting (figure 115). We call it *The Avignon Pietà*, since it was found near Avignon, in the south of France. "Pietà" is the Italian word for "pity," but it also has come to mean the image of the dead Christ in the lap of His mother. In our picture the Madonna is flanked by Saint John and Saint Mary Magdalene. The figure kneeling on the left is the man who ordered the painting.

The *Pietà* does not tell a story; it is meant, rather, to make us share the silent grief of the Virgin by reminding us that a younger and hap-

127. JEROME BOSCH / *The Garden of Worldly Delights* / About 1500. The Prado, Madrid. *The three panels are so densely filled with detail that their full beauty and imaginative power can be grasped only at close range (see figures 113, 114). The entire work demands to be "read" slowly, like a long religious poem such as Dante's* Divine Comedy, *and its meaning is just as complex. Bosch must have worked from a very exact plan, even though many of his images are hard to decipher today.*

pier Madonna once held the Infant Christ on her lap in much the same way. There are many things in our picture that recall Roger van der Weyden, but its design is very much simpler, and in this simplicity lies its strength. It has a "bigness" about it that makes us think of Giotto. And we may not be altogether wrong: Avignon is closer to Italy than to Flanders, so that our master might well have been touched by Italian art even though his *Pietà* remains entirely Late Gothic in feeling.

At the end of the century, the most important French painter was again an artist of uncertain name; we call him the "Master of Moulins." The young princess (figure 122) whose picture he painted about 1490 could not have been more than ten years old. We can tell by her elegant costume and by the castle in the background that she must be somebody important. Fortunately, our painter has not been overawed by her high rank; he shows her as a delicate and gentle little girl, perhaps a bit too serious for one so young. Or could it be that the hint of sadness in her face is just another echo of the style of Roger van der Weyden?

But let us return once more to the Netherlands. Figure 128 was painted by Jerome Bosch, an extraordinary Dutch master who seems closer to the van Eycks than to Roger van der Weyden. Its soft, airy background will remind you of *The Baptism of Christ,* and the jerky gestures and excited expressions of the figures have something in common with the violent Hell scene of *The Last Judgment.* Bosch, too, shows us a kind of hell, but it is a hell of man's own making. His painting was inspired by a popular book, *The Ship of Fools.* It tells us that the world is full of silly people who float through life as if it were a pleasure trip instead of preparing for the day when God will judge their deeds on earth. And yet they don't seem at all happy, despite their frantic merrymaking: in their greed they overeat, get drunk, and fight, while their ship is drifting toward dangerous waters. We can be quite sure that the journey will come to no good end.

128. JEROME BOSCH / *The Ship of Fools* / About 1500. The Louvre, Paris. *The message here is a good deal easier to grasp than in the great altar on the opposite page, but the same gloomy view of human nature can be seen in both works. Sin, to Bosch, was clearly far more real than Salvation.*

The Early Renaissance in Italy

WE MAY LAUGH at the Punch-and-Judy antics of Bosch's figures, but actually they show us a grim, even hopeless, view of human nature and of man's place in the world (compare figures 113, 114). As the Middle Ages came to an end in Northern Europe, there were many people who felt as Bosch did—lost, frightened, longing for a new faith to take the place of the old. But in Italy this mood was not so general. Many Italians welcomed the new era as a "rebirth," for that is what the word "Renaissance" means and they were the ones who coined it. It was, they said, the rebirth of those powers of the human mind that had created the glories of Greece and Rome. The thousand years since the death of Classical Antiquity they called the Middle Ages, the "time in-between," when little of importance had been done in the arts. And the style that had come into Italy from the North they labeled Gothic, because they disliked it so. (The Goths were one of the tribes that had helped to destroy the Roman Empire.) Today we no longer despise the Middle Ages or Gothic art, although we still use the same words.

Of course the Italians did not try to turn themselves into Classical Romans pure and simple. They certainly had no idea of giving up the Christian faith. Still, they believed we ought to rely more on ourselves, instead of depending on God for everything. "Since the Lord has given us such remarkable powers of mind, and such a beautiful world to live in," they asked, "is it not our duty to make full use of these gifts?" The Ancients, they felt, had in many ways done a better job of this than anybody else, so there was a lot to be learned from them. But they thought of themselves as the rivals of Classical Antiquity, not as mere imitators; they took from it what they needed, and left the rest.

Florence, the home town of Giotto, was the birthplace of Renaissance art. In painting, the

129. FRA FILIPPO LIPPI / *Madonna and Child Enthroned* / 1437. National Museum, Tarquinia, Italy. *This panel makes an interesting comparison with the work on the opposite page. The powerful bodies and perspective foreshortening tell us that Fra Filippo was an enthusiastic follower of Masaccio.*

130. MASACCIO / *Madonna and Child with Angels* / 1426. National Gallery, London. *The ancestry of this altar panel can be traced back to Giotto and beyond. The gold background, too, is traditional, but otherwise the picture shows all the revolutionary qualities of Masaccio's Trinity fresco (figure 138).*

131. FRA ANGELICO AND FRA FILIPPO LIPPI / *The Adoration of the Magi* / About 1445. National Gallery of Art, Washington, D. C. (Samuel H. Kress Collection.) *There is still a good deal of the picturesque charm of the International Gothic Style in this panel, with its colorful crowds and well-observed animals. Only a few of the figures betray the influence of Masaccio.*

132. ANDREA DEL CASTAGNO / *The Victorious David* / About 1450-55. National Gallery of Art, Washington, D. C. (Widener Collection.) *This lean, energetic young hero has been "translated" from an ancient statue (see figure 143). Castagno's interest in movement and action points to an important new trend in Early Renaissance art.*

133. PIERO DELLA FRANCESCA / *The Battle of Constantine* (detail) / About 1460. San Francesco, Arezzo. Constantine, the first Christian Emperor of Rome, is holding a small white cross; his pagan enemies (not shown in our plate) flee without a fight from this symbol of the new faith. The subject of the picture, then, is a miracle rather than an ordinary battle, and the firmness and clarity of Piero's forms emphasize its solemn character.

134. ANDREA MANTEGNA / The Crucifixion / 1456-59. The Louvre, Paris. The rich landscape background of this panel, by the greatest Early Renaissance painter of Northern Italy, recalls that of the Van Eyck Crucifixion in figure 108. But the perspective is thoroughly Italian, and so are the tense, vigorous bodies. Mantegna's expressive power can be felt especially in the frozen grief of the women.

135.   GIOVANNI BELLINI / St. Francis in Ecstasy / About 1485. The Frick Collection, New York. *In this early masterpiece of landscape painting, the artist makes us share the mystic rapture of St. Francis before the beauty of the visible world. Note that the Saint has taken off his shoes which are in the lower right-hand corner, since he is standing on holy ground (like Giovanni Arnolfini in figure 109).*

136. DOMENICO GHIRLANDAIO / *An Old Man and His Grandson* / About 1480. The Louvre, Paris. *After the middle of the fifteenth century, the Italians no longer preferred strict profile portraits. Ghirlandaio admired the detailed realism of the Flemish masters, but the human warmth and tenderness of his picture were at that time quite beyond any Northern painter.*

137. SANDRO BOTTICELLI / The Birth of Venus / About 1480. Uffizi Gallery, Florence. The pose of this Venus, like that of Castagno's David, is modeled after an ancient statue. Otherwise, however, the two have little in common. The goddess of love seems as frail and fleeting as a dream; born of the sea, she symbolizes the "rebirth of mankind" which was the great hope of the Renaissance.

new style sprang from the work of Masaccio, a youthful genius who died about 1428 when he was barely twenty-eight years old. We have only a few pictures by his hand, but these show us that he was an even bolder explorer than the van Eycks. The fresco of *The Holy Trinity with Saint John and Saint Mary* (figure 138) owes nothing to the International Style; we can tell from the monumental, bulky figures, and the "bigness" of the design as a whole, that Masaccio has gone back a full hundred years to the style of Giotto. And yet we find a great difference between the two: Giotto's figures remind us of carved stones, while Masaccio's seem to be made of flesh and blood. But then Giotto was, after all, a medieval artist. When he painted a human figure, he thought only of what it would tell us, or how it would make us feel; he was not interested in putting it together the way such figures are put together in real life. Masaccio, on the other hand,

138. MASACCIO / *The Holy Trinity with St. John, St. Mary, and Two Donors* / About 1425. Santa Maria Novella, Florence. *Note how the artist has adjusted the perspective to a beholder whose eyes are on a level with the bottom edge of the fresco, about five feet above the floor of the church.*

139. PAOLO UCCELLO / *The Battle of San Romano* / About 1455. National Gallery, London. *The panel is one of a set of three commemorating a victory won by the Florentine forces in 1432. Here every form, even the landscape, shows the clarity and order—but also the strange "frozen" quality—that reflect the artist's enthusiasm for perspective. Uccello sees the world in terms of solid geometry rather than of light and color. Compare* The Battle of Issus, *figure 44.*

140. DOMENICO VENEZIANO / *Madonna and Saints* / About 1445. Uffizi Gallery, Florence. *This altar panel is as remarkable for its brilliant, sunlit colors as for the harmony of its design. St. John, the second figure from the left, looks directly at the beholder as he points to the Christ Child.*

141. PIERO DELLA FRANCESCA / *Illustrations from the Treatise "De Prospectiva Pingendi"* / About 1480. Biblioteca Palatina, Parma. *View of a cube, with all six sides foreshortened, and the head of a man seen in profile, from above, and from below. See page 101 for a more detailed explanation.*

tried to do exactly that. We might say that he wanted to do Giotto over again, but from nature. You will see what this means if you look, for example, at the Saint John and Saint Mary. Although they are wrapped in heavy cloaks, we can feel the shape of their bodies under the drapery, and this is something we haven't been able to do since we looked at the Roman mural in figure 34. Masaccio had never seen anything like that, but he worked in much the same way as the Ancient painters: he thought of the bodies of his figures first, and then put the clothes on them separately. In order to do that, however, he had to find out

how clothes behave—what kinds of folds you get when you pull a cloak around your shoulders, or bunch it over your arm, or let it hang to the floor. This is why the draperies in the *Trinity* fresco have the natural flow of real cloth.

But Masaccio also needed to know about the forms underneath the drapery; and that was very much more difficult, for it meant that he suddenly had to relearn everything the Ancients had discovered (and the Middle Ages had forgotten) about the workings of the human body. A look at his Christ on the cross will tell you how amazingly well he succeeded in this. The most remarkable thing about the figure is not just that every bone, every muscle is in the right place; it's the way all these details fit together. Masaccio realized that the body is like a complicated and finely adjusted machine, which will run only if all the parts are in working order. That is why all his figures look so strong and full of energy. If you turn back for a moment to the *Christ* of Roger van der Weyden (figure 111), you will find that there, too, the details are well observed, but the "working order" is missing; the joints seem stiff, the muscles weak, and the whole body makes us think of a wooden puppet dangling from invisible strings instead of standing firmly on the ground. (At least that is what Masaccio would have thought.) Late Gothic

figures never look as if they could do anything by themselves; Early Renaissance ones do, even when they are standing, or hanging from a cross.

The *Trinity* fresco also shows us another great discovery. Its architectural background is foreshortened according to a set of rules which we call scientific perspective. Earlier painters had used foreshortening of a sort, too, but they had done so in hit-or-miss fashion, without any rules to guide them. Only scientific perspective made it possible to get a clear and consistent picture of things in space, since it was based on mathematics and the exact measuring of angles and distances. In themselves, the new rules had nothing to do with art or imagination, and yet they were dis-

142. PIERO DELLA FRANCESCA / *The Resurrection* / About 1460. Picture Gallery, Borgo San Sepolcro. *This Christ, unrivaled in Early Renaissance art, has a body as strong and beautiful as that of a classical god, while his gaze recalls the spiritual intensity of the Byzantine Christ at Cefalù (figure 64). To Piero, the miracle of the Resurrection is not a spectacular drama but an event as awesomely simple and direct as the rising of the sun in the stillness of early morning.*

143. *Ancient Statue of a Fleeing Man* / Uffizi Gallery, Florence. *Compare figure 132 and see comment on page 103.*

covered by artists, rather than by scientists, because the artists of the Early Renaissance were so eager to get a firmer grip on the shapes of the natural world.

While Masaccio's bold new style was greatly admired by his fellow artists, it took some time for his ideas to be fully understood. In many other Florentine pictures we can find echoes of the International Style as late as the middle of the fifteenth century. The round panel in figure 131, begun by Fra Angelico and finished by Fra Filippo Lippi about 1445, is of this kind. It shows the Magi—the three wise men or kings from the East—kneeling in adoration before the Madonna and Child. They are accompanied by countless servants and animals, as befits their great wealth. You see this crowd pouring through the city gate on

the left, but there seems to be no end to them, for the people coming down the mountain in the background still belong to the same vast train. All this makes a wonderfully gay and colorful scene but we miss the order, the clarity and simplicity of Masaccio. Just take a look at the buildings—their lines are slanted in a curious, mixed-up way, without regard to scientific perspective. And the graceful peacock on the roof of the barn in the middle of the picture is much too big. On the other hand, we can feel the influence of Masaccio in the dignified Joseph standing next to the Madonna, and in the lively nudes near the city gate.

Among the painters who were willing to follow Masaccio all the way, the greatest was Piero della Francesca. In figure 133 you see part of a mural he did about 1460 in the town of Arezzo, to the

144. ANTONIO POLLAIUOLO / *The Rape of Deianira* / About 1475. Yale University Art Gallery, New Haven, Connecticut. *Hercules, on the right, is shooting at the centaur Nessus, who is abducting his wife. Pollaiuolo's figures, muscular yet graceful, betray the influence of Andrea del Castagno (compare figure 132). Here, strenuous movement and action have replaced the severe, monumental forms of the pioneers of perspective such as Masaccio, Uccello, or Piero della Francesca.*

south of Florence. It shows the Roman Emperor Constantine, who has just become a Christian, at the head of his army; he is holding up a small white cross for his pagan enemies to see, and so great is the power of this symbol of faith that they flee without a fight. (They fill the right-hand half of the picture, not shown in our plate.) Piero has not given his soldiers the kind of costumes and arms they actually used in Constantine's day, even though he could have found out about these things by studying Roman art if he had wanted to. Yet every shape in the painting has so much firmness and clarity that we may well compare Piero's style to the finest Classical works of the Ancients. No other painter ever came as close as he did to the monumental spirit of Masaccio.

Perhaps it will help you to understand the secret of Piero's greatness if you take a look at figure 141, which shows you some illustrations from a famous book he wrote on the rules of perspective for painters. While these are really scientific drawings and not meant to be works of art, they do tell us something about how Piero studied the forms he put into his own pictures. At the top you see a cube, in foreshortened view; this is taken from one of the earlier chapters, which deal with mathematical shapes because they are easier to take apart than the shapes of the natural world. Below, there is the head of a man, seen from the side, from above, and from below. The last two drawings also show the odd outlines you would get if you were to slice through the head at various levels, and the thin straight lines help you to line up the three views with each other. If you now turn to *The Battle of Constantine* once more and look at the rearing white horse on the left, for example, you can see that Piero must have studied its shape by this same mathematical method. But Piero also had a splendid feeling for

145. *Detail of Figure 144. The fine airy landscape in the background of Pollaiuolo's panel—a view of the countryside around the city of Florence—recalls similar vistas by the great Flemish masters (compare figure 104). Northern painting was much admired among Florentine artists at this time.*

146. ANDREA MANTEGNA / *St. James Led to His Execution* / About 1455. Ovetari Chapel, Church of the Eremitani, Padua. *This fresco reveals the artist's tense, expressive style as well as his passionate interest in ancient Roman monuments. For the bold "worm's-eye" perspective, compare figure 138.*

147. ANTONELLO DA MESSINA / *The Crucifixion* / 1475. Royal Museum of Fine Arts, Antwerp. *Antonello, although a Sicilian, was by far the most "Flemish" in style and painting technique among the Italian masters of his time. He must have had close contact with a follower of Jan van Eyck (Petrus Christus?).*

ing. Still, our painters *did* learn from Classical art, by taking ideas from ancient sculpture and fitting them into their own work. In figure 132 you see how this could be done. It shows the victorious David, painted on a leather shield by Andrea del Castagno soon after 1450. While such a shield was meant only for display, not for actual fighting, its owner wanted everybody to know that he would face his enemies as bravely as David. In our picture, David has already won out over Goliath, but he is again wielding his sling and challenging all comers. Perhaps you will remember the Gothic miniature (figure 74) where David appears as a mere child who could never have done what he did if his hands had not been guided by the Lord Himself. That was the medieval way of looking at the story. Castagno obviously thought otherwise: to him, David was an athletic young man whose courage came from God but whose strength and skill were his own.

148. ANDREA MANTEGNA / *Portion of a Ceiling Fresco* / About 1470. Ducal Palace, Mantua. *Here Mantegna, in a lighter vein, has used his mastery of perspective to "open up" the center of the ceiling, so that we feel observed by indiscreet servant girls and threatened by a precariously placed flowerpot.*

design and great power of expression, otherwise our picture would not look so vigorously alive. And he understood the new order of light and air which we first found in the works of the van Eycks. The brisk, clear morning air, the sunlight glistening on the shiny armor—these tell us as much as the forms themselves about the sense of adventure, the wonderful self-confidence of the age of "rebirth."

So far we have seen no direct influence of Classical art on the painters of the Early Renaissance. This is not really so strange: the fifteenth century knew almost nothing about ancient paint-

102

This is why he turned to Classical sculpture for help, since the Ancients had known a great deal more about the human body in action than he did. The statue in figure 143 will show you how Castagno has followed the outlines of his ancient model even to the windblown drapery. Curiously enough, however, the Classical figure is not a hero at all; in fact, he is running away and his hand is raised for protection. Castagno has changed the meaning of the pose from fear to defiance

Castagno's David seems much less solid and bulky than the figures of Masaccio or Piero della Francesca. His forms are more graceful, tense, and nervous. We find a similar style in the dramatic Crucifixion panel (figure 134) by Andrea Mantegna, who was one of the first, and also the greatest, of the Early Renaissance masters in North Italy. He came from the town of Padua, near Venice, and it is likely that he was influenced by Castagno, who had done some murals in Ven-

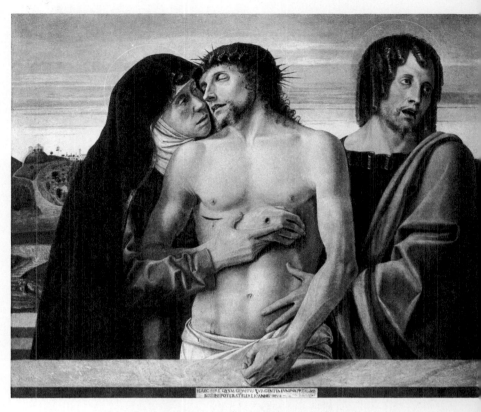

149. GIOVANNI BELLINI / *The Dead Christ between St. Mary and St. John* / About 1480. Brera Gallery, Milan. *In this picture we find the influence of both Montegna (who was Bellini's brother-in-law) and Antonello da Messina. The gentle depth of feeling, however, is Bellini's very own.*

150. GENTILE BELLINI / *Corpus Christi Procession on St. Mark's Square* / 1496. Academy, Venice. *Gentile, although less great an artist than his brother Giovanni, has left us some splendid records of the pageantry of Venetian life. This procession, against the backdrop of the richly decorated façade of St. Mark's, with its Byzantine domes glistening in the sunlight, is a colorful spectacle indeed. The setting of the scene still looks much the same today.*

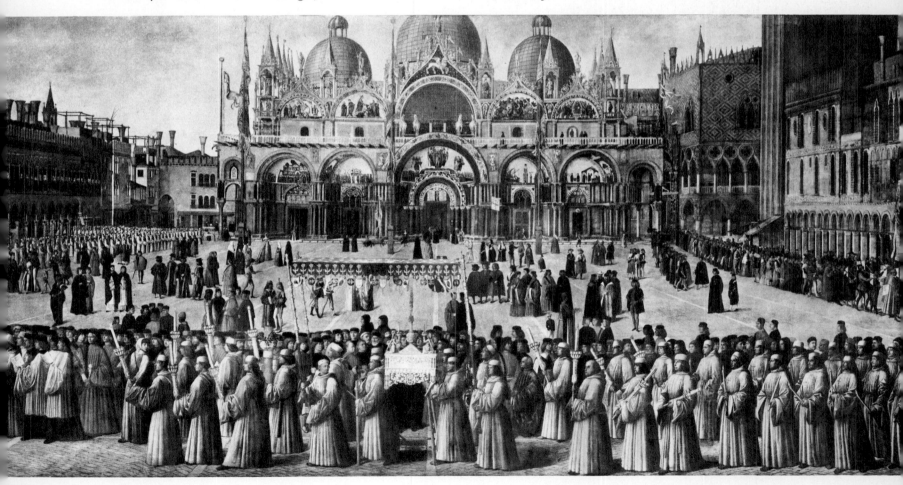

ice during Mantegna's youth. His figures look even more strained than the *David;* the tautly stretched Christ and the mourning group under the cross to the left are so intensely expressive that they make us think of Roger van der Weyden and *The Avignon Pietà,* while the deep, airy background landscape reminds us of the van Eyck *Crucifixion* in figure 108. As a North Italian, Mantegna understood Late Gothic painting better than the Florentine masters did, but he also was a keen student of scientific perspective. Instead of letting us float above the scene, the way the van Eycks had done, he places us on a level with the figures in the picture, so that we are far more directly involved with the tragic story before our eyes.

151. FLORENTINE MASTER / *A Young Lady* / About 1460. Formerly State Museums, Berlin. *Many Italians of the Early Renaissance preferred the cameo-like precision and elegance of strict profile portraits such as this, to the three-quarter view with its more subtle shadings of character.*

152. GIOVANNI BELLINI / *Doge Leonardo Loredano* / About 1501. National Gallery, London. *In this formal portrait of the head of the Venetian Republic, the rigid pose and the elaborate costume emphasize the dignity of the sitter's rank, yet the face is alive with individual character.*

153. MELOZZO DA FORLI / *Sixtus IV and His Familiars* / About 1477. Vatican Gallery, Rome. *Kneeling before the Pope is the humanist Platina, head of the Vatican Library. Melozzo's style combines the monumental spirit of his teacher Piero della Francesca with the expressive force of Mantegna.*

154. DOMENICO GHIRLANDAIO / *The Birth of the Virgin* / About 1490. Santa Maria Novella, Florence. *The cycle of which this fresco forms a part includes many scenes that seem to be taken directly from the life of the artist's own time. The leisurely, detailed storytelling art of Ghirlandaio is the counterpart of Gentile Bellini's in Venice (compare figure 150). Among the group of lady visitors in the foreground we find several fine portrait heads.*

The difference between Late Gothic and Early Renaissance art shows up particularly well in portrait painting. We are not sure who did the elegant young lady in figure 151—an important Florentine master, certainly, of the time around 1460—nor do we know her name, but she must have been one of the famous beauties of her day, and the picture is quite frankly meant to make us admire her. One might almost call her a very refined pin-up girl, who knows her own good looks and is proud of them. Our artist has given her such a self-assured air that the *Young Princess* of the Master of Moulins (figure 122) seems downright timid by comparison.

In figure 136 you see another kind of portrait. This picture of an old man and his grandchild was probably ordered by the little boy's father, and for much the same reason that we today take family snapshots—to remind us of people we love. Domenico Ghirlandaio, who painted it in Florence about 1480, admired the realistic style of the Flemish masters. He has recorded the wrinkles, the warts, the diseased nose of the old man exactly as he saw them. But there is also something here that we don't find in Late Gothic portraits: the picture tells us not only what the old man looked like but what kind of a person he was. We would never think of comparing this face to a landscape (as we did with *The Man in the Red Turban* by Jan van Eyck in figure 103), because it is alive with the glow of love and tenderness. And the little boy looks up to his grandfather so trustingly that we, too, no longer mind the ugly, swollen nose and think only of the warm human feeling with which

155. SANDRO BOTTICELLI / *Primavera* / About 1478. Uffizi Gallery, Florence. *This allegory of springtime, with its wealth of allusions to classical literature and mythology, was designed for the refined taste of a small circle. We, too, enjoy the delicate poetic air of the picture, even if we no longer understand the meaning of every detail. The weightless figures moving with unearthly grace against a background of dark foliage, suggest the decorative pattern of a tapestry.*

the artist has endowed these two people.

Our next pictures bring us back once more to the idea of the "rebirth of antiquity," since their subjects are taken from the religion of the Greeks and Romans. Needless to say, the Church frowned on such pagan stories, and yet we find more and more of them toward the end of the fifteenth century. Needless to say, the artists who painted them, and the patrons who owned them, did not actually believe in the ancient gods. Sandro Botticelli, for instance, who did the famous *Birth of*

156. *Venus, Vulcan, Cupid, and the Three Graces* / From a French Manuscript of about 1480. Bibliothèque Nationale, Paris. *Here a Late Gothic artist has attempted to picture the unfamiliar world of pagan mythology. Compare the delightfully awkward results with the elegance and ease of Botticelli.*

Venus in figure 137, was a deeply religious man; neither he nor anybody else in Florence accepted the goddess of love as "real" the way they accepted Christ or the Madonna. If we want to understand this picture, we must think of it as a sort of poetic dream where Venus, born of the sea like a shimmering pearl, stands for that "rebirth of mankind" which was the great hope of the Renaissance. And she looks as frail as a dream, too—pale, delicate, without weight or bulk, she bends like a reed in the gentle breeze from the mouths of the two wind gods on the left. How solid and powerful the David of Castagno seems as against these gossamer creatures!

Another "pagan" picture (figure 157), painted by Piero di Cosimo, is the very opposite of Botticelli's *Venus:* down-to-earth, gay, and colorful. Here we see Bacchus, the god of wine, and his goat-footed companions, the satyrs, at a sort of picnic on a sunny summer afternoon. The god himself, looking slightly tipsy, stands on the right with his lady love, Ariadne, but most of the satyrs pay little attention to him; instead, they busy themselves about the old willow tree in the center of the scene. If you look closely, you will find that they are all making as much noise as they can by banging their pots and pans, for they have discovered a swarm of bees, and the noise will make the bees settle in a cluster on one of the branches of the tree. The satyrs want to collect the honey, from which they will make a kind of wine. Piero di Cosimo tells us all this as if Bacchus and the satyrs were just plain friendly country folk. And that, in a way, is what he really believed. The ancient gods, he thought, were actually people who had lived in the early days of mankind, before history began. The discovery of honey must have been very important to these simple people;

157. PIERO DI COSIMO / *The Discovery of Honey* / About 1498. Worcester Art Museum, Massachusetts. *Piero, although a Florentine, seems more akin in some ways to the Late Gothic miniature of figure 156 than to Botticelli in his approach to classical subject matter. He was, in fact, a great admirer of Flemish painting. But perhaps it would be more accurate to say that he wanted to give Bacchus and the satyrs the same air of everyday reality as in Ghirlandaio (compare figure 154).*

158. LUCA SIGNORELLI / *The Damned Cast into Hell* / About 1500. Cathedral, Orvieto. *This fresco, one of the crowning achievements of the Early Renaissance, echoes both the discipline of Piero della Francesca and the physical energy of Pollaiuolo. In contrast to the nightmarish tortures and grotesque monsters of Late Gothic art (figures 102, 114), Signorelli does not rob the Damned of their dignity as human beings; he depicts their fate as a tragedy, rather than as a horror story.*

it was, after all, a first step toward civilization. That is why they honored the memory of the first beekeepers by making gods out of them. Thus Bacchus and his companions in our picture stand for "man's slow progress through the ages"—a less poetic idea than Botticelli's dream of "mankind reborn," but a far more realistic one. Piero's style, too, is more realistic. Like Ghirlandaio, he was interested in Flemish painting; the fine airy landscape background of his picture shows this North-

ern influence particularly well. But the landscape is not merely pleasant to look at, it also helps to drive home the "lesson" of the story. The rough, barren hill on the right stands for the primitive early days of man's life on earth, while the one on the left, with its little town and steeple, tells us of the blessings of civilized living. Thus the entire panel reflects the hopeful outlook of the Early Renaissance.

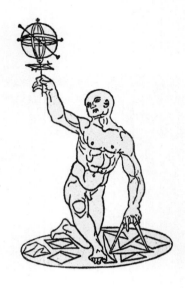

The Age of Genius

As we enter the sixteenth century, we almost come to feel that the idea of "rebirth" was more than an idle dream. There were so many great men that they seemed like a new race of giants, gifted with creative powers such as the human mind had never known before. At first glance, this Age of Genius may strike us as a much happier era than our own troubled times. In actual fact, however, it would be hard to find a century more unstable, more difficult to live in, than the sixteenth. It was a time of never-ending conflicts, both of arms and of ideas, for the discoveries of the previous hundred years had by now thoroughly upset the old order of things everywhere. The wealth of America and of other new-found lands across the ocean started a scramble for power among the nations of Western Europe, with colonies and overseas trade as the stakes. These wars, in turn, were all mixed up with the great religious crisis, which disturbed people more than anything else that happened during those trying days. In the countries north of the Alps, great reformers such as Martin Luther and John Calvin declared themselves independent of the authority of the Pope and established Protestant Churches of their own. The fact that they found so many followers shows that there was a

need for this Reformation of faith; but the struggle between the two opposing camps was so cruel and bloody that it made quite a few people lose their trust in religion altogether.

How, we may wonder, could great masterpieces of art be created in the midst of all this turmoil? It is indeed difficult to say why we find so many men of genius in some periods, and so few in others. Still, let us keep in mind that the sixteenth century was also an age of challenge, when old barriers were breaking down and new horizons were opening up everywhere. Perhaps this gave men a better chance to stretch their minds, and to accomplish great things, than they could have found in a more orderly world.

159. LEONARDO DA VINCI / *Sketch of a Flying Machine* / About 1495. Institut de France, Paris. *The pilot moves the four wings by means of pulleys. Leonardo was the first to find a rational approach to this age-old dream of man. He later realized that our muscles are too weak for powered flight and proposed gliders instead.*

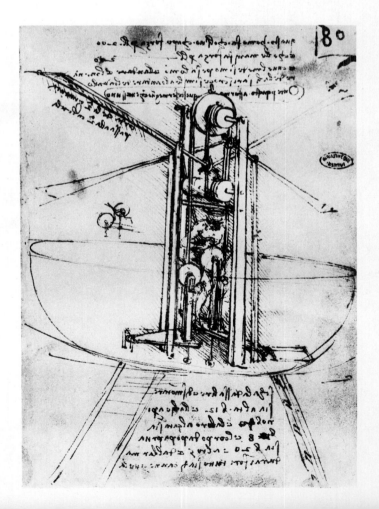

The High Renaissance in Italy

161. LEONARDO DA VINCI / *The Virgin of the Rocks* / About 1485. The Louvre, Paris. *This is the earliest of the pictures Leonardo is known to have completed. The dusky half-light of the grotto blends the colors and softens the outlines so that they appear as if seen through a thin veil of mist.*

AMONG THE ARTISTS of this time, three are so famous that their names have become household words: Leonardo da Vinci, Michelangelo, and Raphael. They lived during the High Renaissance in Italy, a glorious period at the beginning of the century that was like the Classical Age of Ancient Greece. Leonardo da Vinci came closer to being an all-around genius than any other man in history; he thought of himself first and foremost as an artist, but his notebooks and drawings show that his idea of art took in a lot of things that we would call natural science today. He believed so strongly in the eye as the perfect instrument for exploring the natural world that to see and to know meant the same to him. Artists, he said, are the best scientists; not only do they observe things better than other people—they think about what they see, and then tell the rest of us about it in pictures. Nowadays scientists prefer to put their knowledge into words (they have had to invent a great many new ones for this purpose), but in the Renaissance a good picture was still "worth a thousand words."

Leonardo's own drawings are so clear and full of life that even if we don't know how to read his notes we can grasp his ideas by just looking. No matter what we may be particularly interested in, we are apt to find that Leonardo was interested in it, too. He was the first man to design flying machines (figure 159) and to make exact pictures of the inside of the human body (figure 173),

among many other things. His scientific mind can also be seen at work in one of the studies he did for a big battle picture about 1504 (figure 162). The point of the drawing is that animals and men have the same sort of expression on their faces when they are moved by the same strong emotion.

160. *Detail of Figure 161. The angel turns toward us with a tender smile, as if he had just become aware of our presence. By this glance (and his pointing gesture) he asks us to follow the example of the Infant St. John in adoring the Christ Child.*

162. LEONARDO DA VINCI / *Sketches for the "Battle of Anghiari"* / About 1504. Royal Library, Windsor Castle. (Crown copyright reserved.) *Leonardo became interested in the facial expressions of animals because he wanted the horses, too, to fight each other in his battle scene, along with the men.*

In this case it is rage, and the man, the lion, and the horses are all baring their teeth and snarling. Here we really have one of the earliest studies in psychology, which we like to think is something very modern.

Leonardo never finished the battle scene, but during those same years he did his most famous painting, the *Mona Lisa* (figure 164). If we compare it with earlier portraits (figures 136, 151), we will see immediately that Leonardo's seems more complete, more rounded. The figure, the low wall behind her, and the distant landscape are no longer set off against each other as separate things; the picture as a whole has now become more important than any of its parts. This new harmony was one of the aims of the High Renaissance.

163. PETER PAUL RUBENS / *Drawing after Leonardo's cartoon for the "Battle of Anghiari"* / About 1605. The Louvre, Paris. *These horsemen fighting for the battle standard were the center of Leonardo's composition. The violence of the action is particularly striking when compared with the "slow-motion" battles of Uccello (figure 139). Yet even here Leonardo aims at harmony of form; the explosive energy of the figures remains firmly within the lozenge-shaped outline of the design.*

164. LEONARDO DA VINCI / *Mona Lisa* / About 1505. The Louvre, Paris. *See comment on opposite page. An uncanny, haunting quality seizes the imagination of every beholder, however prejudiced. The* Mona Lisa *simply won't leave us alone. This, rather than the well-advertised smile, is its real mystery.*

HIEREMIAS

165. MICHELANGELO / "The Prophet Jeremiah," from the Sistine Ceiling / 1508-1512. Vatican, Rome. *The stormy temper of Michelangelo's genius is summed up in this brooding figure, whose tremendous energy seems turned inward upon the dark thoughts that fill his mind. See figure 175 for a view of the interior of the chapel.*

166. RAPHAEL / *Madonna with the Infant Christ and the Infant St. John* / 1507. The Louvre, Paris.
While he was influenced by both Leonardo and Michelangelo, Raphael here appears far closer to the
calm beauty of the Mona Lisa than to the melancholy gloom of the Jeremiah.

167. GIORGIONE / *The Concert / About 1510. The Louvre, Paris. Giorgione's picture might be termed a worldly, High Renaissance counterpart of Giovanni Bellini's St. Francis (figure 135). Here, too, the artist is absorbed in re-creating, through light and color, the beauty of a "golden moment" when man is completely attuned to the poetic mood of nature.*

168. TITIAN / The Entombment of Christ / About 1525. The Louvre, Paris. The early work of Titian owes a great deal to Giorgione, but the figures are more powerfully built and more expressive. In this scene, the darkening sky, the rapidly fading sunlight make the grief of the mourners seem particularly moving and real as they carry the dead Saviour to his grave.

169. PAOLO VERONESE / *Christ in the House of Levi* / 1573. Academy, Venice. Huge canvases such as this often took the place of murals in Venice. Veronese's main purpose here is to create a feast for the eyes. The rich, colorful costumes and the splendid architecture suggest a banquet in the palace of a Venetian lord rather than the austere setting of a Biblical event.

170. CORREGGIO / *The Virgin Adoring the Christ Child* / About 1523. Uffizi Gallery, Florence. *The soft half-light, the hazy atmosphere, and the tender smile of the Virgin recall Leonardo's Virgin of the Rocks (figure 161), while the color reminds us of the great Venetians, conveying a rapturous joy that is quite beyond the limits of High Renaissance art.*

171. ALBRECHT DURER / *The Four Apostles* / 1523-1526. Pinakothek, Munich. *Dürer's most monumental work, done under the direct impact of the Reformation movement. At the bottom are various quotations from the German Bible of Martin Luther. Here at last a Northern painter has achieved the simple grandeur of Masaccio.*

172. LEONARDO DA VINCI / *Coastal Landscape in a Storm* / About 1510. Royal Library, Windsor Castle. (Crown copyright reserved.) *His interest in the order of the natural world led Leonardo to study the formation of rocks and the movement of water and air. Toward the end of his life, he put all he had learned into a series of magnificent drawings of "nature in action"—thunderstorms, tidal waves, and earthquakes. That is how he imagined the end of the world.*

Leonardo has achieved it here not only by composing the picture more carefully but by painting it as if everything were seen through a slight haze that swallows up the small details, softens the outlines, and blends the shapes and colors together. In this way he leaves a good deal to our imagination, and that is why the *Mona Lisa* strikes us as so wonderfully alive. This is true both of the landscape (where Leonardo suggests to us how the earth "grew" from rocks and water) and of

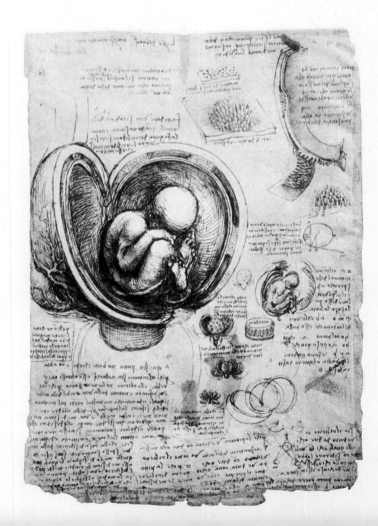

173. LEONARDO DA VINCI / *Child in the Womb* / About 1510. Royal Library, Windsor Castle. (Crown copyright reserved.) *This drawing, a milestone in the history of science, shows especially well what Leonardo had in mind when he said that "to see" and "to know" are the same.*

174, 175. MICHELANGELO / *Interior of the Sistine Chapel and Detail of "The Last Judgment"* / 1534-1541. Vatican, Rome. *A quarter of a century—and the great crisis of the Reformation—separates* The Last Judgment *from the Sistine Ceiling. It is therefore not only the subject but also the artist's advanced age and a general change in spiritual climate that account for the somber mood of the later work. Michelangelo has been greatly impressed with Signorelli's fresco (figure 158).*

the face, with its mysterious smile. What is the *Mona Lisa* thinking about? That really depends on what *we* are thinking about as we look at her. Perhaps Leonardo himself was a bit like that; people always found him even-tempered and friendly, but nobody ever knew for sure what was on his mind.

Michelangelo was in many ways the exact opposite of Leonardo. He, too, had many different strings to his bow—he was a sculptor, architect, and poet, as well as a painter—but he took no interest in science. Leonardo could compare a man's face with that of a lion or a horse because human beings to him were simply part of nature as a whole. For Michelangelo, on the contrary, man was a unique and almost godlike thing; and the artist was not a calmly observing scientist but a creator under whose hands dead materials suddenly came to life. In order to do this, the artist needed more than a brilliant mind—he had to be inspired, and inspiration could come only from God, since the artist was, in a way, competing with Him. Michelangelo himself never knew whether to regard his gift as a blessing or a curse. His violent personality, always torn between hope and despair, filled those who knew him with such awe that they really felt there was something superhuman about him. He has done more than any other man to shape our idea of what genius is like, so that even now we still tend to think of genius as a strange, uncontrollable power that holds the artist in its grip.

Michelangelo's masterpiece is the huge fresco covering the entire ceiling of the Sistine Chapel in the Vatican (figure 175). He did it between 1508 and 1512 for Julius II, the great Pope during whose reign Rome became the center of Italian art. Figure 177 shows you one of the main scenes, *The Creation of Adam*. It will remind you of the monumental style of Giotto and Masaccio, but there is a forcefulness of action and feeling here such as we have never seen before. These mighty creatures, stronger and more perfectly formed

176. MICHELANGELO / *The Resurrection* / About 1535. The Louvre, Paris. *For contrast compare this drawing with The Resurrection by Piero della Francesca (figure 142). Michelangelo's Christ, instead of solemnly facing the beholder, leaps from the tomb like a prisoner suddenly set free.*

than any man, come to us not from the *real* world of nature but from the *ideal* world of Michelangelo's imagination. The figure of God rushing through the sky is nothing less than creative energy itself. Adam, in contrast, still clings to the earth from which he has been molded. Their hands reach out to each other, and we can almost feel the breath of life flowing into Adam. No other

177. MICHELANGELO / *"The Creation of Adam," from the Sistine Ceiling* / 1508-1512. Vatican, Rome. *See comment above. In the view of the interior of the Chapel on the facing page, this section is visible just below the top of the picture. The drama of the scene appears even greater once we realize that Adam is straining not only toward his Creator but also toward the unborn Eve, who glances at him from the shelter of God's left arm.*

178. RAPHAEL / *Self-Portrait* / About 1497. Ashmolean Museum, Oxford. *Even in his teens Raphael already was a masterful draftsman. He appears here as a youth of almost feminine gentleness, with the dreamy eyes of a poet. His personal charm cast its spell on all who knew him during his brief life.*

179. RAPHAEL / *The Dream of Scipio* / About 1500. National Gallery, London. *This tiny panel, only seven inches square, shows the hero facing a choice between a life of pleasure and of virtue. Even the landscape is "moralized": the rocky road of virtue leads away from the plain of pleasure.*

artist has ever equaled Michelangelo's vision of this fateful moment. Around the main scenes on the ceiling there is a framework with seated figures in niches. One of these, the Prophet Jeremiah, is shown in figure 165. His body has even greater bulk and strength than those in *The Creation of Adam*, yet all his energy is turned inward upon the dark thoughts that fill his mind. Michelangelo has portrayed something of his own character in this gloomy figure.

How different are the paintings of Raphael! Younger than Leonardo and Michelangelo, he was the happiest and least complicated of the three. He, too, came to Rome at the request of Julius II, but he had already seen Leonardo's work in Florence and had learned a great deal from it. In the lovely *Madonna* of 1507 (figure 166), the softness of the modeling and the calm

beauty of the Virgin show the influence of the *Mona Lisa*. Yet Raphael has none of those disquieting mysteries that make Leonardo so hard to understand.

In Rome, the Sistine Ceiling made a deep impression on Raphael. This phase of his style may be seen in *The Expulsion of Heliodorus* (figure 182), one of the frescoes he painted in the Vatican Palace. It illustrates the story of a pagan Greek soldier who had brashly entered the Temple in Jerusalem in order to carry off its treasures. In the center of the picture, the High Priest at the altar is asking the Lord's help, and his prayer brings the three armed messengers of God, on the right, who are chasing Heliodorus and his men away. These figures are as powerfully built as those in the Sistine Ceiling, and even more agitated. But with Raphael there is no "battle of feelings" with-

in the figures, such as we saw in Michelangelo's style. What we admire most about *The Expulsion of Heliodorus*, however, is its masterly composition. Only a genius could have made a stable, well-balanced whole out of so many figures doing different things. The way the architectural framework forms the backbone of the entire picture reminds us of Masaccio's *Trinity* mural (figure 138), except that Raphael's design is far richer and full of movement.

After the death of Julius II in 1513, Rome did not long remain the great center of art it had been. Meanwhile, a new school of painting had grown up in the rich seafaring and trading city of Venice. The first master of the Venetian High

180, 181.   RAPHAEL / *The School of Athens* / 1509-1510. Vatican, Rome. *The fresco was painted on one of the walls of the library of Pope Julius II. It shows the "Athenian school of thought"—a great assembly of Greek philosophers, each of them in a characteristic pose or activity, with Plato and Aristotle at the center. Raphael conveys the harmony of the classical world of ideas through the lofty architecture as well as the lively yet disciplined grouping of the figures.*

182. RAPHAEL / *The Expulsion of Heliodorus* / 1511-1514. Vatican, Rome. *In keeping with the subject, Raphael here adopts a far more dramatic style than in* The School of Athens, *full of sweeping movement. The impressive figure being carried into the temple on the left is none other than Julius II, who saw himself as a modern successor to the High Priest in the story, successfully calling upon Divine aid in order to expel the foreign powers who had invaded Italy at that time.*

183. RAPHAEL / *Galatea* / About 1514. Villa Farnesina, Rome. *The style of this fresco is close to* The Expulsion of Heliodorus. *Its subject, the nymph Galatea standing* **on a shell**, *recalls Botticelli's Venus (figure 137) but Raphael's sculptural, rounded forms create a very different effect.*

184. RAPHAEL / *A Young Lady with a Veil, "La Donna Velata"* / About 1513. Pitti Palace, Florence. *Raphael has left us a large number of splendid portraits. La Donna Velata, although more opulent than the Mona Lisa, shows how strongly Raphael had been impressed by Leonardo's picture.*

185. ANDREA DEL SARTO / *The Holy Family* / 1525. Cloister of the Annunziata, Florence. *Andrea, the youngest of the Florentine High Renaissance masters, was influenced—and to some extent overawed—by the work of the "big three": Leonardo, Michelangelo, and Raphael. This fresco, with its breadth of form, its air of dignified repose, shows him at his very best. It is also one of the last examples, in either Florence or Rome, of the true High Renaissance style.*

Renaissance was Giorgione, who died in 1510 when he was still in his early thirties. Yet he is ranked among the greatest painters in history, for it was he who brought to Venetian painting most of the special qualities that set it apart from all the other styles of the sixteenth century. In his splendid *Concert* (figure 167), we find it hard to tell what kind of story the artist had in mind. All we can say is that the figures seem happy in each other's company. Perhaps the difference between the two young men gives us a clue to the riddle: one is a barefoot boy, very simply dressed, while the lute-player sports an elegant and colorful costume. Could Giorgione have wanted to contrast country life and city life? The two women must have a Classical meaning of some sort; they are probably nymphs or similar woodland spirits as imagined by the Ancients.

Oddly enough, not knowing the story seems to make little difference to us. The charm of the picture, we feel, is in its mood rather than its action, as if the artist had conceived a poem—calm and gentle, with a hint of melancholy—and then painted it instead of writing it down. Now, Giorgione was not the first painter to be interested in mood, but with him it became more important than anything else. Michelangelo and Raphael had created an ideal world through their mastery of form; Giorgione created *his* ideal world—a warmer and more human one than theirs—out of light and color. Instead of making us stand in awe, he invites us inside to share it with him. In *The Concert*, the golden rays of a setting sun bring all the details into harmony. If we could only make this wonderful moment last forever! But the shadows are deepening, and night will be here soon.

Giorgione's new way of painting was explored further by Titian, who outlived him by a great many years and became the most brilliant and famous of all Venetian artists. Titian, however, also knew something of the work of Michelangelo and Raphael. In *The Entombment of Christ* (figure 168), which he did about 1525, the figures are far more powerfully built and more expressive

127

186. GIORGIONE / *The Tempest* / About 1505. Academy, Venice. *The poetic feeling for the moods of nature that we met in the St. Francis of Giovanni Bellini (figure 135) reaches a new height in this work of Bellini's star pupil. The figures here are mere incidents in the landscape.*

than those of Giorgione, and the design is more monumental. Even so, we are again touched more deeply by the mood of the scene than by the action; and this mood depends on the kind of lighting and color we saw in *The Concert*. The darkening sky, the rapidly fading sunlight make the grief of the mourners seem particularly real—they cannot bear the thought of leaving the dead Saviour, and yet they must place him in the grave before evening turns into night. So the men force themselves to finish their task while the women take a last look at the limp, pitiful body.

Titian's greatest fame was as a painter of portraits. All the important men of his day, from the Pope and Emperor on down, were eager to have their pictures done by him. You will understand why if you look at the *Man with the Glove* (figure 187). With quick, feathery strokes of the brush, Titian captures the "feel" of the materials so completely that they seem richer and more precious to us than they would be in real life. And the sitter, too, we suspect, looks more attractive than

187. TITIAN / *Man with the Glove* / About 1520. The Louvre, Paris. *See comment above. The dreamy, intimate quality of this portrait, the soft outlines and deep shadows, echo the style of Giorgione, who influenced the early work of Titian to such an extent that the two are often hard to tell apart.*

188. TITIAN / *Paul III and His Grandsons* / 1546. National Museum, Naples. *Titian's keen insight into human character is strikingly evident here; the tiny figure of the Pope, shriveled with old age, shows a truly awesome dominance over his tall companions. For contrast, see Melozzo da Forlì (figure 153).*

189. TITIAN / *Bacchus and Ariadne* / About 1520. National Gallery, London. *In a warmly lit Giorgione-like landscape, Bacchus leaps from his chariot to offer his love to the frightened girl. The impulsive yet controlled movement of these figures stems from the High Renaissance art of Florence and Rome, which Titian had just come to know at that time. His glowing colors, on the other hand, and the richly sensuous treatment of the entire scene, are thoroughly Venetian.*

he actually was—not more beautiful, perhaps, but more interesting, more sensitive. Lost in his own thoughts, the young man seems quite unaware of us. It is this slight touch of sadness that gives him such unusual appeal.

The new broad manner of using oil paint introduced by Giorgione and Titian no longer demanded the smooth surface of wooden panels. The Venetians now preferred to do their pictures on canvas. This was so much cheaper and more

convenient that painters have been using canvas ever since. It also allowed the Venetians to make oil paintings as large as murals. *Christ in the House of Levi* (figure 169), done in 1573 by Paolo Veronese, is a splendid example of such a wall decoration. The sparkling, colorful costumes and the rich architectural setting make us think of a gay party in the palace of some Venetian lord, rather than of a story from the Bible. But if the picture does not strike a very religious mood, Veronese gives us a wonderfully vivid account of the festive scene, as if he had staged this pageant of Venetian life for our special benefit.

Florence, Rome, and Venice were the main centers of Italian art in the sixteenth century. But we also find some important painters in smaller places (see figures 195, 196, 200, 201). The most original of these was Correggio, from the town of Parma. In his *Holy Night* (figure 197), the bold lighting looks very Venetian, while the figures show that he must have known something of Leonardo, Michelangelo, and Raphael. And yet the picture as a

190, 191. TITIAN / *Christ Crowned with Thorns* / About 1565. Bavarian State Collection, Munich. *During the final phase of his career, Titian began to paint in an amazingly free and personal way, spreading thick masses of pigment with broad, quick strokes of the brush. In this picture we see this style carried to its furthest limits: there are no longer any solid, light-reflecting surfaces here—the forms emerging from the darkness seem to glow from within.*

192. GIAMBATTISTA MORONI / *A Tailor* / About 1570. National Gallery, London. *In the mid-sixteenth century the North Italian towns of Brescia and Bergamo were noted for a group of painters who had grown up under the influence of Giorgione and Titian but whose work shows a more straightforward realism. Moroni's* Tailor *looks like a piece of vigorous prose as compared to the poetry of Titian's* Man with the Glove *(figure 187).*

195. GIROLAMO SAVOLDO / *St. Matthew* / About 1535. Metropolitan Museum of Art, New York. *Here is another instance of "North Italian realism" (Savoldo came from Brescia). This night scene is remarkable for the dramatic effect of the lamplight, which helps to convey a strong sense of religious devotion.*

193, 194. PAOLO VERONESE / *Ceiling Fresco and Detail* / About 1567. Villa Giacomelli, Masèr, Italy. *This painted vault recalls Mantegna's ceiling in Mantua (figure 148), but the perspective illusion has now been carried to far greater length: it includes the circle of mythological figures seated on clouds in the center, as well as the startlingly real ladies peering down on us from their painted balcony. Veronese was no mere decorator. He created a festive world that still enchants us today.*

196. GAUDENZIO FERRARI / *Detail of a Ceiling Fresco* / 1535. Santa Maria dei Miracoli, Saronno. *Perhaps you will detect an echo of Leonardo da Vinci (compare figure 160) in these sumptuous angel musicians, on the dome of a pilgrimage church not far from Milan.*

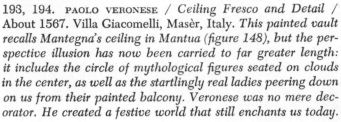

whole is quite unlike any of theirs. First of all, the figures don't stay put inside the frame but keep bursting into the picture from outside, like the huge shepherd on the left or the whirling cloud of angels above him. Obviously, Correggio is much less interested in balanced design than in making us feel the excitement of the story. He shows us the birth of Christ as a great miracle, but one that looks real and natural, too. That is why he has made it a night scene lit up by the newborn Child, just as Gentile da Fabriano had done (figure 100). In his own day Correggio was not regarded very highly. But a century later many other painters took over his sensational style, and he became as famous as the great masters of Rome and Venice.

197. CORREGGIO / *The Holy Night* / About 1530. State Picture Gallery, Dresden. *Correggio's style no longer belongs to the High Renaissance, even though his figures may remind us of Leonardo, Michelangelo, and Raphael. His sweeping compositions are prophetic of the Baroque.*

198. CORREGGIO / *Detail of a Ceiling Fresco* / About 1525. Cathedral, Parma. *These ecstatic angels are part of the Assumption of the Virgin, which covers the dome of the church. Correggio's interest in perspective illusion comes directly from Mantegna, whose pupil he had been. Here he "opens up" the whole curved surface and transforms it into a single great vision of Heaven filled with figures freely soaring in space. How restrained Veronese's ceiling looks in comparison!*

199. CORREGGIO / *Jupiter and Io* / About 1532. Kunsthistorisches Museum, Vienna. *In Correggio, it is impossible to distinguish the pleasures of the senses from spiritual joy. Io, melting in the embrace of a nebulous Jupiter, is the direct kin of the jubilant angels in the master's religious works.*

200. LORENZO LOTTO / *The Birth of Christ* / About 1526. Picture Gallery, Siena. *Although a Venetian, Lotto was strongly tinged with "North Italian realism." In this charmingly domestic Nativity, the Infant Christ, for once, actually looks like a newborn child, even to the dangling umbilical cord.*

201. GIOVANNI ANTONIO PORDENONE / *Ceiling Fresco* / 1520. Cathedral, Treviso. *Unlike most Venetian painters, Pordenone did his finest work in fresco. Here he has borrowed Michelangelo's image of the Lord from the Sistine Ceiling (figure 177) and projected it onto a dome. Quite independently, Pordenone often achieves effects like Correggio's.*

The Northern Renaissance

AROUND 1500 THE PAINTERS of Northern Europe showed a growing interest in Italian art. The Late Gothic style, however, was still very much alive, and there followed a long tug-of-war between the two until the Italian influence finally won out. We can get a good idea of this "battle of styles" by comparing the two greatest Northern painters of that time, Matthias Grunewald and Albrecht Dürer. Both were Germans whose backgrounds had much in common; and yet their aims were as different as could be. Grünewald's masterpiece, the *Isenheim Altar,* was done just about the time Michelangelo finished the Sistine Ceiling. Its four huge wooden wings are painted on both sides (figure 207 shows you the altar with the outer panels opened up; in figure 203 you see the outside of these panels). Grünewald had already felt the influence of the Renaissance: he knew more about perspective than he could have learned from Late Gothic art alone, and some of his figures, too, are surprisingly solid and vigorous. But his imagination is still completely Late Gothic, and he uses Italian ideas only in order to make this world of dreams and visions more real, more exciting than ever before. The *Isenheim Altar* is the final outburst of this particular kind of creative energy—an energy so intense that

202. MATTHIAS GRÜNEWALD / *St. Dorothy* / About 1516. Formerly State Museums, Berlin. *Grünewald's interest in light and color is evident not only in his painted works but also in drawings such as this. Compare its delicate shadings with the clear-cut lines of Dürer (figures 214, 216).*

everything in these panels twists and turns as though it had a life of its own. Compare the *Annunciation* in figure 207, for instance, with the earlier panel by Roger van der Weyden (figure 111). Roger's Christ enters so quietly that he hardly seems to move at all, while Grünewald's angel is blown into the room by a tremendous gust of air that makes the Virgin reel backward. On the two center panels a fairy-tale orchestra of angels entertains the Madonna and the newborn Child. There is a great burst of light above the clouds from which God the Father, in all His glory, gazes upon the young mother and her babe. In this tender and poetic vision, heaven and earth have truly become one. Only the *Holy Night* of Correggio arouses similiar feelings, different as it is in every other way.

In *The Resurrection,* on the right, an even more awesome miracle happens before our eyes: Christ leaves the earth and becomes God once more. But He does not merely *rise* from the grave—He *explodes* upward in a spiraling rush, still trailing His shroud and shining with a light as brilliant as the sun against the midnight sky, while the guardians of the tomb, the forces of death, blindly grope along the ground in utter defeat. Here the strange

203. MATTHIAS GRÜNEWALD / *The Crucifixion, from the Isenheim Altar* / 1509-1511. Musée Unterlinden, Colmar. *Here we see the somber aspect of the altar, as against the joyous spirit of the inner wings (figure 207). This Christ is both God and man; never have the agonies of His flesh been more starkly revealed, yet his great size is far beyond human scale. The bystanders reflect His double nature—those on the left mourn Him as a man; St. John acclaims Him as Saviour.*

genius of Grünewald has created its most unforgettable image.

Little is known about Grünewald's life. In the case of Dürer, on the other hand, we can trace his development almost year by year. Figure 216 shows you a drawing he made of himself when he was only thirteen and had just started his training under a painter in his home town of Nuremberg. Even then, Dürer could draw with great delicacy and assurance, but the style of the portrait is still entirely Late Gothic. Its sensitive yet curiously timid look will remind you of the *Young Princess* by the Master of Moulins (figure 122). If we now turn to the painted self-portrait (figure 217) done in the year 1500, we can't help wondering whether this impressive, almost Christ-like figure is really the same person as the naïve boy of the drawing. During those sixteen years, everything about Dürer had changed: his style, his ideas, and his way of looking at himself. On his

204. LUCAS CRANACH THE ELDER / *Rest on the Flight to Egypt* / 1504. Formerly State Museums, Berlin. *Cranach came from Franconia, the same region that produced Grünewald and Dürer. The Flight to Egypt is here a tender idyl in a fairy-tale forest where tiny angels, playful as nature sprites, minister to the Holy Family.*

205. HANS HOLBEIN THE YOUNGER / *George Gisze* / 1532. Formerly State Museums, Berlin. *Despite the countless small objects, all of them demanding to be explored and recognized, the picture as a whole breathes a spirit of well-planned order. The unhurried precision of these details only serves to emphasize the calm self-assurance of the sitter.*

206. PIETER BRUEGEL / *The Land of Cockayne* / 1567. Pinakothek, Munich. *The monumental design of this painting, in the shape of a great wheel turned on its side, proves that the artist must have thought his subject serious and important. The strongly foreshortened figures remind us of fallen soldiers on the battlefield—casualties of the "battle of the stomach."*

207.   MATTHIAS GRÜNEWALD / *Annunciation, Virgin and Child with Angels, Resurrection, from the Isenheim Altar* / About 1511-
12. Musée Unterlinden, Colmar. *In contrast with the grim drama of the Crucifixion (figure 203), the opened altar overflows with
scenes of joy—the Glad Tidings of the Annunciation, the Heavenly Concert of the central panels, and the triumphant Risen Christ.*

208. PARMIGIANINO / *The Madonna with the Long Neck* / About 1535. Uffizi Gallery, Florence.
*Although Parmigianino greatly admired Raphael, his figures do not acknowledge the classic standards
of the High Renaissance, but have a fascinating arbitrariness, characteristic of the Mannerist style.*

209. TINTORETTO / *Presentation of the Virgin* / About 1550. S. Maria dell' Orto, Venice. *Tintoretto, the greatest Mannerist painter of Venice, is reported to have said that he wanted to combine the draftsmanship of Michelangelo with the color of Titian. Yet when we look at his work we are struck, first of all, by a peculiar excitement reflecting his own powerful personality.*

210.   EL GRECO / *Assumption of the Virgin* / 1577. Art Institute of Chicago. *Though the picture still betrays El Greco's Venetian background, it already shows the ecstatic gestures, the compressed space, and the brittle "tin-foil" draperies of his later, Mannerist work (see figure 241).*

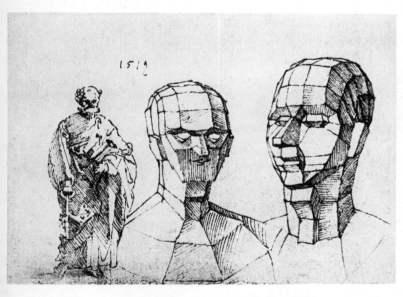

211. ALBRECHT DÜRER / *Two Heads Divided into Facets (pen drawing)* / 1519. Formerly Sächsische Landesbibliothek, Dresden. *Such "cubist" studies of scientific perspective show that this was indeed the earliest system of abstraction, since it demanded that reality be reduced to geometric shapes.*

212. ALBRECHT DÜRER / *Young Hare (water color)* / 1502. Albertina, Vienna. *This appealing and meticulous "portrait" of the little animal represents the Late Gothic, Eyckian side of Dürer's art: his infinite humble respect for every detail of the visible world.*

213. ALBRECHT DÜRER / *Alpine Landscape (water color)* / Probably 1495. Ashmolean Museum, Oxford. *Dürer inscribed this view, "Italian mountains"; he probably did it, along with several others, on the way home from his first Italian journey. The lightly brushed, delicate tints have a freshness that give the scene an amazingly modern look. Perhaps we should be grateful to whatever chance event kept the artist from "finishing" the sheet*

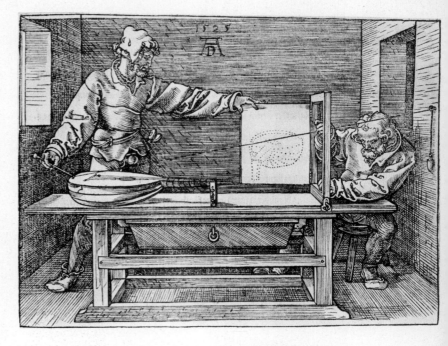

215. ALBRECHT DÜRER / *Demonstration of Perspective Drawing of a Lute* (woodcut, from the artist's treatise on geometry) *1525. This apparatus produces scientifically correct foreshortened views on a purely mechanical basis. How it works is explained on page 149.*

214. ALBRECHT DÜRER / *The Artist's Mother (charcoal drawing) / 1514.* Formerly Kupferstichkabinett, Berlin. *There is an expressive force in these features that makes us think of Grünewald. The ravages of old age upon body and mind have rarely been recorded with such frightening directness.*

216. ALBRECHT DÜRER / *Self-Portrait (silverpoint drawing) / 1484.* Albertina, Vienna. *Dürer did this remarkable drawing at the age of 13, "out of a mirror," as the inscription notes. The idea, as well as the demanding technique, he probably took from his goldsmith father.*

217. ALBRECHT DÜRER / *Self-Portrait / 1500.* Pinakothek, Munich. *The deliberate resemblance to Christ reflects the Renaissance idea that the artist of genius is endowed with a God-given authority, since his creative power derives from the creative power of God.*

218. ALBRECHT DÜRER / *Knight, Death, and Devil (engraving) / 1513. Here Italian and Northern elements are strikingly combined; see page 150.*

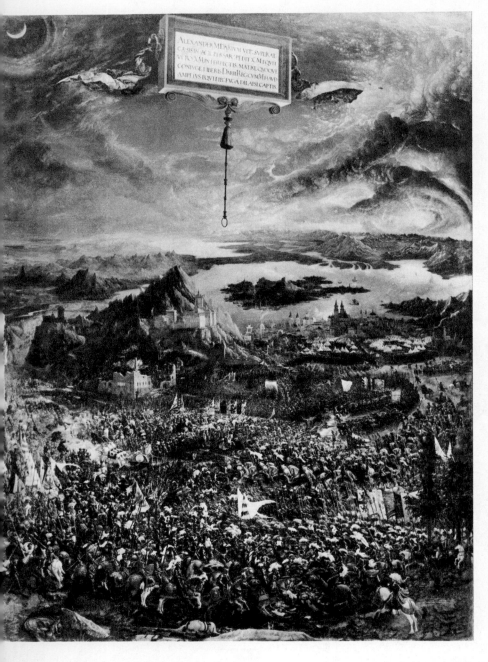

first visit to Italy, Dürer discovered both a new kind of art and a new kind of artist. He had been brought up to think of painters as modest craftsmen; in the South, he found, they enjoyed the same respect as scientists, scholars, and philosophers. So he decided not only to make the Italian style his own, but to educate himself in all the fields of learning that went with this new approach to art. More than that, he felt called upon to spread his own knowledge among his fellow artists, like a missionary preaching a new faith. In the self-portrait of 1500, he sees himself in this important new role; it is an idealized picture of the artist, much as the *Mona Lisa* is an idealized portrait of a woman.

Dürer's "mission" was helped a great deal by the fact that he was the finest print-maker of his time. These prints were of two kinds: engravings, where the lines of the picture are cut into a sheet of copper with a steel point; and woodcuts, where the spaces between the lines are carved out of the surface of a wooden block, leaving a raised design. Both copperplates and woodblocks can then be inked and many copies printed from them. Such prints, needless to say, are much cheaper

219, 220. ALBRECHT ALTDORFER / *Alexander the Great Defeating Darius, and Detail* / 1529. Pinakothek, Munich. *Even though his work is full of Renaissance detail, Altdorfer never shared Dürer's enthusiasm for Italian monumentality. His fame rests on his wonderfully poetic landscapes, such as the setting of this picture. The masses of tiny soldiers clashing in the foreground seem far less exciting than the cosmic drama of the sunrise "defeating" the moon.*

221. LUCAS CRANACH THE ELDER / *The Judgment of Paris* / 1530. Staatliche Kunsthalle, Karlsruhe. *The playful charm of the artist's* Rest on the Flight *(see figure 204) can still be found, twenty years later, in his delicious but utterly un-classical pictures of mythological subjects.*

222. ALBRECHT ALTDORFER / *Landscape with Satyr Family* 1507. Formerly State Museums, Berlin. *Here again we are reminded of the fairy-tale spirit of Cranach's* Rest on the Flight. *These satyrs in their forest refuge look very much like a pagan counterpart of the Holy Family.*

than paintings, so that a great many more people can afford to buy them. The woodcut in figure 215 is from a book Dürer wrote about scientific perspective (this was another idea he got from Italy—Piero della Francesca had written a book on the same subject). It shows a device for making correctly foreshortened pictures in a purely mechanical way. The two men are "drawing" the lute on the table as it would appear to us if we looked at it from the spot on the wall where you see a little hook with a string passing through it. Dürer knew, of course, that such pictures were not works of art but simply records of a scientific

223. WOLF HUBER / *Landscape (pen drawing)* / About 1530. Print Collection, Library, University at Erlangen, Germany. *The drawings of Huber, a south German like Altdorfer and akin to him in many ways, show an energetic "handwriting" and a passion for movement that make us think of Van Gogh (compare figure 430).*

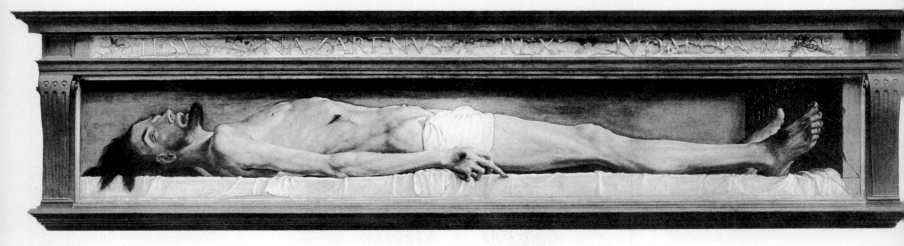

experiment. He just wanted to prove that "correct" perspective did not depend on anybody's skill or judgment. Still, devices like this led people to invent better ways of making mechanical pictures. Soon the hook-and-string was replaced by the *camera obscura,* a box with a lens at one end and a screen of oiled paper at the other. The image projected by the lens could then be traced directly on the paper, or, as in the camera of today, recorded on film.

But Dürer did not imitate Italian art slavishly. He picked what he thought interesting and impressive and then combined it with his own ideas, in the spirit of his own time and place. In his splendid engraving, *Knight, Death, and Devil* (figure 218) the horse and rider have the calmness, the monumental form of similar Italian works, such as the mounted soldiers of Piero della Francesca (figure 133), while Death and the Devil show the same weird imagination that we know

224. MAERTEN VAN HEEMSKERK / *Family Portrait* / About 1530. State Collections, Kassel. *This Dutch family group, solid, dignified, yet lively and good-humored, has much in common with Holbein's portrait of George Gisze (see figure 205). The pose of the nude child is taken from Italian art.*

225. NICHOLAS HILLIARD / *A Young Man Among Roses* / About 1588. Victoria & Albert Museum, London. (Crown copyright.) *Such miniatures, hardly larger than our figure, were popular in Elizabethan England. Ours was probably ordered by the sentimental élégant as a keepsake for his ladylove.*

226. *At left:* HANS HOLBEIN THE YOUNGER *The Dead Christ* / 1521. Öffentliche Kunstsammlung, Basel. *In this early masterpiece, which is also his most powerful religious work, Holbein has combined Italian clarity with an expressiveness that can be compared only to Grünewald.*

227. HANS HOLBEIN THE YOUNGER / *Erasmus of Rotterdam* / 1523. The Louvre, Paris. *Holbein here gives us not only a sensitive character portrayal, he endows the great humanist with an intellectual authority formerly reserved to the Evangelists or the Fathers of the Church.*

228. HANS HOLBEIN THE YOUNGER / *Henry VIII* / 1540. Corsini Gallery, Rome. *This portrait conveys the authority of the sovereign ruler "by the Grace of God," but the picture makes us feel that Henry VIII owed his position as much to his own ruthless, commanding personality.*

· ANNO · ETATIS ·   · SVÆ · XLIX ·

151

229. PIETER AERTSEN / *A Meat Stall* / 1551. Museum of Art, Uppsala University, Sweden. *Despite a few earlier examples, the history of still life as an independent subject begins with pictures such as this. In the background we often find a tiny Biblical scene, as a sort of excuse. There is as yet little interest in selection or arrangement; the objects, piled in huge heaps, are meant to overwhelm us with their sensuous reality.*

230. MARINUS VAN ROYMERSWAELE / *The Virgin and Child* / About 1540. The Prado, Madrid. *Here is another striking example of Netherlandish realism: an "authentic" Madonna based on a Jewish model. She may have been one of the refugees from Portugal who settled in Flanders after 1536.*

from the Van Eyck *Last Judgment* (figure 102). The contrast between the two styles helps to make Dürer's idea clear: his Knight is the exact opposite of those idle pleasure-seekers in Jerome Bosch's *Ship of Fools* (figure 128). He "knows where he is going"; his journey through life follows the road to Heaven (represented by the city in the distance) no matter how frightful the dangers along the way. The words of the famous hymn, "Onward, Christian Soldiers," might well serve as a title for Dürer's picture.

Hans Holbein the Younger was the last of the great German masters of this period. His best known works are the portraits he did in England, where he spent his later years as court painter to King Henry VIII (figure 228). The portrait of George Gisze (figure 205) strikes a happy balance between the Northern European love of fine detail and the solidity and dignity of Italian Renaissance art. While the sitter has not been idealized in any way, his pose has something of the restful, harmonious quality of the *Mona Lisa;* and compared to Late Gothic portraits, this young merchant seems to have a new confidence in himself and in his own worth. Holbein shows him in his office, surrounded by business papers, seals, writing equipment, even a vase of flowers. These things only add to the feeling of quiet pride conveyed by the picture as a whole.

At the time Holbein came to England, the religious Reformation movement was already widespread in Northern Europe, and artists felt its

231. PIETER BRUEGEL / *Alpine Landscape (pen drawing)* / About 1553–55. The Pierpont Morgan Library, New York. *This majestic view shows how deep an impression the Alps had made upon Bruegel when he visited Italy in 1553. Could he have seen Leonardo drawings such as figure 172?*

232. PIETER BRUEGEL / *The Return of the Hunters* / 1565. Kunsthistorisches Museum, Vienna. *The painting is part of a set that echoes the "calendar landscape" of Late Medieval art (see figure 85). But now the seasonal activities of man have become mere incidents within the great annual cycle of death and rebirth that is the breathing rhythm of all nature. In our picture "the dead of winter" can be sensed in the very air.*

233. PIETER BRUEGEL / *Peasant Wedding* / About 1565. Kunsthistorisches Museum, Vienna. *This is the artist's most famous painting of peasant life. Shown as simple-minded, even crude folk, the peasants also strike us as grave and dignified, perhaps because every shape in the picture has so much weight and roundness. Most impressive of all, however, is the composition, which is as monumental as that of any Italian master.*

effect more directly, perhaps, than anyone else. The new forms of faith all agreed on one point: religious art, they claimed, tempted people to worship statues and pictures rather than God himself. Wherever the Reformers won out, the Church no longer demanded the sacred subjects that had been the mainstay of medieval art. As a result, religious pictures became much less important than before, since painters had to turn to other subjects in order to make a living. Holbein, as we have seen, concentrated on portraits. In figure 206 we meet a different kind of new subject. The picture was painted in 1567 by the great Flemish master Pieter Bruegel, at a time when the Netherlands, under the banner of the Reformation, was fighting a bloody war of independence against Catholic Spain. It shows the *Land of Cockayne,* a fool's paradise where we find tables always laden with tasty dishes, houses with roofs made of pies, and other wonders. Bruegel, of course, wants to teach us a moral lesson, but he no longer needs religion for this. The men under the tree are not unhappy sinners in the grip of evil; they *could* act as responsible human beings but, like most people, they are not wise enough to know what is best for them in the long run. By becoming slaves to their appetites, they have given up all ambition, all self-respect, for the sake of a kind of animal happiness: the knight has dropped his lance, the farmer his flail, and the scholar, on the right, has given up his books. "Beware of the fool's paradise," Bruegel seems to say, "it's more dangerous than hell because people *like* going there."

Mannerism

IN ITALY, the home of the Catholic Church, the Reformation did not touch the artists directly. Yet there, too, the great crisis of faith had a deeply unsettling effect upon their work. After 1520, the confidence of the High Renaissance in the almost divine powers of the human spirit was no longer shared by the younger artists; to them, man seemed once again at the mercy of forces over which he had no control. So they began to show the human figure in strange new ways, twisting it into ever more complicated poses and pulling it

out to unnatural height. Some of them even developed a strange taste for the Late Gothic. This disturbing phase of Italian art used to be looked down upon as the "decay of the Renaissance"; that is what the term Mannerism meant. But we now accept it as an important style in its own right, and the highly personal flavor of the best of the Mannerists seems particularly exciting to us—perhaps because we, too, no longer believe in fixed ideals in art. You can see the beginning of the new style in the extraordinary *Self-Portrait* (figure 236) by a young painter from Parma called Parmigianino. It shows the artist exactly as he saw himself in one of those round, convex mirrors, so that his hand looks monstrously large and the walls and ceiling of the room are bent into curves. Why was Parmigianino so fascinated by these distorted shapes? Was it merely scientific curiosity, or had he come to feel that there was no such thing as a steady, "correct" reality, that everything depended on your personal point of view?

In Parmigianino's picture the artist still faces the outside world, even if he does it "through the

234. NICCOLO DELL'ABBATE / *Landscape with the Story of Eurydice* / About 1555. National Gallery, London. *The figures reflect the Mannerist elegance of Parmigianino, while the sweeping landscape suggests Flemish influence (Niccolò spent the latter part of his life in France).*

235. PONTORMO / *Study of a Young Girl (chalk drawing) /* About 1526. Uffizi Gallery, Florence. *Pontormo and Rosso were the first Florentines to break away from the High Renaissance style. The fragile, withdrawn look of this portrait hints at the artist's own inner anxiety.*

looking glass." The early Mannerists working in Florence went even further; they depended far less on nature than on their own private worlds of dreams and visions. This is certainly true of the drawing by Jacopo da Pontormo (figure 235) and of the *Descent from the Cross* in figure 239, which was done by a painter known simply as Rosso. The spidery, angular figures, their frenzied gestures and expressions, the weird, unreal light —all these give the picture a ghostly, frightening quality that is not soon forgotten. Rosso's men and women are no longer acting, they are being acted upon; their garments, and their very bodies, have turned brittle, as though frozen by a sudden blast of cold. Nothing could be more remote from the Classical balance of the High Renaissance than this nightmarish, "anti-Classical" style.

In Venice, Mannerism did not appear so quickly, but by the middle of the century we find it firmly established in the work of Tintoretto, the most important Venetian master after Titian. His *Presentation of the Virgin* (figure 209) is less "anti-Classical" than Rosso's *Descent*; the vigorous poses of some of the figures may remind you

236. PARMIGIANINO / *Self-Portrait* / 1524. Kunsthistorisches Museum, Vienna. *Here the "anti-classical" spirit shows itself in the artist's too-complete acceptance of what he sees in the mirror; before this, only Northern art had produced such "duplicates" of reality (see figure 107).*

237. AGNOLO BRONZINO / *Eleonora of Toledo and Her Son Giovanni* / About 1550. Uffizi Gallery, Florence. *This coldly elegant portrait of the wife of Duke Cosimo I of Tuscany against a deep-blue evening sky has the same unapproachable air as Holbein's* Henry VIII *(figure 228).*

238. JEAN CLOUET / *Francis I* / About 1525–30. The Louvre, Paris. *The "International Court Portrait Style" that came to the fore in London under Henry VIII and in Florence under Cosimo I, may have existed even earlier in France, as suggested by this very polished example.*

239. ROSSO FIORENTINO / *Descent from the Cross* / 1521. Picture Gallery, Volterra, Italy. *See comment on facing page. In this great pioneer work of Mannerism, Rosso launched the ecstatic, visionary style that was to be carried to its furthest limits by El Greco (compare figures 210, 241).*

240. TINTORETTO / *Moses Raising the Brazen Serpent* / 1576–81. Scuola di S. Rocco, Venice. *Many of the poses here recall Michelangelo's Last Judgment (see figure 174), but instead of individual figures we see whirling masses and a flickering pattern of highlights and shadows.*

of Michelangelo, whom Tintoretto admired greatly. Even so, you can feel the Mannerist spirit in the odd perspective, in the unsteady light with its sudden bright flashes and deep, inky shadows, and in the agitated gestures of the figures as they watch the twelve-year-old Mary going up the steps to the Temple. What matters most to Tintoretto is not the simple, straightforward story from the life of the Virgin but the tense, excited air he has given to the scene, as if it were some tremendous drama.

This style of painting fitted in well with a new trend in the Catholic world. In defense against the Reformation, the Church had begun to stress the mystical and supernatural parts of religious experience. This Counter Reformation was at its strongest in Spain, and in Spain, too, we find the last and most striking of the Mannerist painters. He is known today simply as El Greco, "the Greek," since he came from the island of Crete. His style of painting, however, was formed in Venice, under the influence of Tintoretto and other

241. EL GRECO / *Opening of the Fifth Seal* / About 1604–14. Metropolitan Museum of Art, New York. *In this scene from the Revelation of St. John (he is the large, ecstatic figure on the left), the souls of the martyred saints are clothed in robes, before the Last Judgment.*

242. EL GRECO / *Cardinal Niño de Guevara* / 1596–1601. Metropolitan Museum of Art, New York. *El Greco's only full-length portrait is a truly frightening picture—frightening because this wielder of vast authority seems so tense and insecure, despite his coldly intelligent glance.*

243. GIUSEPPE ARCIMBOLDO / *Summer (vegetable still life in the shape of a bust)* / 1563. Kunsthistorisches Museum, Vienna. *Double images such as this spring from the same taste for "eccentric realism" that we met in the painted mirror-image of Parmigianino (figure 236).*

masters. He went to Spain as a mature artist and settled in the town of Toledo, where his first great success was the *Assumption* (figure 210), of 1577. It shows the Virgin Mary being carried to Heaven after her death, in the presence of the Apostles. The sudden flashes of light and the curiously unreal colors will remind you of Tintoretto, but in spirit the work seems closer to Rosso's *Descent*. Here again we find the sharp-edged, "frozen" draperies, the angular, frantic gestures, the drawn-out limbs. And El Greco handles space in an even more personal way than Rosso; he uses foreshortening, but without perspective, so that we cannot tell from what level we are viewing the scene. Then, too, there is a good deal of modeling in the figures, and yet they look like cardboard cutouts placed one over the other, with no space between them. Thus El Greco makes it quite impossible for us to separate the real from the unreal, the world of feeling from the world we can see and touch.

The Triumph of Light

I T IS NOT EASY TO DEFINE the spirit of seventeenth-century art. We often speak of it as the Baroque, but nobody seems to be quite sure what this means, or ought to mean. The word itself might be compared to the term Gothic, which at one time meant simply that Late Medieval art was poor, although it has become thoroughly respectable since then. Baroque, too, started out as an insulting tag for certain kinds of seventeenth-century art; but because it did not come into general use until recent times, its negative meaning has not yet worn off completely. Quite a few people still feel that it's all-right to call *some* seventeenth-century artists Baroque but not others. In this book we shall be less cautious; we shall use Baroque for the last

244. ANNIBALE CARRACCI / *Detail of a Ceiling Painting* / 1597–1601. Farnese Palace, Rome. *Shortly before 1600, two great "anti-Mannerists" appeared in Rome: the revolutionary realist Caravaggio (see page 165), and the cautious reformer Annibale Carracci. Both felt that art must draw closer to nature, but Annibale approached this aim by studying classical antiquity and such modern classics as Raphael, Michelangelo, Correggio, and Titian.*

245. CARAVAGGIO / *The Conversion of St. Paul* / 1600–01. Sta. Maria del Popolo, Rome. *Here, even more than in figure 246, it is the light alone that creates a sense of dramatic action. By "freezing" all body movement, Caravaggio stresses the inward character of St. Paul's experience.*

explorers like Columbus setting out to bring back the riches of unknown lands. These were now followed by colonists, such as the Pilgrim Fathers who settled in New England in 1620. The countries along the Atlantic coast of Europe—England, Holland, France, and Spain—had all gained important overseas territories and grew more prosperous and powerful than they had been before, while Germany and Italy became less so. In the sciences, we no longer find all-around geniuses like Leonardo and Dürer opening up new fields of knowledge all at once. They had taught the specialists how to use their eyes, but it remained for the latter to describe the workings of nature in an orderly and systematic manner. So now there were men such as Galileo and Newton, who summed up the behavior of moving bodies in a few simple laws that held good for every kind of motion, whether of the earth circling around the sun or of an apple dropping from a tree. These important scientists of the Baroque age laid the foundation for the technical marvels of our own day.

The struggle between the Reformation movement and the defenders of the old faith had now reached a stalemate, so that there was less open conflict than before. The Catholic Church, its strength revived by the Counter Reformation, could feel secure once more, and the city of Rome again became the goal of artists from all over Europe. They came, of course, to study the great masterpieces of Classical Antiquity and of the High Renaissance; but they also learned from the Italian artists of their own time, and these, in turn, picked up ideas from them. Seventeenth-century Rome was a sort of melting pot of styles, where North and South, past and present, flowed together in an endless and bewildering stream. Every visitor came away from it with different impressions, yet the experience gave all of them something in common—enough, at any rate, to make us feel that the Baroque was an international style, however much it might vary from one place to the next.

phase of the Renaissance era (after Early Renaissance, High Renaissance, and Mannerism), just as Gothic means the last phase of Medieval art. If you think of it like that you will understand more easily how seventeenth-century art could be as rich and varied as it was and yet have a decided character of its own.

In many ways the Baroque age is a summing up of all the different trends we have seen since the early fifteenth century. People were no longer so upset by the exciting new ideas and discoveries that had brought the Medieval world to an end; they had learned how to live with them and what to do with them. Earlier, we had found daring

246. CARAVAGGIO / *The Calling of St. Matthew* / About 1597-98. S. Luigi dei Francesi, Rome. *Despite its everyday realism, this scene is filled with deep religious feeling. While Christ appears as a humble "man of the people" in contrast to the richly dressed group on the left, his commanding gesture is borrowed directly from Michelangelo's Creation of Adam (figure 177).*

248. PETER PAUL RUBENS / *The Abduction of the Daughters of Leucippus* / About 1616. Pinakothek. Munich. *Rubens was a genius even in his borrowings from other masters. Here he echoes Leonardo as well as Titian and Raphael (see figures 163, 168, 182), yet all these diverse "quotations" have become an organic part of Rubens' own style.*

AT LEFT:

247. PETER PAUL RUBENS / *Marie de Medicis, Queen of France, Landing in Marseilles* / About 1622. Pinakothek, Munich. *Oil sketches such as this are small-scale "models" of large pictures, and often far more attractive, since they were done entirely by the master's own hand in a quick, transparent technique that captures the full sweep of his inventive genius.*

249. FRANS HALS / *Yonker Ramp and His Sweetheart* / 1623. Metropolitan Museum of Art, New York. *The new awareness of "timing" pioneered by Caravaggio (see figure 250 on opposite page) reaches its climax in works such as this; the dashing brush strokes almost make us believe that "the hand is quicker than the eye."*

Italy and Flanders

251. CARAVAGGIO / *Victorious Cupid* / About 1602. Formerly State Museums, Berlin. *By giving this mischievous cupid the pose of Michelangelo's* Victory *(vignette at left), Caravaggio, also baptized Michelangelo, saluted his famous namesake, while poking fun at the Michelangelo cult of conservatives.*

Tʜᴇ ғᴏʀᴇɪɢɴ ᴀʀᴛɪsᴛs who arrived in Rome toward the year 1600 found the Italians all excited about a young painter from Northern Italy named Caravaggio, who had himself come to the city only a few years before. A look at his *Cardsharps* (figure 250) will make you realize how little his work has in common with the art of the Mannerists. Caravaggio had learned a good deal from the Venetian High Renaissance style (compare figures 167 and 168), but his own out-

250. CARAVAGGIO / *The Cardsharps* / About 1593. Private Collection. *See comment above. In Rome, where Caravaggio painted this picture soon after his arrival, people were struck by its bright colors, and spoke of it as being "in the manner of Giorgione." Our artist, however, must also have been impressed with the works of later North Italian masters such as Savoldo, whose St. Matthew (figure 195) is placed as close to us as the cardsharps and shows a similarly dramatic lighting.*

252. ORAZIO GENTILESCHI / *Rest on the Flight to Egypt* / About 1630. Kunsthistorisches Museum, Vienna. *One of the most appealing followers of Caravaggio, Gentileschi carried the new realism to Northern Europe. This picture differs greatly from older interpretations such as figure 204: the Holy Family rests against a stark gray wall; no angels comfort them; Joseph has collapsed with exhaustion. They are humble folk who share the plight of all the "displaced persons" of our own day.*

look was naturalistic, which means that he wanted to show the world just as he saw it in everyday life. In our picture he has painted some soldiers such as one might meet in any Roman tavern, playing a crooked game of cards: the young scoundrel on the right has some extra cards hidden behind his back and is about to spring them on his victim, following a signal from the older man. Will they get away with this, we won-

der, or is there going to be a fight? Caravaggio does not tell us; he only builds up the suspense. Clearly, there is no moral lesson to be learned here. At first people were shocked at this kind of subject—they claimed it was neither noble nor beautiful enough for a large painting. Yet they could not but admire the way Caravaggio had made the group come to life. Two things impressed them particularly: Caravaggio's new sense

253. ANNIBALE CARRACCI / *Landscape with the Flight into Egypt* / About 1600. Doria Gallery, Rome. *Here Annibale has created a truly classical landscape: an idealized, "composed" view of nature which nevertheless shares the intimate pastoral mood of Venetian landscapes (compare figures 167, 186).*

254. GUIDO RENI / *Aurora* / About 1613-1614. Ceiling fresco, Casino Rospigliosi, Rome. *The art academy of the Carracci in Bologna produced a number of talented painters, of whom Reni became the most famous. His Aurora clearly betrays his admiration for the classical ideals of Raphael (compare figure 183), yet the onrushing motion is Baroque rather than High Renaissance in spirit. Nor, we may be sure, would Raphael ever have chosen dappled horses for Apollo's chariot.*

255. GUERCINO / *Aurora* / 1621-1623. Ceiling fresco, Villa Ludovisi, Rome. *Although Guercino, too, had studied at the Carracci academy in Bologna, his Aurora shows none of the classicism of Reni's. The latter resembles a framed picture placed overhead; Guercino's, in contrast, covers the entire ceiling as well as the walls, using all the perspective tricks of Veronese (see figure 193) and Correggio (figure 198) to argue away the difference between illusion and reality.*

256. ADAM ELSHEIMER / *Landscape with the Temple of the Sibyl* / About 1608. National Gallery, Prague. *A German who lived in Italy, Elsheimer harmonized many approaches to landscape painting: German, Flemish, Venetian, and the classical one of Annibale Carracci (see figure 253).*

257. PETER PAUL RUBENS / *Self-Portrait with Isabella Brant* / 1609-10. Pinakothek, Munich. *This early work of the greatest Flemish Baroque painter still has a curiously "Elizabethan" air that recalls the elegant* Young Man Among Roses *of Nicholas Hilliard (figure 225).*

258. PIETRO DA CORTONA / *Detail of a Ceiling Fresco* / 1633-39. Palazzo Barberini, Rome. *With this ceiling—of which we see here only a small corner—Roman Baroque decoration reaches an overpowering climax. Yet, incredibly, Pietro derived his scheme from the Farnese Gallery (figure 244).*

of timing, which let him catch his characters at exactly the right moment; and his dramatic use of light and dark. He was the first painter who spotlighted his pictures like a stage director, contrasting brilliant highlights with sharply outlined, deep shadows, in order to make every face, every gesture as expressive as possible.

In *The Calling of Saint Matthew* (figure 246), Caravaggio has taken an even bolder step: he paints a story from the life of Christ as if it were happening right then and there in a Roman street. These men sitting at a table outside a cheap, drab tavern clearly belong to the same disreputable class of soldiers as the *Cardsharps*. Matthew, who sits with this group, points questioningly at himself as the Saviour approaches from the right with one of His disciples. They are obviously poor and humble people—both of them are barefoot, and their simple dress makes a strong contrast with the colorful costumes of the others. As Christ

259. PETER PAUL RUBENS / *Crucifixion Altar* / 1620. Royal Museum of Fine Arts, Antwerp. *The Baroque spirit can transform even the Crucifixion into a scene of dramatic action. Rubens has done so by depicting the moment when the Roman centurion pierces Christ's side with a lance. Christ endures the wound with heroic calm, while the thief on the right seems to recoil in fear. There is a sudden flash of light, for the thrust of the lance also reveals to the centurion that Christ is the Messiah.*

260. PETER PAUL RUBENS / *Helene Fourment* / About 1638. Kunsthistorisches Museum, Vienna. *In this glowingly sensuous picture, the aging artist celebrates the beauty of the young woman whom he had married in 1630 and who had become his favorite model. The pose is derived from a painting by Titian.*

261. ANTHONY VAN DYCK / *James Stuart, Duke of Lennox* / About 1635. Metropolitan Museum of Art, New York. *Van Dyck, Rubens' most brilliant pupil, lacked his master's vitality. This portrait, done after he had settled in England, breathes "class-conscious" elegance rather than human warmth.*

raises His arm in a beckoning gesture, a golden beam of sunlight carries His call across to Matthew. It seems a perfectly natural kind of light, but the way it points at Matthew and lets the hand and face of Christ suddenly emerge from the dark, gives it a symbolic meaning, too. As a matter of fact, this beam is by far the most important thing in the picture. Take it away, and all the magic, all the expressive power, disappears with it. You will understand now how Caravaggio

could translate an important Biblical story such as this into the workaday reality of his own time and yet fill it with the deepest religious feeling; it is his discovery of light *as a force* that raises his tavern scene to the level of a sacred event.

Caravaggio's naturalism seemed less strange to visiting foreigners than it did to the Italians. But then the human, everyday approach to religious subjects had been familiar to Northern artists ever since Gothic times. While he was not exactly a prophet without honor in his own country, it was in the Netherlands, in France, and in Spain that Caravaggio left the deepest impression. His ideas influenced all the important masters of Baroque painting, even those who became far more famous than he did.

The first of these, Peter Paul Rubens, was from Flanders, the southern part of the Netherlands that had remained Catholic and under Spanish rule when Holland, the northern half, gained its independence. As a young man Rubens spent eight years in Italy, eagerly studying the works of the great painters from the High Renaissance to his own day. By the time he returned home to Antwerp, he had learned very much more about Italian art than any Northern artist before him. It might well be said of him, in fact, that he finished what Dürer had started to do a hundred years earlier—to break down the barriers of taste and style between North and South. The wonderful *Crucifixion* in figure 259 shows you how much Rubens owed to the Italians: here you find the powerful bodies of Michelangelo and Raphael, the sparkling color of Titian, the sweep of Correggio, the naturalism, the drama, and the spotlighting of Caravaggio, along with a force of expression that will remind you of Grünewald. The amazing thing about Rubens' genius is that he was able to digest all these different sources so that we don't even know they are there unless we make a special point of looking for them. If he borrows the "words" of other artists, he gives them a new sound and a new meaning, so that they become part of his own personal "language." And what an exciting, colorful language it is! For Rubens, nothing ever stands still; all his forms are alive with a flowing, swirling movement that sweeps through the picture like a windstorm. A Rubens scene is never complete in itself—it spills over the edges of the canvas on every side (just compare his *Crucifixion* with the one by Mantegna in figure 134). The idea of composing pictures in this way came, of course, from Correggio, but Rubens carried it a great deal further. "After all," he seems to be

262. PETER PAUL RUBENS / *Chalk Drawing for a Figure in "The Garden of Love"* / About 1632. Stadel Institute, Frankfurt.
263. PETER PAUL RUBENS / *The Garden of Love* / 1632-34. The Prado, Madrid. *Here Rubens pays perhaps his finest tribute to the pleasures of life. His richly dressed young couples mingle so naturally with the assaulting cupids that we can no longer distinguish myth and reality, which even Titian, whom Rubens admired so much, never merged so completely.*

264. JACOB JORDAENS / *The Four Evangelists* / About 1620. The Louvre, Paris. *Jordaens, next to Rubens the most important master of the Flemish Baroque, never went to Italy; yet, as this picture shows, his art owes as much to the realism of Caravaggio as it does to the opulence of Rubens.*

telling us, "in the real world there are no limits to space or time; life as we know it means change, movement, action. Why should things be different in the world of art?"

We can see all this even better in figure 247, which is a small sketch for a very large painting, one of a series Rubens did for the Queen of France. It shows her arrival in Marseilles (she was Italian and had come to France by boat). Not a very exciting story, you might say—but Rubens turns it into a glorious spectacle of a kind we have never seen before. As the Queen walks down the gangplank, the winged figure of Fame flying overhead sounds a blast on his trumpets, and Neptune, the god of the sea, emerges from the deep with his fish-tailed crew; they have guarded the Queen's ship during her journey, and are overjoyed at her safe landing. In this festive scene everything flows together: heaven and earth, fantasy and reality, motion and emotion—even drawing and painting. For in our sketch these two have become the same thing. Rubens could not plan the design of the picture without thinking of light and color from the very start, just as in real life there are no forms apart from light and color. It is this unified way of seeing that makes his work, and Baroque art in general, so different from all earlier styles.

265. HENDRICK TERBRUGGHEN / *The Calling of St. Matthew* / 1621. Central Museum, Utrecht. *While the picture clearly derives from Caravaggio, it also suggests memories of Marinus van Roymerswaele (compare figure 230), and the head of the old man on the right somehow recalls certain faces by Bosch.*

266. ADRIAEN BROUWER / *A Tavern Brawl* / About 1630. Pinakothek, Munich. *Here the cardsharps of Caravaggio have come to blows, but the dupes are now Dutch peasants, whom the artist has observed with an acute but hardly sympathetic eye. Such pictures were popular in both Holland and Flanders.*

267. REMBRANDT / *The Story of Balaam's Ass* / 1626. Musée Cognacq-Jay, Paris. *Balaam, unaware of the angel, strikes his balky ass until the animal speaks to him in a human voice. The dramatic action, the vivid contrast of light and dark, betray the strong—if indirect—impact of Caravaggio upon the young Rembrandt.*

268. REMBRANDT / *The Polish Rider* / About 1655. The Frick Collection, New York. *Compared to such early paintings as* Balaam's Ass, *this mature work impresses us with its subtlety of color and design. Everything seems to be in a state of transition here—the light, the mood, even the movement of horse and rider.*

269.   JAN STEEN / *The Eve of Saint Nicholas* / About 1660-65. Rijksmuseum, Amsterdam. *Among the Dutch painters of daily life, none was as sharp—and good-humored—an observer as Jan Steen. Perhaps the fact that he also kept an inn, to supplement his earnings as a painter, helps to explain his keen insight into human behavior.*

270.   JAN VERMEER / *The Artist in His Studio* / About 1665-70. Kunsthistorisches Museum, Vienna. *Unlike Steen, Vermeer had no gift as a storyteller. His is an art of silence and order, of beautiful shapes and colors revealed through the action of light. To us, he seems the most "modern" of all Dutch artists of his time.*

271, 272. FRANS HALS / *The Women Regents of the Old Men's Home at Haarlem, and Detail* / 1664. Frans Hals Museum, Haarlem. *In contrast to the color and excitement of* Yonker Ramp *(figure 249), the last works of Hals have an austerity of mood and a depth of insight into human character matched only by the Rembrandt of the 1650's and 1660's (see pages 180, 181). Hals was more than 80 years old when he did this magnificent group portrait.*

Holland

WHILE RUBENS became the most famous artist of his time in the Catholic half of Europe, the first great painters of the Protestant world appeared in Holland. As a wealthy nation of merchants and seafarers, proud of their hard-won freedom, the Dutch developed such an appetite for pictures of themselves and of their way of life that their artists had quite enough to do even without working for the Church. In fact, Holland probably had more painters, and more art collectors, than any other country during the seventeenth century. Pictures were as popular then as movies or sports are today, so that many Dutchmen were lured into becoming painters by hopes of success which all too often failed to come true. At times even the greatest artists of Holland found themselves suddenly out of favor with the public and hard-pressed for a living. Actually, this boom only lasted for about half a century, but these years are one of the most important chapters in the history of painting.

Not many Dutch painters traveled to Rome. However, in the early years of the century there were several who did. They are known as the Utrecht School, after the name of their home town. In Rome, these men were so impressed with the style of Caravaggio that they looked at little else. *The Calling of St. Matthew* by Hendrick Terbrugghen (figure 265), the most talented member of this group, is a direct echo of Caravaggio's

version of the same subject; the naturalism, the light, the "timing," all remind us of the earlier picture. These were the things Terbrugghen and his friends brought home with them to Holland, for other painters to see and get excited about. They thus became the connecting link between Caravaggio and the great masters of their own country, who knew better than they did how to put the new Italian ideas to work.

This is what has happened in the wonderfully lively portrait of *Yonker Ramp and His Sweetheart* (figure 249), which was done by Frans Hals, the leading painter of the town of Haarlem. It is hard to imagine Titian's young nobleman or Holbein's George Gisze wanting to have himself shown like this, drinking and carousing; yet the young Dutch cavalier of our painting did not mind posing as the main figure in a gay tavern

273. REMBRANDT / *The Anatomy of Dr. Tulp* / 1632. Mauritshuis, The Hague. *Through this picture, his first monumental group portrait, Rembrandt established himself in Amsterdam. It shows a public performance by the great anatomist—who wears a hat, as a sign of authority—before the members of the surgeon's guild. Two of them (at the top and on the extreme left) were added somewhat later, unbalancing the original design.*

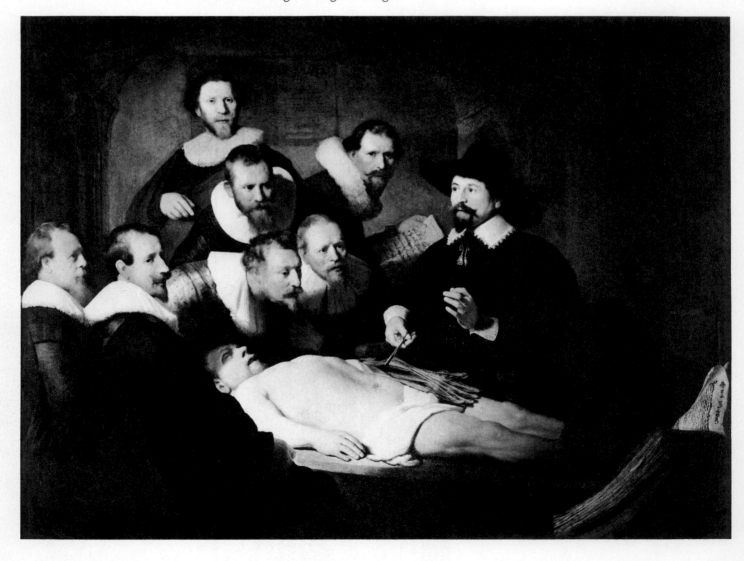

scene. Apparently he wanted liveliness rather than dignity, and Frans Hals has given him more of that than even Caravaggio could have done. Everything here is keyed to the mood of the moment: the laughter, the raising of the wine glass, and—most important of all—the way the picture is painted. Frans Hals works in broad, dashing strokes of the brush, never really "finishing" any of the details, so that the completed picture keeps the freshness of a first sketch (compare the one by Rubens, figure 247). We can almost see the artist battling against time, making every split second count. How happy he would have been with a modern camera! Or so, at least, it seems to us; actually it took Frans Hals hours, not minutes, to do a life-size painting such as this. What matters is that he wants us to *think* he did it in the wink of an eye.

Frans Hals was among the most prosperous portrait painters of Holland, but as he grew older the public turned away from him, and he found himself "out of fashion." A similar fate fell to Rembrandt, the greatest genius of Dutch art. In figure 274 you see one of his earlier pictures, done in 1633, soon after he had settled in Amsterdam. For about a decade, it was the height of fashion for the wealthy people of this great seaport city to have their portraits painted by Rembrandt (see figure 273). He himself, however, was more interested in religious scenes, of which he did a great many, although for private collectors rather than for churches. The subject of ours is *Christ in the Storm on the Lake of Galilee*. Here Rembrandt comes close to Rubens: the forces of wind and water are clashing so fiercely that they almost seem to merge into one, crushing the boat between them. For the Dutch, who often knew the threat of the sea from personal experience, as sailors or as lowland dwellers, this scene had a very

276. REMBRANDT / *Christ Preaching (etching)* / About 1652. *This print shows the gentler light and the more subtle mood of the artist's mature years. Some of the people listening to Christ are based on models Rembrandt had found in the ghetto of Amsterdam.*

274. REMBRANDT / *Christ in the Storm on the Lake of Galilee* 1633. Isabella Stewart Gardner Museum, Boston. *See comment below. Much of Rembrandt's work before 1650 shows the vigorous movement and the dramatic contrasts we think of as the more obvious qualities of the Baroque.*

275. REMBRANDT / *Christ Carrying the Cross (pen and wash drawing)* / About 1635. Formerly Kupferstichkabinett, Berlin. *Here again we see a Baroque intensity of action and feeling, conveyed by violent, sweeping strokes, by extremes of light and dark, and by a design that bursts the frame.*

direct bearing on their daily lives; they could easily imagine themselves in the same boat with Christ, especially since Rembrandt has painted a fishing boat of the kind actually in use during those days. And the followers of Christ are just as frightened as ordinary men (one of them is even being seasick). But the most remarkable thing in the picture is the light, which reveals the entire scene to us in a single flash, as though it came from a terrific bolt of lightning. This is Caravaggio's dramatic timing again, put to work by Rembrandt and raised to a new pitch of excitement.

As Rembrandt grew older he became less and less interested in scenes of violent action. Instead, he gained a new insight into the drama of people's thoughts and feelings. *The Polish Rider* (figure 268) was done some twenty years after the *Christ in the Storm,* in this more personal style. We do not know for sure whether the rider is Polish (the title was given to him later), only that he is dressed in a strange, Eastern-looking costume. Nor can we tell exactly what meaning Rembrandt had in mind for him, although we can make a pretty good guess. Like Dürer, Rembrandt was a maker of prints, so he probably knew and admired the famous engraving, *Knight, Death, and Devil* (figure 218). *The Polish Rider* is another "Christian Soldier," bravely riding through a perilous world; but here the dangers along the way, and the goal as well, are left to our imagination, instead of being spelled out as in Dürer's print.

277. REMBRANDT / *Saul and David* / About 1660. Mauritshuis, The Hague. *The magnificent breadth and freedom of the brushwork here recalls the late work of Titian (figures 190, 191). Rembrandt's use of Jewish models sprang in part from a desire for "authenticity" (compare figure 230) but also from the special sympathy he felt for a people in whose faces he read the spiritual heritage as well as the sufferings of a great past.*

278. REMBRANDT / *Family Portrait* / About 1668. Municipal Museum, Brunswick, Germany. *In his late years, Rembrandt showed a growing awareness of Renaissance art. Here he has patterned his composition after a family portrait of more than a century before (see figure 224). He also enriched the golden-brown tone of his pictures with bright greens and reds, which he spread in heavy yet somehow transparent layers against the velvety darkness of the background.*

The gloomy landscape and the somber colors suggest that our "knight" is not having an easy time; his serious, alert glance also tells us of unseen dangers, while the determined set of his mouth makes us feel that he will face them with courage.

If *Christ in the Storm* made us think of Rubens, *The Polish Rider* reminds us of Giorgione and Titian. Like them, Rembrandt has now become a poet of light and color, a maker of moods rather than of stories. And yet *The Polish Rider* remains a Baroque picture. Giorgione (figure 167) respects the limits of his canvas, he makes all his forms stay within the frame; with Rembrandt, on the contrary, the frame does not hold anything in place. His horseman is merely "passing through" and will soon be out of sight. And since he moves in the same direction as the light in the picture, we almost come to feel that the light is a kind of force which helps him along. The language of Rembrandt's late style, then, is not so different

279. REMBRANDT / *Self-Portrait* / About 1660. The Iveagh Bequest, Kenwood, London. *Throughout his life, Rembrandt was his own favorite model. No other painter reveals himself so completely in his self-portraits. This example combines great dignity with simple directness.*

181

280. HERCULES SEGHERS / *Mountain Landscape* / About 1630–35. Uffizi Gallery, Florence. *This sweeping view, by the greatest Dutch landscapist of the early seventeenth century, recalls the grandeur of Pieter Bruegel (see page 153) as well as the dramatic lighting of Rembrandt (see figure 274). Rembrandt admired the somber poetic genius of Seghers: he probably owned this particular picture and may have added the small figures at the lower left.*

from that of Rubens after all; he just uses it to say other things.

The magic of light plays an even greater part in the religious works of Rembrandt's old age, such as the unforgettable *Saul and David* (figure 277). The Bible tells us that after his victory over Goliath, David was taken into the royal household, but that King Saul grew jealous when people praised the young hero more highly than him. One day, while David was playing the harp, he suddenly hurled his spear at the boy. Here is a subject ready-made for Rubens: what a splendid action picture he would have made of it! Rem-

brandt, on the other hand, shows us not the story itself but the meaning behind it. His Saul is not simply the victim of an evil passion, but a sad and lonely man so overcome with feeling that he forgets all about his royal dignity—he uses a curtain to wipe away his tears. What is it, we wonder, that moves him so deeply; has David's playing filled him with remorse at his guilty thoughts? Or is he mourning the loss of his own youth, now that a new leader has arisen? Whatever it is, David remains quite unaware of it; he is just a young musician busily plucking his harp. Rembrandt's attention and sympathy are centered on the unhappy king. Through the wonderful play of light on Saul's face, he tells us all he has learned in his lifetime about the strange ways of the human spirit.

281. JAN VAN GOYEN / *Fort on a River* / 1644. Museum of Fine Arts, Boston. *See comments on facing page. It was Van Goyen who discovered the pictorial beauty of the Dutch countryside, with its moisture-laden atmosphere and looming gray skies reflected in rivers and canals.*

Paintings like this demand a lot of thoughtful attention if we want to understand them completely. At any rate, most of the art buyers of Holland found them too difficult for their taste. They much preferred pictures of familiar things and experiences, such as the *Fort on a River* by Jan van Goyen (figure 281), with its view of a distant town, its sailboats and windmills. There is nothing remarkable about this scene—it might be almost anywhere along the Dutch coast—and people loved it just because they knew it so well. Van Goyen, however, is less interested in the details than in the special mood of these low-lying "nether lands" that are always at the mercy of

282. JACOB VAN RUISDAEL / *View of Haarlem* / About 1670. Formerly State Museums, Berlin. *This landscape shares the low horizon of Van Goyen's pictures but creates a very different mood through the dramatic, wind-swept sky and the alternating streaks of sunlight and shadow.*

283. JACOB VAN RUISDAEL / *The Jewish Graveyard* / About 1655. Picture Gallery, Dresden. *See comment on following page. The landscape with ruins is a characteristic invention of Baroque art, for it involves an awareness of time. Elsheimer's classical ruin in its idyllic setting (figure 256) evokes the lost golden age of Greece and Rome, while Ruisdael's medieval ruin in storm-tossed, deserted country is a grim reminder that All Is Vanity.*

wind and water. His vast gray sky seems calm enough, yet it holds the threat of those same forces whose fury we had seen unleashed in Rembrandt's *Christ in the Storm*.

Like so many artists of seventeenth-century Holland, Van Goyen was a specialist; most of his works are landscapes of the type we have just seen. Other Dutch landscape painters favored different moods and different kinds of scenes. Figure 283, *The Jewish Graveyard*, is by the most famous of them all, Jacob van Ruisdael. Here the forces of nature are again the main theme, although the setting is frankly imaginary. The thunderclouds passing over the wild and deserted countryside, the ruined building, the rushing stream that has forced its way between the ancient graves, all help to create a mood of deepest gloom. Nothing endures on this earth, Ruisdael tells us; time, wind, and water will grind it all to dust—not only the feeble works of man but trees and rocks as well. He must have felt that way about his own life, for he has put his name on the tombstone nearest to us.

Another group of specialists were the "painters of things," whose works we call still lifes. In figure 284 you see a very fine one by Willem Claesz Heda, painted in 1634. Earlier masters had been interested in things, too (look at Holbein's *George Gisze*, figure 205), but only as part of a human subject. Why, then, did the Baroque painters regard still lifes as good enough to put a frame around, and how did they decide what to put into such pictures? In our painting, the silver dish and the great glass goblet are fine and expensive pieces, interesting in themselves; the oysters go with the wine in the goblet, and the lemon goes with the oysters. Are we perhaps meant to wonder why this elegant lunch was left uneaten? The silver dish has been upset, and one of the goblets is broken, but the arrangement as a whole is too tasteful and well balanced to fit any kind of a story. What really "explains" it is the artist's interest in light and its reflections on these varied surfaces. It is this that stamps our still life not only as Baroque but as Dutch Baroque of the 1630's. Compare it with Rembrandt's *Christ in the Storm* of 1633: it may seem hard to believe that two paintings so different could have anything in common, yet they share a peculiar silvery tone—the light "feels" the same in both.

284. WILLEM CLAESZ. HEDA / *Still Life* / 1634. Boymans Museum, Rotterdam. *See comment above. The origins of the "banquet still life" (as this type is often called) can be found in such pictures as Heemskerk's* Family Portrait *(figure 224), which includes a table with food and drink.*

285. JAN DAVIDSZ. DE HEEM / *Flower Still Life* / About 1665. Ashmolean Museum, Oxford. *For another still life by the same artist see figure 447. What gives this picture such appeal is not only the rich variety of shapes and colors but the Baroque energy and vitality of every flower.*

286.   JAN VERMEER / *The Girl with a Red Hat* / About 1660. National Gallery of Art, Washington, D. C. (Mellon Collection.) *This tiny picture, here shown in about the size of the original, is a fascinating study of the nature of light and its effect on color and form (note how the highlights are rendered as glistening "droplets").*

288. DIEGO VELAZQUEZ / *The Maids of Honor* / 1656. The Prado, Madrid. *In this master-piece of his late years, Velazquez combines splendid portraiture with a poetry of light and shade that shows his kinship with the best of the Dutch genre painters (compare figures 270, 296).*

289. NICOLAS POUSSIN / *The Abduction of the Sabine Women* / 1636-37. Metropolitan Museum of Art, New York. *Poussin, who felt more at home in Italy than in France, became the greatest guardian of the classical tradition in a Baroque world—a tradition reaching back from Reni and the Carracci to Raphael and Ancient Roman art.*

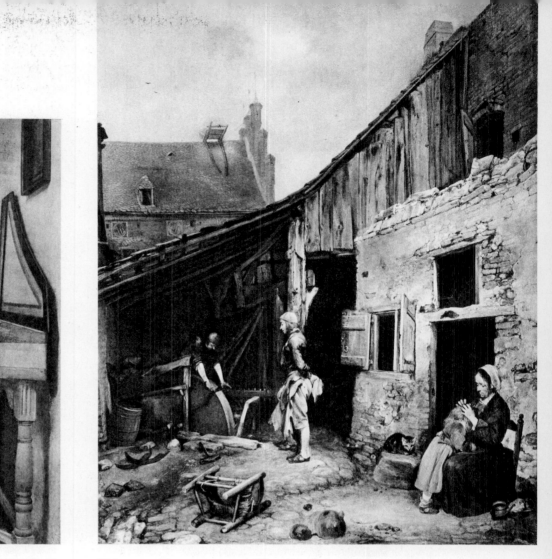

290. GERARD TERBORCH / *The Concert* / About 1655–60. Formerly State Museums, Berlin. *In rendering the sheen of silk or the softness of velvet, Terborch had no rivals. Yet he was no mere virtuoso of textures; The Concert also impresses us with its finely balanced design and the delicacy of its mood.*

291. GERARD TERBORCH / *The Grinder's Family* / About 1635–40. Formerly State Museums, Berlin. *Terborch had been trained as a painter of low life genre (compare figure 266); but here, instead of telling a story, he views the back-yard world of the poor with seriousness and sympathy.*

Before we leave Holland let us have a quick look at the genre specialists, the painters of daily life. *The Eve of Saint Nicholas* by Jan Steen (figure 269) shows a family at Christmas time. Nicholas has just visited the children, dealing out toys, candy, and the traditional Dutch honey-cake; everybody is having a fine time except the bad boy to the left, who has received nothing but a birch rod (for punishment) in his shoe. Jan Steen has told this story with great relish, embroidering it with all sorts of warm human touches and delightful details. It all looks very much like the

292. VERMEER / *The Letter* / About 1666. Rijksmuseum, Amsterdam. *Of all Vermeer's pictures, this one is the most "modern." The interlocking of shapes is so precise, so daringly original, that its closest relatives would seem to be in twentieth-century rather than in nineteenth-century art.*

293. CAREL FABRITIUS / *Self-Portrait* / About 1643. Pinakothek, Munich. *Rembrandt's most gifted pupil, who died in Delft at the age of 32, was the teacher of Vermeer. This picture, although still close to Rembrandt, already shows his distinctly individual style.*

294. DIEGO VELAZQUEZ / *The Water Carrier of Seville* / About 1619. Wellington Museum, London. (Crown copyright reserved.) *When he painted this canvas, the 20-year-old Velazquez probably had never seen an original by Caravaggio; yet he grasped all the essentials of Caravaggio's style.*

295. EMANUEL DE WITTE / *Interior of a Church* / 1668. Boymans Museum, Rotterdam. *Medieval church interiors were one of the many special fields in Dutch painting. This example shows an imaginary view combining features from several buildings so as to yield the richest interplay of light and shade.*

296. PIETER DE HOOCH / *The Young Mother* / About 1660. Formerly State Museums, Berlin. *At their best, the interiors of De Hooch have the same cool, steady light and some of the same geometric sense of order we find in Vermeer, but with greater emphasis on description and sentiment.*

scene that is still acted out in our own homes every year. Few artists can make us feel the pleasures —and pains!—of family celebrations quite so well as this one does.

After the cheerful din of Steen's Christmas party, we are struck by the silence and order of *The Artist in his Studio* by Jan Vermeer (figure 270). Both pictures were done about the same time—in the 1660's—but this only helps to stress the basic difference between them. Steen, the storyteller, has the vivid sense of timing we know from Frans Hals. Vermeer, in contrast, shows us a time-less "still life" world, where nothing stirs, not even the figures. And yet, strange to say, they do not look at all frozen; it is rather as if this room, and everything in it, had been gently becalmed by some magic spell. The cool, clear daylight filtering in from the left provides all the action there is, and all that is needed, as it glances

off the model's bright blue gown, sets the brass chandelier aglow, or settles in tiny, dew-like "droplets" on the curtain in the foreground. And now we realize the meaning of the spell: it makes us aware of the miracle of sight. Looking at this picture, we feel as if a veil had been pulled from our eyes, so that everything shines with a freshness and beauty we never knew before. In his early years Vermeer had learned a good deal from the painters of the Utrecht School; through them, he owes a debt to Caravaggio. But the quiet perfection of his style reminds us of something else—of Hubert and Jan van Eyck, the first great "discoverers of reality." In one sense, Vermeer completed what they had begun; yet he is also an important discoverer in his own right. Neglected until quite recently, he seems today far more modern in spirit than any other Dutch painter of his time.

297. FRANCISCO DE ZURBARAN / *A Franciscan in Prayer* / About 1639. National Gallery, London. *In Zurbaran, the same Caravaggio influence that inspired the everyday scenes of the young Velazquez (figure 294) gave rise to an art of austere and exalted religious feeling.*

298. JUSEPE RIBERA / *The Martyrdom of St. Bartholomew* 1639. The Prado, Madrid. *Although he spent most of his life in Naples, Ribera here remains unmistakably Spanish, both in his human types and in the tough-minded directness with which he renders physical cruelty.*

299. DIEGO VELAZQUEZ / *Infante Carlos* / About 1625. The Prado, Madrid. *This portrait, painted not long after he had settled in Madrid, still has the clean outlines, the precise separation of light and shade, and the solemn dignity of the artist's Sevillian works (see figure 294).*

Spain, France

IN ALL OF SEVENTEENTH-CENTURY art, there was only one other painter as completely devoted to the wonders of seeing as Vermeer: Diego Velazquez, the greatest master of the Spanish Baroque. He, too, had been influenced by Caravaggio (figure 294); after he was appointed court painter to the King of Spain, he came to know Rubens and studied the works of Titian. His mature style, however, is unlike any of these. It can no more be "explained" than that of Vermeer. Most of Velazquez' works are royal portraits that had to follow set patterns (see figure 299), but every once in a while he would do a picture entirely on his own, such as *The Maids of Honor* of 1656 (figures 288, 301). It might also be called "the artist in his studio," for it shows Velazquez himself at work on a huge canvas, probably the very picture we see before us. In the center is the little Princess Margarita with her playmates and maids of honor. Her parents, the King and Queen, have just stepped into the room; their faces are reflected in the mirror on the back wall, which means that they saw the scene exactly as we do. In other words, Velazquez has painted a "king's-eye view" of his studio. But could the King and Queen really have seen *as much* here as Velazquez shows us? Were they as struck as we are by the soft, shadowy depth of the room? Did they sense the drama of the sunlight flooding the foreground the way we do? Velazquez' brushwork may at first glance remind you of Frans Hals, but you will find it a great deal more varied and subtle, for its aim is

300. *Detail of Figure 287. The fluid brushwork and atmospheric depth of this vista show us how deeply Velazquez was affected by the works of Titian and Rubens he saw in the collections of the King of Spain.*

not to catch figures in motion but, rather, the movement of light *over* the figures. Light, to Velazquez, is what *makes* color and form; that's why he puts so many kinds of light into his picture—to find out how different they make things look; how the colors of a gown can change from warm to cool, and its "feel" from crisp to soft. If we had to pick a single work to sum up the "language" of Baroque painting, we could hardly make a better choice than this.

Moving on from Spain to France, we find a very different taste at the royal court at Paris. King Louis XIV liked to be called the "Sun King," because he wanted it known that everything in France depended on his will, just as all life on earth depends on the sun. He even wanted to control the way French artists painted, and he did this through the Royal Academy, an official school for painters and sculptors. In the past, young artists had always been trained by working in the shops of older men; during the Baroque era, this was still the usual method. But since the Renaissance, as we have seen, practical skill and experience were no longer enough for the artist. He needed to know a good deal of science and theory, too, so certain masters had founded private academies where they taught these things to groups of young artists. At the Royal Academy of Louis XIV, practice and theory were combined into a complete system of instruction, with the aim of giving the student an approved standard of style and beauty. This program became the model for all the later academies, and its echoes can still be felt among the art schools of today. Even so, it never worked very well. The most important thing in art, after all, is imagination, and it is pretty hard to make rules about that. Artists are by nature "unruly," so the best of them usually stayed outside the academies. In fact, the man on whose work the "ideal style" of the Royal Academy was based, preferred to live in Rome at a safe distance from the pressure of the Court. He was Nicolas Poussin, the greatest French painter of the seventeenth century. *The Abduction of the*

301. *Detail of Figure 288. Even a small area such as this contains a vast variety of brush stroke effects—creamy smooth, feathery, jabbing, twisting—designed to capture not the actual surface textures but the light they reflect.*

302. ESTEBAN MURILLO / *A Girl and Her Duenna* / About 1665–75. National Gallery of Art, Washington, D.C. (Widener Collection.) *The Sevillian tradition of genre painting (see figure 294) survived in the work of Murillo. This charming picture may have impressed Goya (see figure 346).*

303. GEORGES DE LA TOUR / *The Education of the Virgin* / About 1635–40. Private collection, Paris. *Like Vermeer, La Tour is far more famous now than he was in his own day. His pictures, indirect echoes of Caravaggio, combine clarity of form with a touching tenderness of feeling.*

Sabine Women (figure 289) will show you why the Academy considered him such a perfect example for its students. The subject is a famous event of Early Roman times. In the beginning, there was a great shortage of women in Rome, since the city had been founded by an adventurous band of men from across the sea. The Romans tried to find wives among their neighbors, the Sabines, but the Sabine men would not let them. So they used a trick—having invited the entire Sabine tribe into the city for a peaceful festival, they suddenly fell upon them with arms and took the women away by force. Poussin was, of course, interested in this scene as a drama involving many different kinds of action and emotion. At the same time, however, he felt that it must be treated in a noble and heroic manner, so instead of trying to imagine how ordinary people would behave in such a situation he modeled his figures after Classical statues and after the masters of the Roman High Renaissance (compare Raphael's *Heliodorus* mural, figure 182). Still, Poussin was far from blind toward the art of his own day.

304. LOUIS LE NAIN / *Peasant Family* / About 1640. The Louvre, Paris. *Here we see the impact of Caravaggio, but Louis Le Nain has less in common with La Tour than with the low life scenes of the young Velazquez (see figure 294). Two centuries later, the dignity and humanity of his poverty-stricken peasants was to inspire Courbet and Millet (see figures 380, 381, 385) and, through them, the early Van Gogh (see figure 420).*

305. NICOLAS POUSSIN / *Landscape with the Burial of Phocion* / 1648. The Louvre, Paris. *This austerely beautiful picture stems from the "classical landscape" of Annibale Carracci (see figure 253). Poussin's view of nature, and of man's place in it, was a nostalgic vision of harmony and stability—nostalgic because he knew it to be forever beyond our grasp. The opposite extreme is represented by* The Jewish Graveyard *of Ruisdael (figure 283).*

The flowing movement in his picture reminds us of Rubens, and the light has some of the sharpness of Caravaggio's. Drawing and modeling were obviously more important to Poussin than painting —he believed in form as something apart from light and color—yet there is a fine color sense in the *Sabine Women,* and the soft and airy background landscape seems almost Venetian. The entire picture suggests an artist who knew his own mind almost too well. Poussin's style did not

306. NICOLAS POUSSIN / *Self-Portrait* / 1650. The Louvre, Paris. *While Poussin's view of himself may seem lacking in human warmth and intimacy, it is in its own way as revealing as we could wish; here, clearly, is a man for whom the pursuit of art has become an ascetic discipline.*

307. NICOLAS POUSSIN / *Cephalus and Aurora* / About 1630. National Gallery, London. *Poussin's devotion to classical form —that is, to ancient art and Raphael—is counterbalanced, in his earlier years, by an enthusiasm for the light and color of Titian (compare figure 189).*

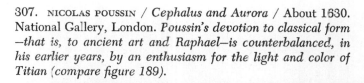

308. HYACINTHE RIGAUD / *Louis XIV* / 1701. The Louvre, Paris. *The Baroque splendor of this official portrait of the "Sun King," with its great flourishes of drapery, is closer to Rubens (who had glorified another French monarch in the 1620's, see figure 247) than to Poussin.*

just happen; it grew from conscious effort. His aim, it seems, was an art of the "golden middle ground" where form and color, thought and feeling, truth and beauty, the ideal and the real are in harmony with each other. Since all this involved much discipline and self-control, Poussin's style was considered more "teachable" than that of any other important master. Poussin himself wrote about his work at great length in his letters to friends or patrons. Sometimes he would discuss a single picture, explaining in detail exactly what he had done, and why; or he would set down theories and ideas about painting in general, always confident that art could be reasoned out like any other subject. The teachers at the Academy followed the same method of taking a picture apart as if it were an intricate piece of machinery. One of them even made up a sort of scoreboard of the great painters of all periods with definite grades for each one in composition, drawing, color, and "expression" (in the last Caravaggio got a zero, the lowest mark!). All this, of course, never produced another Poussin, yet we still admire his work and respect his ideals.

309. CLAUDE LORRAIN / *A Clump of Trees (brush drawing)* / About 1650. Teyler Museum, Haarlem. *Claude, like Poussin, chose to spend most of his life in Rome, where he became the most famous painter of "classical landscapes." Today, these seem less impressive than his drawings from nature, which reveal a freshness of eye and a poetic sensitivity to the changing moods of light and atmosphere unmatched by any other artist of his time.*

Toward Revolution

WHEN WE THINK OF the eighteenth century, the events that come to our mind are, first of all, the American Revolution of 1776 and the French Revolution of 1789. We are also apt to remember that it was the Age of Enlightenment, the time of the great social thinkers who believed that all human affairs ought to be ruled by reason and the common good—a revolution of the mind that started many years before the political revolutions. This is all true enough, yet it gives us a somewhat one-sided view of the times. It was indeed an age of change, but most of the changes happened slowly, rather than from one day to the next, and until the late years of the eighteenth century, life was not so very different from what it had been in the seventeenth. In art, too, the trends that had begun during the Baroque era continued for quite a long time without

310. *Detail of Figure 326. Watteau's couples move with the studied grace of actors, but their radiant charm is fresh and natural. Here the enchanted world of Rubens' Garden of Love (figure 263) has come to life again. If Watteau lacks some of the full-bodied vitality of the great Flemish master, he has an elegance and subtlety of touch all his own.*

311. FRANÇOIS BOUCHER / *Shepherd and Shepherdess* / 1755. The Louvre, Paris. *In Boucher we find both the virtues and the shortcomings of Rococo painting; we enjoy its refined sensuousness, but its charm, having lost the human warmth of Watteau, strikes us as shallow and cloying.*

any violent breaks. Since we have seen before how freely new ideas in art could cross from one country to the next, it will no longer surprise us to find that we can trace the pageantry of Rubens, the realism of the Dutch masters, the severe ideals of Poussin, even when they appear in other places and under different circumstances.

In France, the early years of the century saw a really striking change of public taste. During the reign of Louis XIV, the Royal Academy had controlled much of the art life of the country, and the "Sun King" had kept a stern eye upon his courtiers. When he finally died in 1715, it was as if the entire French Court had decided to go on a holiday. The nobles deserted the Royal Palace of Versailles, where they had been forced to live before, and built themselves elegant private town

312. FRANÇOIS BOUCHER / *Madame de Pompadour* / About 1755. National Galleries of Scotland, Edinburgh. *Boucher enjoyed the particular support of Madame de Pompadour, who even took drawing lessons from him. Here he shows the favorite of Louis XV reposing amidst a gorgeous array of textures—silk, lace, brocade, flowers both real and artificial—to set off her powdered beauty. Her real personality remains discreetly hidden behind the fashionable ideal she embodies.*

313. JEAN BAPTISTE GREUZE / *The Village Bride* / 1761. The Louvre, Paris. *It is hard to understand today how Greuze could be hailed as the apostle of a return to nature, in contrast to the "decadent" Rococo style. To us, his pictures seem no less theatrical than those of Boucher, and the sentiment no less contrived. The self-conscious pathos of this scene makes us suspect that Greuze actually knew very little about the way people feel and behave in real life.*

houses in Paris. These they had decorated by artists who had broken with the old tradition of the Academy. Their hero was no longer Poussin but Rubens, who to them represented all the things the Academy had frowned upon: color, light, movement, and a frank pleasure in living. Antoine Watteau, who came from the northern border of France near Flanders, was the first and by far the most gifted painter of this new era, which we often call the Rococo. His *Mezzetin* (figure 325) shows us Watteau's favorite subject, a character out of the popular comedy theater of

314. JEAN ETIENNE LIOTARD / *A Turkish Lady with Her Servant (pastel)* / About 1740. Musee d'Art et d'Histoire, Geneva. *Liotard was the most subtle pastellist of his day. This fresh and cool-toned study, the fruit of a five-year stay in Turkey, betrays his admiration for the Dutch genre painters.*

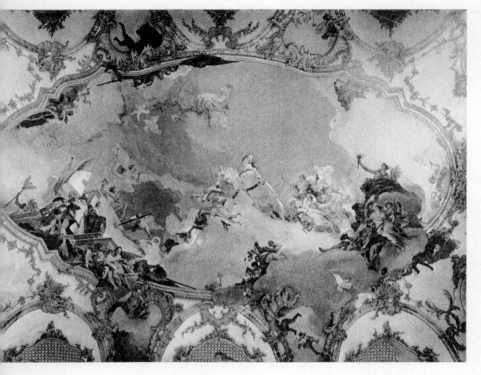

315, 316. *Above and below, at left:* GIOVANNI BATTISTA TIEPOLO / *Ceiling Fresco, and Detail* / 1751. Episcopal Palace, Würzburg. 317. *Above, at right: River God and Nymph (pen-and-wash study for the ceiling painting)* / Metropolitan Museum of Art, New York. *The Würzburg frescoes, Tiepolo's masterpiece, are the last great achievement of the Italian tradition of decorative wall painting. Gay, opulent, and facile, they celebrate the final triumph of the Baroque imagination.*

the time. The easy, flowing brushwork and the splendid color leave no doubt in our minds about the influence of Rubens, even though Watteau lacks the sweeping energy of the great Fleming. Instead we find delicate, slender forms and a mood, half gay and half sad, that may remind you a bit of Giorgione's *Concert*. Watteau, however, has made the situation more pointed: Mezzetin is doomed to serenade his lady love without hope, both on the stage and in real life—we recognize him as a relative of those sorrowful clowns that have survived till today in such popular successes as the opera *I Pagliacci*.

Watteau's love of the theater gives us a clue to the spirit of Rococo society. It was, for the nobles at any rate, an age of play acting—of pretending that their life was as free from worry as that of François Boucher's shepherd and shepherdess (figure 311), who live in a delightful world where the sheep never stray, so that they can devote all their time to the pursuit of love. Marie Antoinette, the last Queen of France, actually had a model farm built on the grounds of the Palace of Versailles, where she and her friends could play at being milkmaids and field hands when they tired of the formality of court life.

There was, however, another side to French eighteenth-century painting, especially during the thirty years right before the Revolution. It reflects the growing importance of the common man, who, as the "citizen" of 1789, was to become the ruler of France. In 1761, while Boucher was still catering to the taste of the nobles with his powdery shepherds and shepherdesses, Jean-Baptiste Greuze did *The Village Bride* (figure 313), a subject drawn from the daily life of the people, which won him the praise of all the leading critics. He had been trained in the Rococo style, but here he turns to the realistic genre painters of Holland for inspiration. His reasons for picking a scene like this, however, were quite different from those of the Dutch masters. Steen's *Eve of Saint Nicholas* strikes us as a real event, observed with humor and sympathy, while *The Village Bride* is "staged" by actors. The bride looks too bashful, her mother too tear-stained, the

grandfather too venerable to be quite convincing. We feel that Greuze wants to pull our heartstrings at all cost—"just look how touching, how sincere these poor people are!" he seems to say. Everything in the picture plays a part in this message, even such apparently unrelated details as the hen with her chicks in the foreground; one of them has left the brood and is sitting alone on the saucer to the right, just the way the bride is about to leave *her* "brood." Strangely enough, *The Village Bride* was acclaimed as a masterpiece, and the loudest praise came from the most "enlightened" minds—from the advocates of the rule of reason. These men liked the fact that everything in Greuze's picture "meant" something, and that the artist wanted to appeal to our moral sense instead of just giving us pleasure like the Rococo painters. They overlooked, of course, that a worthy moral is not enough—in fact, it is not even necessary—to make a great work of art.

318. FRANCISCO GOYA / The Parasol / 1777. The Prado, Madrid. *This gay and charming "pre-revolutionary" work of Goya, designed for the royal tapestry factory, contains more than a faint echo of Tiepolo's style. Tiepolo spent the last eight years of his life in Madrid and died there in 1770. About that time Goya, then 24 years old, set out on his trip to Italy; was he prompted by a desire to see more works by the great Venetian?*

We can learn this lesson from the *Kitchen Still Life* by Jean Siméon Chardin (figure 327). Its meaning is similar to Greuze's, but Chardin conveys it to us without preaching or acting, and yet far more effectively. He, too, admired Dutch painting, and his picture comes from such earlier still lifes as the one by Willem Claesz Heda (figure 284). However, instead of using expensive silver dishes and handblown glass, he picked a few plain, sturdy kitchen pieces and some uncooked meat and fowl—the household things of the common man. Chardin has found so much beauty in these everyday objects, he treats them with such respect and understanding, that they suddenly become important as symbols for a way of life. Somehow, we feel, this quiet and unassuming picture has all the dignity and simplicity that Greuze tried, in vain, to put into *The Village Bride*. And the reason is that Chardin speaks to us in the painter's own language—through color, light, and form—instead of borrowing the language of the stage.

During those years many Frenchmen had a great admiration for England. The English had gone through a time of political revolution in the seventeenth century; they had forced the King to hand most of his powers over to Parliament, so that the "common Englishman" already had a voice, although a limited one, in his own government. As a result, England became the envy of

319. WILLIAM HOGARTH / *The Orgy (Scene III from the series "The Rake's Progress")* / About 1734. Sir John Soane's Museum, London. *This picture makes an instructive comparison with Greuze (figure 313), who has been called, with undue flattery, "the French Hogarth," and who was surely indebted to the inventor of these pictorial morality plays. Hogarth's sermon is so full of the spice of life that we can enjoy it without taking its lesson at face value.*

320. THOMAS GAINSBOROUGH / *Robert Andrews and His Wife* / About 1750. G. W. Andrews, Redhill, Surrey, England. *Despite some echoes of Ruisdael (compare figure 282), there is an intensely English flavor in this landscape and in the relaxed, natural pose of the country gentleman and his lady. Some years later, Gainsborough was to adapt his portraits to an ideal of aristocratic elegance based on Van Dyck (compare figures 261, 321).*

321. *Below:* THOMAS GAINSBOROUGH / *Mrs. Siddons* / 1785. National Gallery, London.   322. *At right:* SIR JOSHUA REYNOLDS / *Mrs. Siddons as the Tragic Muse* / 1784. Henry E. Huntington Library and Art Gallery, San Marino, California. *Gainsborough shows her as the coolly elegant lady of fashion; Reynolds casts her in a "noble" role of his own invention. Here two aspects of British painting are reflected.*

the continental nations. Its wealth was growing rapidly, the overseas colonies prospered, and the British navy and merchant fleet ruled the seas. Last but not least, the English had begun to play an important part in the fine arts.

Since the time of the Reformation, there had been little painting in England except portraits, and the leading artists had been foreigners: Holbein under Henry VIII, Flemings and Dutchmen later on. Even in the eighteenth century, when English artists came to the fore again, portraits were all they could count on for a steady living; but many of them did other subjects as important sidelines, so that these, too, found a home in England. William Hogarth was such a painter. His particular interest lay in realistic scenes from daily life, similar to those of the Dutch genre masters. Hogarth, however, gave a keen satirical edge to these pictures and strung them together into series that told a story in many separate "installments" (see figure 319). His sense of humor, as well as his fresh and observant eye, may also be seen in the delightful portrait of the Graham children (figure 331). It will remind you of Jan Steen, even though Hogarth's colors are brighter

and his brushwork freer. The picture is, of course, not meant to be a genre scene. We can surmise from the fine costumes that the parents of these children must have been very well-to-do; they probably expected our artist to paint quite a formal portrait, with poses borrowed from adults. Hogarth has done that, but he has also found ways of relieving the stiffness of such a group. The two girls, we feel, are just having fun pretending to be ladies, and over on the right he tells us a little story—the boy is cranking his music box for the bird in the cage, but a large cat has jumped onto the back of the chair, and the poor bird is so afraid of its greedy stare that instead of singing it only flaps its wings and shrieks.

The most famous portrait painter of eighteenth-century England, Thomas Gainsborough, had a sideline, too: he did wonderful landscapes. In his *Robert Andrews and His Wife* (figure 320), the outdoors setting is as important as the sitters. The cloudswept view will remind you of Dutch landscapes, such as those in figures 282 and 283, but now the forces of nature seem gentle, rather than threatening. This land belongs to the country squire and his lady, and they, in a sense, be-

323. THOMAS GAINSBOROUGH / *The Market Cart* / 1786. Tate Gallery, London. *In this fluidly painted woodland idyl, with its atmospheric haze and deep, soft shadows, Gainsborough has created an imaginative, poetic landscape far removed from the Dutch tradition.*

324. JOSEPH WRIGHT OF DERBY / *An Experiment with the Air Pump* / 1768. Tate Gallery, London. *The subject of this picture is as remarkable as the bold use of candlelight; it records the intense concern with science that brought about England's leadership in the Industrial Revolution.*

325. ANTOINE WATTEAU / *Mezzetin* / About 1715. Metropolitan Museum of Art, New York.
This stock character of Rococo comedy, painted in a fluid, sensuous technique borrowed from Rubens,
has so much human appeal that we find it hard to tell theatrical pathos from genuine passion.

326. ANTOINE WATTEAU / *Embarkation for Cythera* / 1717. The Louvre, Paris. *See also the detail, figure 310. Here we see the same poetic mixture of allegory, myth, and reality as in Rubens' Garden of Love (figure 263). With this picture Watteau became a full member of the French Royal Academy as "painter of gallant fetes."*

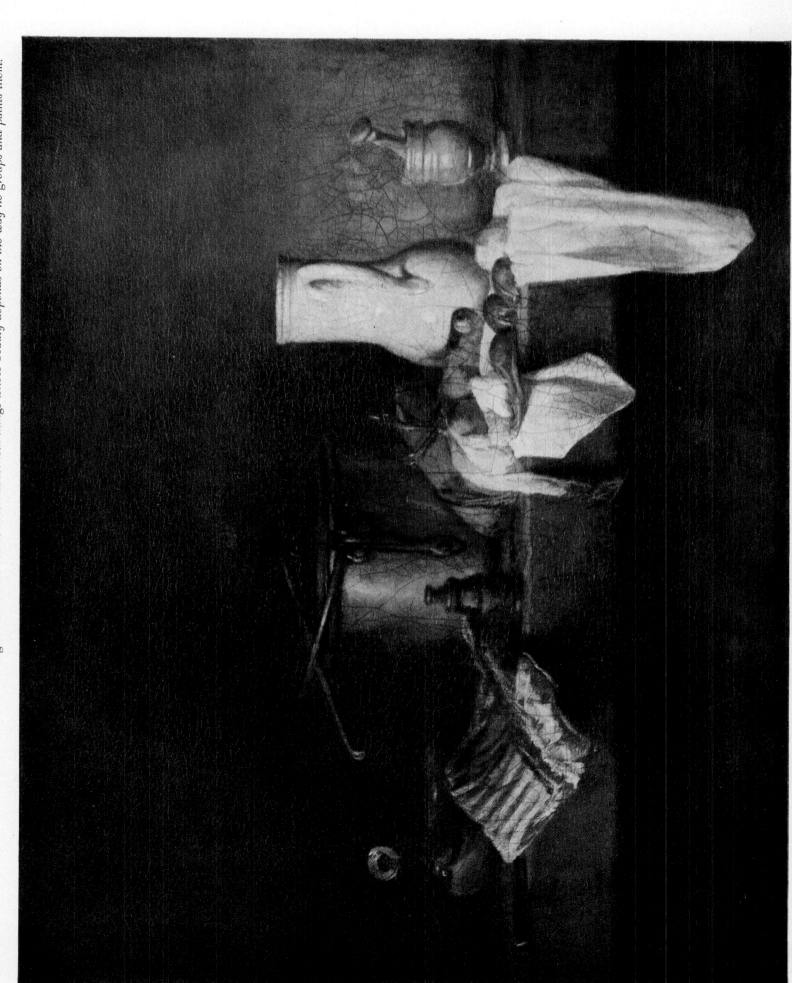

327. JEAN SIMEON CHARDIN / Kitchen Still Life / 1735. Museum of Fine Arts, Boston. Although Chardin is clearly inspired by Dutch still lifes such as that in figure 284, he no longer chooses objects that are interesting in themselves but common household things whose beauty depends on the way he groups and paints them.

328. JEAN SIMEON CHARDIN / *Back from the Market* / 1739. The Louvre, Paris. *Here again Chardin has taken over a Dutch tradition (compare figure 296) and invested it with a new feeling for the dignity of everyday life.*

329. JEAN HONORE FRAGONARD / *The Bathers* / About 1765. The Louvre, Paris. *The spirit of the Rococo—its levity, grace, and frank indulgence in the pleasures of the senses—is summed up perfectly in this enchanting picture, which on a smaller scale recaptures so much of the vitality, the heightened sense of life of Rubens (compare figures 247, 248).*

331.   WILLIAM HOGARTH / *The Graham Children* / 1742. Tate Gallery, London. *Hogarth's sense of humor, his fresh and observant eye, remind us of Jan Steen (figure 269), even though this is not a genre scene but a formal portrait. Fortunately, the artist did not force his sitters to take their conventional, mock-adult poses too seriously.*

At left:

330.   GIOVANNI BATTISTA TIEPOLO / *The Triumph of Religion* / About 1760. The Louvre, Paris. *This oil sketch for a ceiling fresco similar to that in figure 315, again shows the vast, light-filled space that no other master knew how to paint with such sweeping ease and assurance. Even Correggio and Veronese seem strangely earthbound in comparison.*

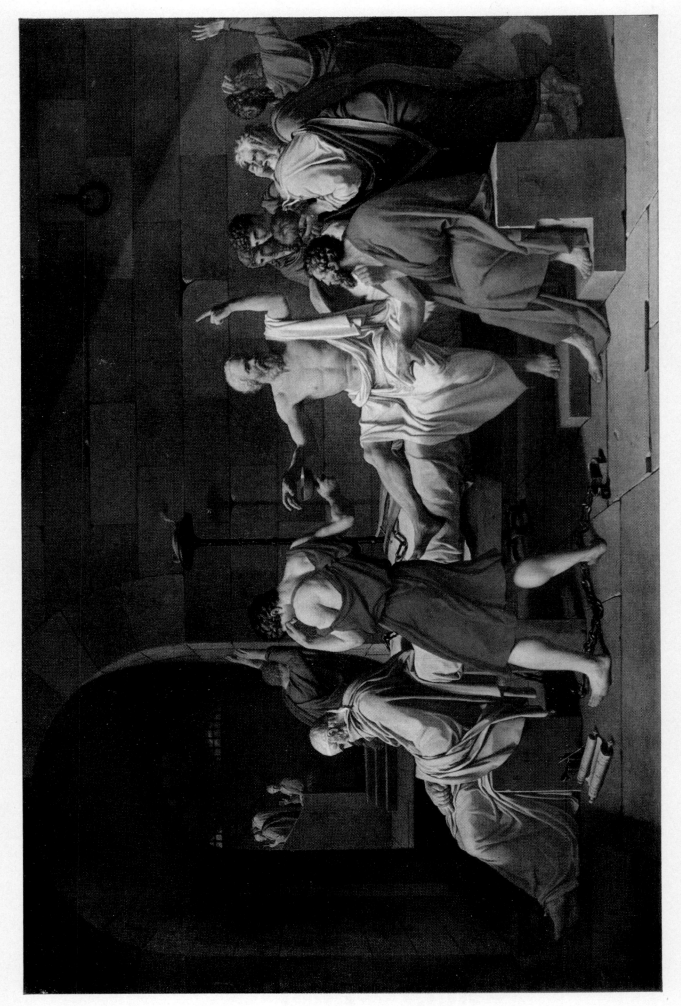

332. JACQUES LOUIS DAVID / *The Death of Socrates* / 1787. Metropolitan Museum of Art, New York. *Painted on the eve of the French Revolution,* The Death of Socrates *represents a return to the severe ideals of Poussin. Its heroic theme and relief-like, Neo-Classic design are a protest against the sensuous, pleasure-loving art fostered by Rococo society.*

long to it. Gainsborough here suggests the charm of a country life that is real, not make-believe as in Boucher's picture.

The North American colonies were by now old enough to have some fine painters of their own. The two most gifted ones, however, did not remain at home long enough to witness America's coming-of-age. Benjamin West, a Pennsylvania Quaker, and John Singleton Copley, from Boston, had gone to London a few years before the American Revolution. They had such success there that they stayed on for good, and West even became court painter to King George III and president of the British Royal Academy of Painting. This Academy was patterned on the principles of Poussin, but its ideals were much less severely Classical; in fact, they were broad enough to include the art of Rembrandt. West's portrait of *Colonel Guy Johnson* (figure 334) is bathed in a light of Rembrandt-like warmth, although we miss the Dutch master's expressive force. The poses of the figures, on the other hand, seem a bit self-consciously heroic, as if the two were Ancient Romans, while the costumes, and all the other trappings, are faithfully observed down to the last detail. Colonel Johnson was one of our first superintendents of Indian affairs. He is shown here with his trusted friend, Thayendanegea, who looks very much like "the noblest redskin of them all." West must have been quite proud of his

334. BENJAMIN WEST / *Colonel Guy Johnson* / About 1775. National Gallery of Art, Washington, D.C. (Mellon Collection.) *See comment on this page. Before settling in London, West went to Rome, to study the classics. Reportedly, he said of a famous Apollo statue: "How like a Mohawk warrior!"*

333. ALEXANDER COZENS / *Landscape Made of Ink Blots (aquatint)* / 1784-86. British Museum, London. *That we sometimes see images in accidental blots had already been noted by Leonardo. Cozens made a method of it, by developing landscapes such as this one from a series of blots he had splashed on the paper more or less by chance. His idea, which earned him much ridicule, has proved of great value to modern artists (see figure 500).*

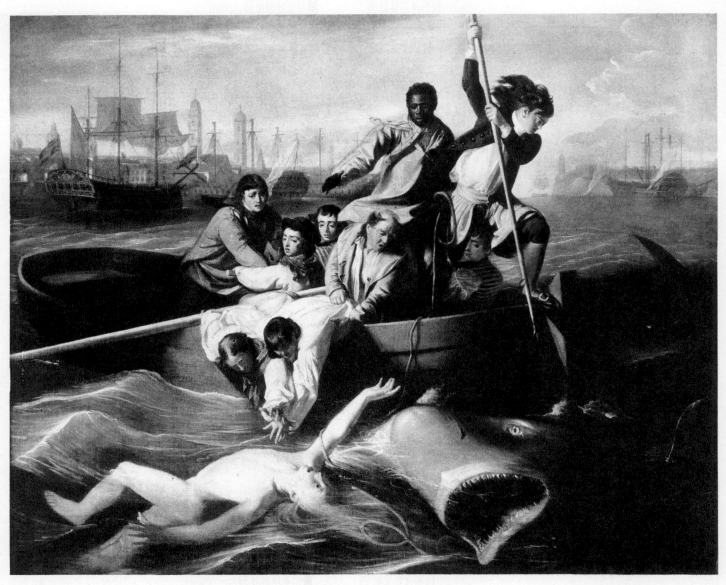

335. JOHN SINGLETON COPLEY / *Watson and the Shark* / 1778. Museum of Fine Arts, Boston. *See comment below. Copley painted this picture in the hope of gaining full membership in the Royal Academy. Far more than a showpiece, it re-creates Mr. Watson's misadventure with such genuine passion that it becomes the modern counterpart of the heroic tales of the ancients. In raising a private ordeal to this level of general significance, Copley blazed a path for many later artists.*

American background, since he stresses all the little touches of frontier life (including the Indian encampment on the left) which no European painter could have known so well.

This sense of adventure may be found even more strikingly in Copley's *Watson and the Shark* (figure 335). The picture is based on Mr. Watson's own account of his gruesome experience, which happened in the harbor of Havana and cost him a leg before he was pulled aboard the boat. Of course the scene did not look exactly as we see it here, but then Copley did not really

336. JOHN SINGLETON COPLEY / *Mrs. Seymour Fort* / About 1776. Collection Wadsworth Atheneum, Hartford, Connecticut. *In colonial America, portraits were the only kind of picture steadily in demand. The young Copley had helped to coin a "colonial" portrait style, less elegant but also less conventional than that of England (compare figure 321).*

214

mean to reconstruct it detail by detail. What he wanted was to make it as thrilling as possible, and he has used every trick of the Baroque style to this end. Caravaggio himself could hardly have "timed" it better. Yet behind all this we feel an imagination that carries the flavor of the New World rather than of the Old.

The American Revolution was fought for much the same reasons that were to bring on the Revolution in France: unfair taxes imposed on the people by a government in which they had no voice. Ironically enough, the French King aided the Colonists' struggle for freedom, since he saw it as a chance to weaken the power of England. Their success may well have been the last bit of fuel that brought his own pot of political troubles to a boil. Criticism of the weak and corrupt government, and attacks on the holders of special

privilege had been growing for a long time in France. We saw signs of this in Greuze's *Village Bride*, where the honesty and goodness of the poor is meant to show up the moral decay of the aristocrats. Other painters went even further: they depicted the stories of heroic defenders of freedom in Ancient Athens or Rome, conveying the idea of "give me liberty or give me death" (see figure 332). Even the style of these pictures carried a moral message. It was based on the severe, "ideal" style of Poussin, as a rebuke to painters like Boucher, who had modeled themselves on Rubens and were now looked down upon as mere pleasure-seekers with nothing worthwhile to say (it was at this time that the terms Baroque and Rococo came into use as unflattering labels). But the "anti-Rococo" painters were far more rigid than Poussin in their admiration for Ancient

337. JACQUES LOUIS DAVID / *Marie Antoinette on Her Way to the Guillotine* / 1793. The Louvre, Paris. *As a violent anti-royalist, David had no pity for the former Queen in her final hour. Yet his stark little sketch does not show her as devoid of human dignity, even though it stresses her plainness.*

338. JACQUES LOUIS DAVID / *View of the Luxembourg Gardens* / 1794. The Louvre, Paris. *This, David's only landscape, shows the view from the Luxembourg Palace, where he was imprisoned after the fall of Robespierre. Here we see him as a painter pure and simple, stripped of all theories.*

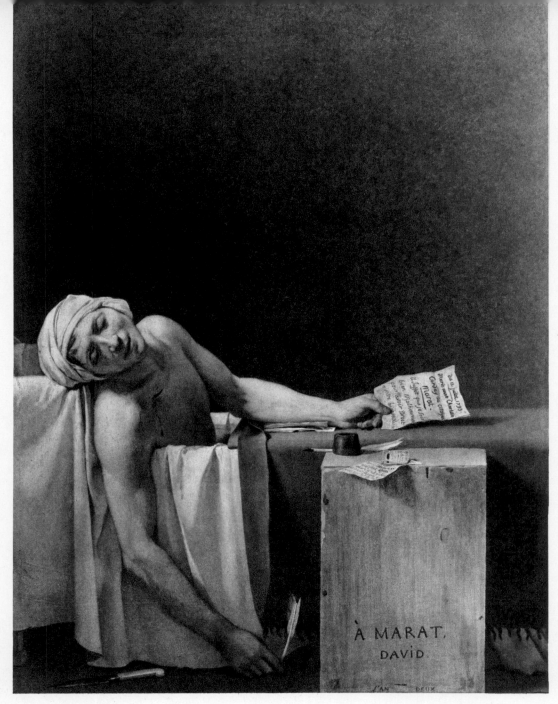

339. JACQUES LOUIS DAVID / *The Death of Marat* / 1793. Royal Museums of Fine Arts, Brussels. *See comment below. The picture, painted "to avenge the murder of Marat," was placed in the meeting hall of the Deputies. In 1795, its removal was forced by a decree forbidding the public display of any portrait whose subject had not been dead for at least ten years. Eventually the canvas followed the artist to Brussels, where he had taken refuge after the downfall of Napoleon.*

art, so that we speak of their work as Neo-Classic. Just as the artists of the Renaissance had helped to bring about a new era in science, so the Neo-Classic artists had a share in paving the way for the new political era that began with the French Revolution.

The most important among them was Jacques Louis David, who took an active part in the Revolution and became its "official" painter. His picture of the *Death of Marat* (figure 339) is a memorial to one of the heroes of the struggle. David's deep emotion has made a masterpiece out of a

scene that would have embarrassed many lesser artists, for Marat had been murdered in his bathtub. He liked to do his paper work that way, with a wooden board serving as his desk. One day a young woman named Charlotte Corday burst in, handed him a personal note, and while he read it plunged a knife into his chest. Whatever her side of the story—and Marat was hated by many —David makes us feel that this is no ordinary murder but something close to the death of a saint who gives his life for his faith—a saint of flesh and blood, like those of Caravaggio.

The Age of Machines

THE FRENCH REVOLUTION had replaced the King with a republican government. The Republic, however, lasted only a decade. Before the century was out, France was again ruled by one man. Napoleon Bonaparte had risen to power as the leader of the republican armies when the nation was attacked by its neighbors, who feared that the slogans of the Revolution—Liberty, Equality, and Fraternity—would soon catch on with their own people. The military genius of Napoleon conquered them all, except for England. He then made himself Emperor, a thousand years after Charlemagne. But in another ten years, in 1814, his army was beaten, and he was taken prisoner, by the united forces of England, Germany, and Russia.

Napoleon is one of the bitter jokes of history. In order to defeat him, the other countries had to take over a good part of the revolutionary ideas they had been so afraid of. For Napoleon did not undo the results of the Revolution; he simply used them for his own ends. His was the first modern army—a mass army of citizen soldiers fired by a feeling of patriotic duty. His enemies, who fought him at first only with soldiers hired for money, had to create mass armies, too; and having asked this common sacrifice of everybody, they found it more and more difficult to resist people's

demands for more rights. Under Napoleon, a man rose in rank because of what he could do, not because he came from a noble family; here again the Emperor set an example to those countries where personal ability was less well rewarded. No wonder, then, that after the Napoleonic wars the common man felt greater confidence in his own powers and asserted his claim to those hard-won rights that Americans had been enjoying ever since 1776.

Napoleon fancied himself an Ancient Roman Emperor re-born. And the painters who, before and during the Revolution, had preached the he-

340. ANTOINE GROS / *Napoleon at the Battle of Arcole* / 1796. The Louvre, Paris. *This splendid though frankly hero-worshiping portrait, painted when Gros was 25 and Napoleon 27, recaptures the color and drama of the Baroque. A tide of emotion has swept away David's Neo-Classic doctrines.*

roic virtues of the Ancient republics, now took the elegance and splendor of Imperial Roman art as their model. David himself had been one of the earliest and most ardent admirers of Napoleon, but he no longer held the same commanding position as before; a number of younger artists, who had grown up with the Revolution, were now taking the lead. They included David's star pupil, Jean Auguste Dominique Ingres, whose wonderful portrait of *Madame Rivière* you see in figure 348. Notice how women's fashions have changed—instead of the billowing skirts of Baroque and Rococo days (compare figures 312, 320), Madame is wearing a slim, "classic" gown that follows the natural outlines of the body. While not exactly like the costume of the Roman lady in the Boscoreale mural (figure 34), it does

remind us of her. You will find these comparisons interesting in other ways, too. As a faithful believer in the Neo-Classic theories of David, Ingres regarded himself first of all as a draftsman and designer. Since he thought color and light less essential than form, he carefully avoided the broad, flowing brushwork of the Baroque masters. Yet he was much more of a "painter's painter" than he thought. In his *Madame Rivière*, the colors are of extraordinary beauty, the surfaces have a delicate pearly sheen, and the poetic mood is as important as the finely balanced design in holding the picture together. Compared to the Boscoreale lady, our portrait seems almost photographic in the exact rendering of every detail. Here Ingres shows a concern for "truth" that also comes from David—we saw it in the *Death of*

341. ANTOINE GROS / *Napoleon Visiting Plague-Stricken Soldiers at Jaffa* / 1804. The Louvre, Paris. *The incident had taken place five years earlier, during the Egyptian campaign; in order to allay the spread of panic among his troops, Napoleon boldly touches the sores of one of the victims of the dread disease. Here again, although his painting technique is less free than in figure 340, Gros has used the dramatic devices of the Baroque to persuade us that we are witnessing a kind of miracle.*

342. DOMINIQUE INGRES / *Odalisque* / 1814. The Louvre, Paris. *The Near East, always fascinating to the West (see figure 314), was even more so after the Egyptian campaign of Napoleon. This odalisque—a Turkish word meaning a harem slave girl—breathes the enchantment of* The Thousand and One Nights. *Cool yet sensuous, her petal-smooth limbs framed by rich silks, she embodies an ideal of beauty strangely reminiscent of Parmigianino (figure 208).*

343, 344. DOMINIQUE INGRES / *Pencil Drawing for "Louis Bertin"* / 1832. Whereabouts unknown. *Louis Bertin* / 1832. The Louvre, Paris. *Here we see why Ingres was the greatest portraitist of his day: precise, detached observation in the drawing, massive force of personality in the finished picture.*

345. FRANCISCO GOYA / *Self-Portrait* / About 1817–19. The Prado, Madrid. *This canvas, painted when he was in his early seventies, shows Goya as a man of astonishing vigor for his age. Its frankness and depth as a character study are matched only by Rembrandt (compare figure 279).*

346. FRANCISCO GOYA / *Majas on a Balcony* / About 1810–15. Metropolitan Museum of Art, New York. *The subject here harks back to the artist's youth (see figure 318), but now Rococo gaiety has given way to a dramatic contrast between the alluring women and the sinister, cloaked men.*

Marat—and that in lesser hands could easily become a danger. This desire of the time for exact likenesses had a good deal to do with the invention of photography between 1820 and 1840, when Ingres was at the height of his fame.

Meanwhile the Baroque-Rococo style, with its

347. FRANCISCO GOYA / *The Witches' Sabbath* / 1819-23. The Prado, Madrid. *Goya painted this fantastic scene—the devil in the shape of a goat preaching to a horde of his devotees—for the dining room of his villa. Its nightmarish intensity bespeaks the gloomy mood of the artist's last years in Spain under the repressive rule of Ferdinand VII. In 1824, at 78, Goya fled to Bordeaux, where he died four years later.*

348. DOMINIQUE INGRES / *Madame Rivière* / 1805. The Louvre, Paris. *With Ingres, Neo-Classicism lost its revolutionary flavor. His work became, in fact, the very model of conservative, "official" painting, even though his imitators never grasped his masterful clarity of form or his subtle sense of color.*

349.   FRANCISCO GOYA / *The Third of May, 1808* / 1814-15. The Prado, Madrid. *In painting this massacre of citizens of Madrid who had revolted against the occupation troops of Napoleon, Goya has endowed it with all the expressive force of a scene of religious martyrdom. His picture is a memorial to all the resistance heroes of modern times.*

350. THEODORE GERICAULT / *Mounted Officer of the Guard* / 1812. The Louvre, Paris. *Here we see a sort of ideal portrait of the Napoleonic soldier, filled with the color and excitement of violent action, by one of the earliest Romantic painters. Goya had still been raised in the tradition of Baroque art; Géricault revived it, as the style best suited to his own temper.*

351. EUGENE DELACROIX / *The Death of Sardanapalus* / 1844. Collection Henry P. McIlhenny, Philadelphia. *Delacroix had to go farther afield than Géricault for subjects that excited his imagination. Visions of barbaric Oriental splendor such as this one held a particularly strong appeal for him, since they invited him to give free rein to his passionate Neo-Baroque style.*

352. THEODORE GERICAULT / *The Madman* / 1821–24. Museum of Fine Arts, Ghent. *A sympathetic interest in the insane was characteristic of the Romantic era, so intensely concerned with the world of emotions. This powerful study is one of a series Géricault did for a doctor friend.*

353, 354. THEODORE GERICAULT / *The Raft of the "Medusa," and Detail* / 1818–19. The Louvre, Paris. *In 1816, the French government ship* Medusa *sank in a storm, and only a few of her men survived after many days on a makeshift raft. Géricault has painted the climax of the story—the sighting of the rescue ship—on the ambitious scale and in the spirit of heroic tragedy hitherto reserved for more "noble" subjects, thus breaking all the rules of Neo-Classicism.*

emphasis on imagination rather than "truth," and on light and color rather than form, had never died out completely. There were artists in Napoleon's day who painted Neo-Classic ideas in a Baroque way, while others took over the Neo-Classic "language" but used it for highly imaginative, even fantastic subjects. One very important painter, the Spaniard Francisco Goya, even managed to turn the Baroque into a "modern" style without being touched by the Neo-Classic trend at all. Like Velazquez, whose art he greatly admired, Goya was the official painter of the Spanish King, although he did a great many things besides court portraits. Perhaps his most powerful works are those devoted to the struggle of the Spanish people against the army of Napoleon, which had occupied the country but never really conquered it. In *The Third of May, 1808* (figure 349) he shows the shooting of a group of Madrid citizens who had resisted the foreign invaders. The blazing color, the broad "handwriting" in paint, the dramatic light, all remind us of the Baroque. Why then do we feel so strongly that the picture belongs to the early nineteenth century in spirit? The subject itself, of course, is new and daring, but the way Goya has treated it

355. EUGENE DELACROIX / *Frédéric Chopin* / 1838. The Louvre, Paris. *Here we see the Romantic conception of the hero in its purest form—a blend of Gros's* Napoleon *(figure 340) and Géricault's* Madman *(figure 352), agonized, rebellious, and burning with the fever of genius.*

356. EUGENE DELACROIX / *The Massacre of Chios* / 1824. The Louvre, Paris. *Like* The Raft of the "Medusa," *this was a contemporary theme, an incident of the Greek struggle for independence against the Turks. Conservative critics called it "the massacre of painting."*

is even more so. David's *Marat* had reminded us of a religious painting; *The Third of May, 1808* makes equally full use of the devices of religious art—Goya had been deeply impressed with the work of Rembrandt—and again people are dying, not for the Kingdom of Heaven but for Liberty. In Goya's view, however, the real tragedy was that the shooting should be done by the French. Like so many others he had thought at first that

the forces of Napoleon would carry the ideals of the Revolution into his own backward country. *The Third of May, 1808* is a memorial to shattered hopes—and to those of countless others in the years to come. This same scene has been repeated so many times since Goya's day, always with a different cast of characters and in countries all over the globe, that it has become a terrifying symbol of our "era of revolutions."

The Romantic Movement

L ET US NOW TURN to the *Mounted Officer of the Guard* (figure 350), to see how a young French painter felt about Napoleon. This life-size picture was done in 1812 by the marvelously talented Théodore Géricault, then only twenty-one years of age, as a sort of ideal portrait of the Napoleonic soldier. Born more than four decades after David and Goya, Géricault had a viewpoint very different from either. For him, politics no longer had the force of a faith; all he saw in the Emperor's military campaigns was the color and excitement of violent action. These, of course, were just the things that could not be well expressed in the Neo-Classic style, so our artist has gone all the way back to Rubens for his source of inspiration (compare the dramatic *Crucifixion* by the older master in figure 259). Goya had still been raised in the tradition of Baroque art; Géricault revived it, as the style best suited to his own temper. With him we meet a new type of painter, and a new movement in art called Romantic.

The word actually comes from the field of literature, where "romances" (that is, stories of adventure) were very popular at that time, so that it describes a state of mind, rather than a particular style of painting. Few Romantic painters came as close to the full-blown Baroque as Géricault in his *Mounted Officer*, but they all shared a similar outlook. Art to them did not mean a fixed ideal, the way it did to the Neo-Classic artists. There was no such thing as a single "perfect" style for them. What mattered in art and in life, they felt, was not the *kind* of experience you had but how strongly you felt about it. One might al-

357. EUGENE DELACROIX / *Arab Attacked by a Lion* / About 1850. Art Institute of Chicago. *Delacroix's love of the Orient can be felt even in the anti-Turkish Massacre; eight years later, he visited Morocco, and brought back a treasury of Arabic motifs, as well as a new brilliance of color.*

358. EUGENE DELACROIX / *Young Tiger Playing with Its Mother* / 1830. The Louvre, Paris. *The union of violence and sensuous beauty that haunts the Oriental scenes of Delacroix can also be felt in his wild animals. These tigers, while realistically observed, are also beasts of myth and fable.*

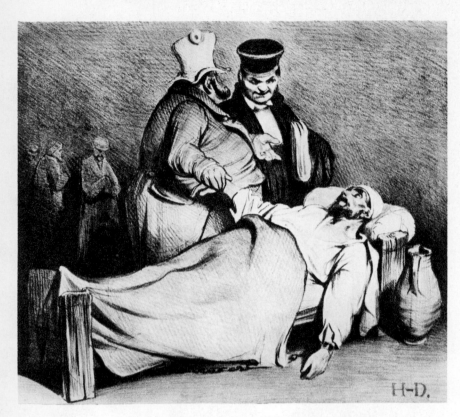

359. HONORE DAUMIER / "It's safe to release this one!" (lithograph) / 1834. Of humble birth and a staunch republican, Daumier began his artistic career as a political cartoonist in 1831; soon after, he spent six months in jail for one of his savage attacks on the King.

most say that the Romantics sought emotion for emotion's sake. They believed in living dangerously, or at least thrillingly (and sometimes theatrically). Géricault, for instance, was an ardent horseman and died after a bad spill at the early age of thirty-three. As born rebels against any kind of set rules or values, the only thing they held sacred was the individual personality; and

360. HONORE DAUMIER / Don Quixote Attacking the Windmills / About 1866. Collection Mr. and Mrs. Charles S. Payson, New York. As a painter, Daumier is a Romantic not only in his broad, expressive technique and dramatic composition but also, at times, in his use of literary themes.

since they could not express anybody's viewpoint but their own, people often found them hard to understand. In fact, the Romantics enjoyed being misfits in the society of their time. Here, then, you see the beginning of a split between artist and public that still persists today.

Just before Géricault's death, another fine Romantic painter appeared on the Paris scene: Eugène Delacroix. He and Ingres were to be the two opposite poles of French painting—"professional enemies," so to speak—until well past the middle of the century. At first Ingres, the great conservative, received all the honors and prizes, although Delacroix caught up with him in the end, when people had grown used to the Romantic movement. His Arab Attacked by a Lion (figure 357), done about 1850, still has a great deal in common with Géricault's Officer. Here again you find the Rubens-like energy of movement, the open, flowing brushwork, the thrill of violent action. By now, however, the glamorous days of Napoleon and his Empire were only a dim memory, so that Delacroix had to go either to literature and history or, as in this case, to remote places for the kind of subject that excited his imagination. He had actually visited the Arabic world of North Africa once, but our scene is freely invented without any models.

In earlier years, both Géricault and Delacroix had been much impressed by English painting. England, where Romantic literature had had its start, had produced an important group of land-

361. Above, facing page: HONORE DAUMIER / The Soup (pen-and-wash drawing) / About 1860–70. The Louvre, Paris. For massive power and monumentality of design, this drawing is matched only by Michelangelo (compare figure 165). These figures have an almost superhuman force and vitality.

362. At right, facing page: HONORE DAUMIER / The Third-Class Carriage / About 1860–70. Metropolitan Museum of Art, New York. Daumier's subject here is the fundamental paradox of modern city life: the loneliness of people in a crowd. There is a depth of compassion in these faces that makes us think of Rembrandt.

363. JOHN CONSTABLE / *Hampstead Heath (oil sketch)* / 1821. City of Manchester Art Galleries, England. *See comment on facing page. When Constable's landscapes were shown in Paris for the first time, in 1824, their freshness and vibrancy of color made a deep impression on Delacroix; he reworked the background of the* Massacre of Chios *(figure 356)—so the story goes—just before sending it to an exhibition.*

364. JOHN CROME / *Slate Quarries* / About 1802. Tate Gallery, London. *Crome, a few years older than Constable, was perhaps the first to discover that the English countryside could yield the same range of poetic moods, from the heroic to the intimate, as Italy or Holland.*

365. RICHARD BONINGTON / *View at Versailles* / 1826. The Louvre, Paris. *An Englishman trained in France, Bonington nevertheless developed a landscape style akin to Constable's in its vivid hues and directness of technique. He, too, was admired by Delacroix.*

scape painters at the beginning of the nineteenth century, all of them Romantic in temper. What Rubens was to the French Romantics, the Dutch Baroque landscape masters were to these Englishmen. In them they found a feeling, similar to their own, for the majestic forces of nature and for man's loneliness and insignificance when faced with these forces. Even so, they did not simply imitate their models, any more than the French copied Rubens. You can tell this from the view of *Hampstead Heath* (figure 363) by John Constable. The picture is one of the countless small oil sketches, none of them much larger than this page, that Constable did of this district, which today is a suburb of London. They were done very quickly and on the spot, a new and unusual idea at the time; that is why our picture looks so different from van Goyen and Ruisdael (figures

281 and 282). The Baroque masters had never painted landscapes out-of-doors, even when they wanted to depict a particular place. They only made drawings, which they could then work up in the studio at their leisure. Constable, however, was so fascinated by the ever-changing moods of nature that these changes became far more important to him than the things that stayed the same about a given view. In our sketch, he has caught a particularly splendid moment—a great sky drama of wind, sunlight, and clouds, played over a vast sweep of countryside. The details on the ground are no more than the "backdrop," so they are barely indicated. Perhaps the scene did not look quite as exciting in reality, but since his is the only account we have, we see it through his eyes and believe him.

With William Turner, the other great English

366. CAMILLE COROT / *Jumièges* / About 1829–30. Smith College Museum of Art, Northampton, Massachusetts. *The English landscapists also stimulated the talent of Corot, whose early work has a morning-bright freshness much like theirs. But Corot at the same time was the heir of Poussin and Claude; in the clear sky and the balanced design of* Jumièges *there is a timeless serenity that is the very opposite of the ever-changing moods of Constable.*

367. CAMILLE COROT / *Self-Portrait* / 1835. Uffizi Gallery, Florence. *Here, in what is probably the first self-portrait ever painted out-of-doors, we find the same clarity and directness, the same precise division of light and shade as in Jumièges.*

368. EUGENE DELACROIX / *Self-Portrait* / About 1836. Uffizi Gallery, Florence. *In striking contrast to the workmanlike simplicity of Corot, Delacroix views himself not as a painter but as a man of the world whose aristocratic bearing blends with his Romantic sensibility.*

369. CAMILLE COROT / *The Interrupted Reading* / 1865–70. Art Institute of Chicago. *The finest works of Corot's later years are large figure pieces such as this, subtly pensive in mood and of a classical harmony of shape and color that was to impress Matisse in the 1920's.*

landscapist of Constable's time, we often find believing rather more difficult. In *The Fighting Téméraire* (figure 372) he shows us a famous old warship, once the pride of the British fleet, being towed to her last berth against the light of a brilliant sunset. These fireworks in the sky suggest a last salute at the burial of a dead hero who is going down in glory, like the sun itself. Let us also take note (because Turner would want us to) of the contrast between the squat, monster-like tugboat and the silvery tallness of the *Téméraire*. All this is a splendid show, but it may make some of us feel a bit uncomfortable. Like an over-zealous organist, Turner has pulled a few stops too many, so that the music becomes deafening.

Landscape painting was perhaps the most origi-

370. HONORÉ DAUMIER / *Crispin and Scapin* / About 1865. The Louvre, Paris. *As a painter, Daumier shares Delacroix's admiration for the Baroque. This scene from a comedy by Molière recalls the eighteenth century not only in subject (see figure 325) but in the broad, fluid handling of light and color (compare figure 329).*

371. JOHN CONSTABLE / *Weymouth Bay* / 1816. National Gallery, London. *In painting this lonely stretch of coastline Constable has captured the precise conditions of light and atmosphere as he found it on a particular day. Never before had a landscape painter achieved such freshness and immediacy in his pictures.*

372.   WILLIAM TURNER / The Fighting "Téméraire" Towed to Her Last Berth / 1838. Tate Gallery, London.
In contrast to Constable, the poet of the Here and Now, Turner was never content with nature as he found her.
Direct observation, while important, was merely the starting point for his brilliantly imaginative visions.

374. CASPAR DAVID FRIEDRICH / *The Wreck of the "Hoffnung" / 1821. Kunsthalle, Hamburg. This picture re-enacts a specific event: the end of an ill-fated expedition in the Bering Strait. It was not only the theme of man's defeat by the forces of nature, always dear to the Romantics, that appealed to Friedrich; the irony of a ship named "Hope" slowly crushed to death in the icy wastes of the Arctic must have struck him as symbolic.*

nal part of the Romantic movement in art. At any rate, it was the most popular. While Constable and Turner, each in his own way, show us the

AT LEFT:

373. GEORGE CALEB BINGHAM / *Fur Traders on the Missouri* About 1845. Metropolitan Museum of Art, New York. *See comment on next page. Scenes such as this show that Americans were becoming aware of themselves as a nation molded by the Middle West and Far West rather than by the Atlantic seaboard alone.*

Romantic view of nature more clearly than anyone else, we find many others all over Europe doing similar things until far into the second half of the century. The New World, too, had its Romantic landscape artists, even though most Americans were far too busy coping with nature in practical ways to pay much attention to the poetry of her moods. There were few painters among the people who settled the wilderness of

the Middle West and Far West. Yet every once in a while these men would do pictures like the *Fur Traders on the Missouri* (figure 373) by George Caleb Bingham, full of the vastness and silence of the wide-open spaces. The two trappers in their dugout canoe with the black fox chained to the prow, soundlessly gliding downstream in the misty sunlight, carry us right back to the river life of Mark Twain's childhood, to Tom Sawyer and Huck Finn.

Winslow Homer's *Breezing Up* (figure 376), done about thirty years later than the *Fur Traders*, was painted "down East" rather than in the frontier country, but it shows just as fine a feeling

375. RAPHAELLE PEALE / *After the Bath* / 1823. Nelson Gallery-Atkins Museum, Kansas City, Missouri. *By tempting us to lift the cloth that hides the nude bather, Peale achieves a witty contrast between the real and the ideal in this "deception" (as he called such pictures).*

376. WINSLOW HOMER / *Breezing Up* / About 1873-76. National Gallery of Art, Washington, D. C. (Gift of the W. L. and May T. Mellon Foundation.) *Homer had started his artistic career as a pictorial reporter. When he began to paint in oils, he retained his sharp eye for the fleeting moment and his freedom from conventional notions of picture-making. The daring off-center design of Breezing Up is extremely effective just because it does not look "composed."*

377. EDWARD HICKS / *The Peaceable Kingdom* / About 1830. Worcester Art Museum, Massachusetts. *The pious Quaker Hicks believed that painting was "one of those trifling, insignificant arts which has never been of substantial advantage to man"; yet, having failed as a farmer, he had no choice but to do what he knew best, though always "within the bounds of innocence and usefulness." He is said to have done close to eighty "Kingdoms."*

for the great outdoors of America. Here we are off the coast of New England at high noon on a fine, windy day, and we can almost smell the salty tang of the sea air as we sail along with the old fisherman and the three boys toward the distant lighthouse on the left, while the schooner follows its own steady course off to the right.

Bingham and Homer were talented professional artists, trained in the big cities of the East. Neither of them, we may be sure, had ever heard of Edward Hicks, the Pennsylvania preacher and sign painter who did *The Peaceable Kingdom* (figure 377). Hicks was a folk artist, a man of simple mind and simple faith, to whom painting was still a craft, and the Bible the Word of God, the way it had been to people in the Middle

Ages. Like them, too, Hicks had a compelling imagination. His picture illustrates the words of the Prophet Isaiah about the coming of peace among men: "The wolf also shall dwell with the lamb, and the leopard shall lie down with the kid. . . . The cow and the bear shall feed . . . together: and the lion shall eat straw like the ox." On the left we see William Penn signing his treaty with the Indians, a practical example of peacemaking, but it is the animals that really impress us. The ferocious lion choking on his mouthful of straw beside the mild-eyed ox, the sly wolf, the leopard spread out like a fur rug, are all doing their best to live up to the sacred text. And if we smile at the way they act out their roles, we are also touched by their seriousness and sincerity.

378. WILLIAM HARNETT / *Old Models* / About 1890–92.
Museum of Fine Arts, Boston. *Harnett's "deceptions," based
on Peale (see figure 375) and Dutch still life, are far more
than the work of a virtuoso; in his choice and arrangement of
objects we find a formal balance akin to modern art.*

379. THOMAS EAKINS / *The Gross Clinic* / 1875. Jefferson
Medical College, Philadelphia. *This challenge to earlier
"Anatomies" (see figure 273) combines relentless realism and
a powerful dramatic sense within a strikingly monumental design. Conservatives called the picture a "degradation of art."*

380. FRANÇOIS MILLET / *The Man with the Hoe*
1863. Mrs. Henry P. Russell, San Francisco.
*Among those who turned to realism after the
crisis of 1848 (see page 242), Millet became the
painter of peasant life. The stark form of this
figure looming up in a bare expanse, embodies
all the hardship of backbreaking labor.*

Realism and
Impressionism

BUT LET US RETURN from the great outdoors to the noise and unrest of the mid-nineteenth century. In the years since the French Revolution, another and even greater revolution had been going on everywhere: the revolution in industry that came with the use of machines. There had, of course, been machines all along, but their usefulness had been limited because they could be run only by wind power (which was unreliable) or water power (which had to be used on the spot). The invention of the steam engine in the late eighteenth century changed all that. Now the knowledge that natural scientists had been gathering ever since the Renaissance could be put to practical use in thinking up machines for an endless variety of purposes. This, in turn, led to more scientific discoveries and more inventions, right down to the technical miracles of our own time.

It is hard for us today to realize how completely steamboats, railroads, and factories unsettled everybody's way of life a hundred years ago. People marveled at the flood of cheap and plentiful goods made or shipped with the aid of machines, but the same machines also caused a good deal of human misery. The trained craftsmen of old were thrown out of work and their places taken by masses of industrial workers, unskilled, badly paid, and crowded together in unhealthy slums. No wonder the machine was welcomed

381.   GUSTAVE COURBET / *The Stone Breakers* / 1849. Formerly Picture Gallery, Dresden. (Destroyed?) *See comment on next page. Courbet's work, lacking the sentiment that made the peasants of Millet acceptable to the public, aroused a storm of criticism in the late 1850's. The artist thrived on controversy; boisterous and forthright, proud of his provincial background, he enjoyed defying the officialdom of art and the custodians of respectability.*

382. GUSTAVE COURBET / *Charles Baudelaire* / 1845. Musée Fabre, Montpellier, France. *This intimate study shows how strongly the young Courbet was influenced by Romanticism, since it casts the great poet and critic in the role of the self-absorbed, lonely Bohemian shivering in his garret.*

by some as a blessing while others called it a curse. Altogether, the rise of modern industry overthrew a great many beliefs, habits, and institutions. It created new tensions and conflicts, yet at the same time it made people more dependent on each other's labor than ever before.

And the painters? What effect did the Age of Machines have on them? The Romantics had put freedom of feeling and imagination above anything else; but others thought this was just an easy way to escape from the realities of the time. They believed that in a period of science and industrial progress, art should only deal with contemporary subjects. In 1848, when a wave of revolutions swept over Europe, inspired by the demand of the lower classes for better living conditions and a more democratic society, these Realists began to portray the life of workers and peasants in a serious spirit. Their leader was Gustave Courbet, whose *Stone Breakers* (figure 381) started an up-

383. GUSTAVE COURBET / *The Edge of the Forest* / About 1850-55. Private collection. *In contrast with the atmospheric softness of the Baudelaire portrait, this landscape has the firm material solidity of Courbet's mature style. The Romantic view of nature, with its searching for poetic effects, has given way to a sturdy, almost "anti-poetic" approach that stresses the tangible qualities of rock, tree bark, and foliage. Yet we also sense the artist's keen enjoyment of the outdoors.*

384, 385. GUSTAVE COURBET / *The Painter's Studio, and Detail* / 1854-55. The Louvre, Paris. *Courbet exhibited this huge canvas in his private Pavilion of Realism at the Paris Exposition of 1855. Subtitled, "A real allegory defining a seven-year phase of my artistic life," it represented his Parisian friends (Baudelaire is at the extreme right), his home town neighbors (detail below), and other figures, all intended to convey his ideas about art and society.*

roar similar to the one caused by Caravaggio two and a half centuries earlier. Here we find no "noble ideals," no flights of fancy, only an old man breaking up rocks, aided by his young helper. We learn little about them as persons, since their faces are turned away from us, yet we immediately feel sympathy and respect for them because they are so firmly and monumentally *there*. The modern artist, Courbet believed, must stay firmly on the ground of everyday life; he must paint only what he can see directly, not what appears in his mind's eye; he should try to rival the old masters, but only in ambition, not by imitating them.

Even so, Courbet's own painting technique still reminds us a good deal of the seventeenth century. He was more interested in the new things he wanted to say than in finding a new way to say them. This new way had to be discovered by another great French painter, Edouard Manet.

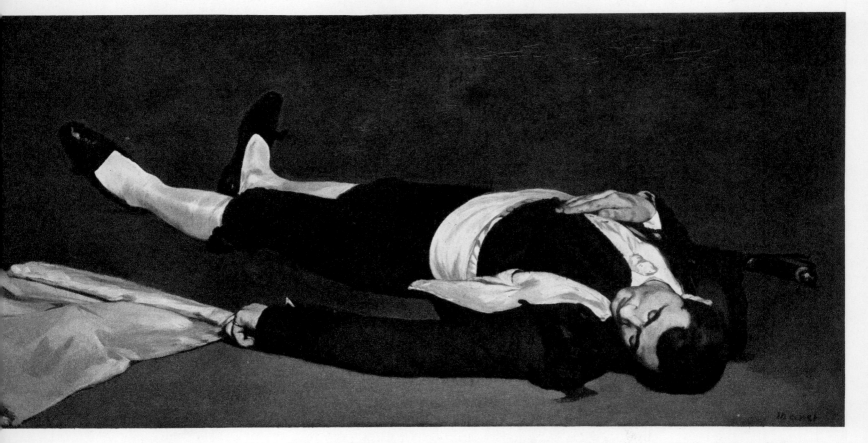

386. EDOUARD MANET / *The Dead Toreador* / 1864. National Gallery of Art, Washington, D. C. (Widener Collection.) *The canvas makes a fascinating comparison with its seventeenth-century model: painting in sharply defined areas of solid color, Manet has transformed the shadowy depth of the cave into a flat vertical plane that counterbalances the strong fore-shortening of the toreador, so that the figure almost looks like a cutout shape glued onto the neutral background.*

He shared Courbet's idea that one should paint only what the eye actually sees, but he felt that in order to do this he first had to re-think the whole language of painting. So he began by learning everything he could about this language; he made copies and studies after the old masters, and for several years these "pictures of pictures" were his main concern (see figures 386, 387). You can see the new language Manet worked out for himself if you compare his *Fife Player* of 1866 (figure 394) with the *Stone Breakers*. Since the Late Mid-

dle Ages when pictures first became "windows," painters had always relied on modeling and shading to make their shapes look round and solid, and the surrounding spaces deep and hollow. Courbet, too, still painted that way. Manet, on the other hand, decided that all this could be done through differences in color alone, rather than through different shades of light and dark. In his *Fife Player*, the light hits the forms head-on, so that we find practically no shadows, and no shading. The whole picture is made up of separate, flat color patches placed next to each other on the canvas. And every patch, whether it stands for a thing (such as a part of the boy's uniform) or just for empty space (like the light grey "patch" around the figure) has a clear-cut shape of its own. What does all this mean? Simply this: that for

387. UNKNOWN MASTER (SPANISH?) / *A Dead Soldier* / Seventeenth century. National Gallery, London. *In Manet's time, the picture was believed to be by Velazquez or Zurbaran, two masters he greatly admired. It is an elaborate allegory, full of symbols of the brevity of man's life (skulls, floating bubbles, and the like).*

388. EDOUARD MANET / *In the Boat* / 1874. Metropolitan Museum of Art, New York. *In this picture, done a decade after* The Dead Toreador, *Manet had adapted his new "language" of painting to a brightly lit, casual outdoor scene that seems to glide past us as we look at it.*

389. AUGUSTE RENOIR / *Le Pont Neuf* / 1872. Collection Mrs. Marshall Field, New York. *The Impressionists discovered a wealth of color in places where earlier painters had seen only neutral darkness. To Renoir the*

390. CLAUDE MONET / *Vétheuil: Sunshine and Snow* / 1881. National Gallery, London. *The silent countryside illuminated by the slanting rays of winter sunlight here yields a harvest of color as rich as Renoir's noonday scene in the center of Paris. Who would ever dare to insist that snow is white after seeing this picture?*

391.   EDGAR DEGAS / *Café Concert: At Les Ambassadeurs (pastel)* / 1876-77. Museum, Lyons. *To Degas, the master draftsman among the Impressionists, colored chalks were a welcome substitute for oil, since they permitted him to draw and paint at the same time.*

Manet the picture has become more important than the things it represents. The limited world of the canvas, he found, has its own "natural laws," and the first of these is that every brush stroke, every color patch is equally "real," no matter what it stands for in nature. Vermeer and Velazquez had come closest to this idea of "pure painting" among the old masters. It remained for Manet, however, to turn the Baroque triumph of light into a triumph of color.

In the Boat (figure 388) shows you the next stage of the revolution Manet had started. Stimulated by younger artists (Claude Monet and others) who had carried his ideas further in their own canvases, Manet had turned to outdoor scenes such as this, flooded with sunlight of a brightness that makes all earlier paintings seem murky by comparison. Color is everywhere, especially in the shadows (if we can call them that!). It is a genre picture, but Manet gives us only a casual glimpse of the two people and what they are doing; his brushwork has become quick

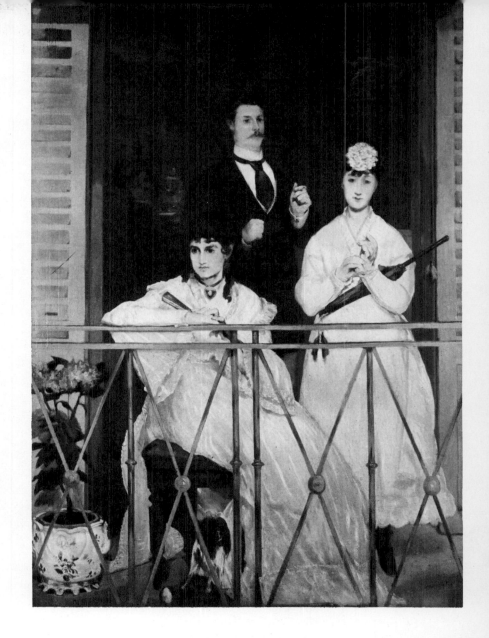

392, 393. EDOUARD MANET / *The Balcony, and Detail* / 1869. The Louvre, Paris. *The design of this picture was inspired by Goya's* Majas on a Balcony *(figure 346); the relation of the two is much like that of Manet's* Dead Toreador *and its Baroque model (see page 244). Again the subject has been drained of emotional content, the composition is now geometrically precise (compare the two gratings!), and the shadows have become as solid as the highlights.*

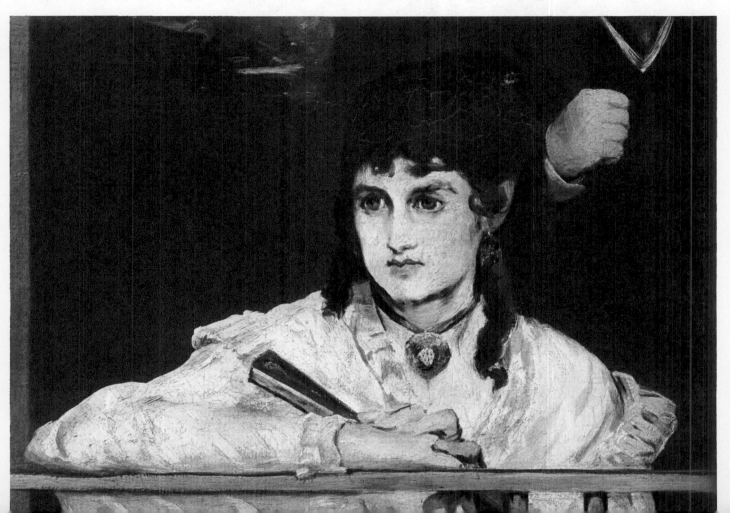

and sparkling like that of Hals or Constable, so that the entire scene seems in motion. It was this that made the conservative critics call the new style Impressionism; to them, such pictures were at best no more than quick impressions, unfinished sketches not worthy of serious attention. Moreover, they complained, the color was so raw that it hurt their eyes (apparently they never went out on sunny days). One of the younger Impressionists, Auguste Renoir, was particularly successful in using Impressionism to catch the bustling life of the Paris streets. His *Pont Neuf* (figure 389) shows one of the bridges over the river Seine in the blazing noonday sun of midsummer, and again it is the wealth and brilliance of color that gives the picture such charm and gaiety. The air

394. EDOUARD MANET / *The Fife Player* / 1866. The Louvre, Paris. *Here Manet repeats the bold experiment of* The Dead Toreador *(figure 386) with even greater emphasis on the flatness of the gray background that frames the boy, and with brighter colors.*

395. CLAUDE MONET / *The Seine at Argenteuil* / 1868. Art Institute of Chicago. *This canvas shows Manet's new way of painting adapted to the outdoors; the entire picture is built up of patches of solid color, and the reflections in the water are no less "real" in this network of patches than the rest. To Monet, reflections were as fascinating as they had been to the Van Eycks (see figure 101!), but for the opposite reason.*

quivers with the heat reflected from the pavement, but the shade seems deliciously cool—altogether, a perfect day for a stroll.

How could anyone have failed to enjoy the wonderful freshness of this scene? Yet for most people during those years the greatest living painter was William Adolphe Bouguereau, whose pictures sold for prices as high as those paid for the rarest of old masters. Figure 400 shows us one of his works, entitled *Youth*. We see a young woman in classical garb leaning against an ancient Roman fountain and playfully beset by two fluttering cupids, the "voices of love." Maybe there is nothing wrong with this idea as such—after all, Botticelli's *Birth of Venus* (figure 137) also has a rather complicated poetic theme, and of a similar kind. If Bouguereau's painting has lost its appeal for most of us, while Botticelli's *Venus* and Renoir's *Pont Neuf* have kept theirs, the reason is that Bouguereau was not very sensitive to the beauty of painted shapes and colors; he was satisfied simply to "photograph" his model, a job that

396. AUGUSTE RENOIR / *Bather with a Griffon* / 1870. Museum of Art, São Paolo, Brazil. *This nude, like some other early works of Renoir, echoes the solid realism of Courbet (see figure 384); yet it also has a rich, sensuous glow matched only by Rubens (see figure 260).*

397. AUGUSTE RENOIR / *Study for "The Bathers"* / About 1885. Formerly Knoedler Galleries, New York. *Renoir did this drawing, with the firm, simple outlines and strongly modeled forms, at a time when a trip to Italy had helped him to rediscover the classical tradition of Raphael and Ingres.*

398. AUGUSTE RENOIR / *The Judgment of Paris* / About 1914. Collection Henry P. McIlhenny, Philadelphia. *In his old age, Renoir united the brilliant rainbow colors of his Impressionist phase with his awareness of classical form in these shimmering, voluptuously rounded bodies.*

399. AUGUSTE RENOIR / *Le Moulin de la Galette* / 1876. The Louvre, Paris. *Café life and other casual forms of amusement were a favorite subject for Impressionism, but only Renoir knew how to capture the human warmth of such scenes; his gay flirting couples under the dappled pattern of sunlight and shadow radiate a sense of happiness shared that is utterly entrancing. Degas' café scene of the same year on the facing page is difficult to endure after this.*

the camera could have done much more conveniently. Maybe that is why people liked his work so: they trusted it the way they trusted the camera, which "never lies," and were quite willing to see inspiration where we today can find only perspiration and cheap sentiment.

Bouguereau shows us the style of the art academies at its worst. He thought of himself as the heir of Ingres and David (and, through them, of

400. *At left:* ADOLPHE WILLIAM BOUGUEREAU / *Youth* / About 1875. Whereabouts unknown. *The theme of this picture by the most famous "official" painter of his time is the same as that of Renoir above. Which is the more successful?*

401. *At right:* EDGAR DEGAS / *The Glass of Absinthe* / 1876. The Louvre, Paris. *Degas' disenchanted couple—or are they complete strangers?—is a typically Impressionist "slice of life"; yet their brooding loneliness, behind the zigzag of empty tables, is as unforgettable as the sunlit charm of Renoir.*

Poussin and Raphael), but he simply did not know how to practice what he preached. Still, the academic "system" out of which he came was not wholly bad; a young artist of real talent could profit from it despite its glaring faults. One of the great masters of Impressionism, Edgar Degas, had gone through this kind of training. He had studied with a follower of Ingres, and had come away with a respect for line and composition that served him well throughout his life. The splendid portrait drawing (figure 402) that Degas made of his friend Manet not long after their first meeting, is far closer to the spirit of Ingres than anything Bouguereau ever did. The pose, to be sure, seems casual and relaxed, as if Degas had caught his sitter unawares, yet the figure is carefully composed, and the lines are so graceful, the forms so

402. EDGAR DEGAS / *Manet (pencil drawing)* / About 1865. Metropolitan Museum of Art, New York. *See comment on the right. The use of pencil, a "dry" and precise tool, is in itself a mark of respect for Ingres (compare figure 343).*

403. EDGAR DEGAS / *Uncle and Niece* / 1862. Art Institute of Chicago. *All Degas' portraits are of people he himself chose to do (he despised portraiture as a trade). This group, admirably composed, shows his intimate feeling for character and for the subtle interplay of personalities.*

404. EDGAR DEGAS / *Two Dancers at Rest (crayon drawing)* About 1890. Owner unknown. *Like Renoir, Degas after 1880 began to develop a style of classic simplicity and breadth. Even now, however, his forms have a tension and controlled power such as only he could achieve.*

405. JAMES WHISTLER / *Nocturne in Blue and Silver: Old Battersea Bridge* / About 1870. Tate Gallery, London. *Even though his own work was no more than a mild echo of Impressionism, Whistler came to personify the new movement in the eyes of the English and American public.*

406. JAMES WHISTLER / *Arrangement in Black and Gray (The Artist's Mother)* / 1871. The Louvre, Paris. *The title proclaims Whistler's belief in Art for Art's Sake; art, he said, means shapes and colors, rather than sentiment. Obviously, he did not quite practice what he preached.*

cleanly set down, that we need not be afraid to compare them with Ingres' *Madame Rivière* (figure 348).

Unlike other members of the group around Manet, Degas hardly ever painted out-of-doors. Among the favorite subjects of this "indoors and nighttime Impressionist" were scenes of the theater and show business, such as the *Café Concert* (figure 391). Here the bright colors of the costumes, the dramatic lighting, the contrast between the "artificial" world of the stage and the "real" world of the spectators, have been woven into a wonderfully rich and vivid pattern. Again we get what seems to be almost a chance view, as if the artist had sketched it in a few minutes' time while passing through the crowded hall. Actually, however, this unstudied, off-center look

hides a lot of exact planning. Notice, for instance, how the string of lanterns to the left of the singer in the red dress helps to draw attention to her outstretched arm; how the neck of the bass fiddle sticking out of the orchestra pit makes us realize the gap in space between foreground and background. The way the picture is put together shows all the care of an Old Master, but an Old Master with a thoroughly modern mind.

407. CLAUDE MONET / *Charing Cross Bridge* / 1904. Courtesy Wildenstein & Co., Inc., New York. *In his later years, Monet became more and more concerned with the way light and color are conditioned by the atmosphere. His pictures now began to look like shimmering, weightless screens.*

408. PAUL CEZANNE / *The Black Clock* / About 1870. Collection Stavros Niarchos. *The creamy, solid surfaces of paint, the clear-cut division of light and dark areas, all remind us of the early Manet (compare figure 393), but the architectural order of the design is uniquely Cézanne's.*

The "Post=Impressionists"

AMONG the earliest admirers of Manet was a rather gruff young man from the south of France named Paul Cézanne. He quickly took over the new language of such pictures as *The Fife Player* and made it the basis of his own work (see figure 408). In the early 1870's Cézanne began to do brightly lit outdoor scenes similar to Manet's *In the Boat* and Renoir's *Pont Neuf*, but he never shared his friends' interest in the "spur of the moment," in movement and change; and toward

409. *At left:* PAUL CEZANNE / *Christ in Limbo* / About 1868–70. Collection Mr. and Mrs. René Lecomte, Paris. 410. *Below:* SEBASTIANO DEL PIOMBO / *Christ in Limbo* / About 1530. The Prado, Madrid. *In this "picture of a picture," done from a reproduction, we again see how strongly Cézanne's ideas about painting were influenced by Manet (compare figures 386, 387), and how well he understood the nature of the "Manet revolution" of the 1860's.*

411. PAUL CEZANNE / *Victor Chocquet Seated* / About 1877. Gallery of Fine Arts, Columbus, Ohio. *In contrast to the somber tones of his early work, Cézanne now uses the rainbow-bright colors of Impressionism. Yet his quest for stability and order is seen in the dovetailing of verticals and horizontals (compare figure 306).*

412.   PAUL CEZANNE / *Fruit Bowl, Glass, and Apples* / 1879-82. Collection Mr. and Mrs. René Lecomte, Paris. *In this still life the artist combines a firm and balanced design with the most subtle color values. The play of light and shade over the surfaces is translated into a richly graded scale of cool and warm tones.*

AT RIGHT:

413.   PAUL CEZANNE / *House in Provence* / 1885-86. The John Herron Art Institute, Indianapolis, Indiana. *Here the near and the far, man-made form and natural growth, are both contrasted and brought into harmony—a harmony the more impressive since it still bears the traces of Cézanne's effort to discipline his own unruly temper.*

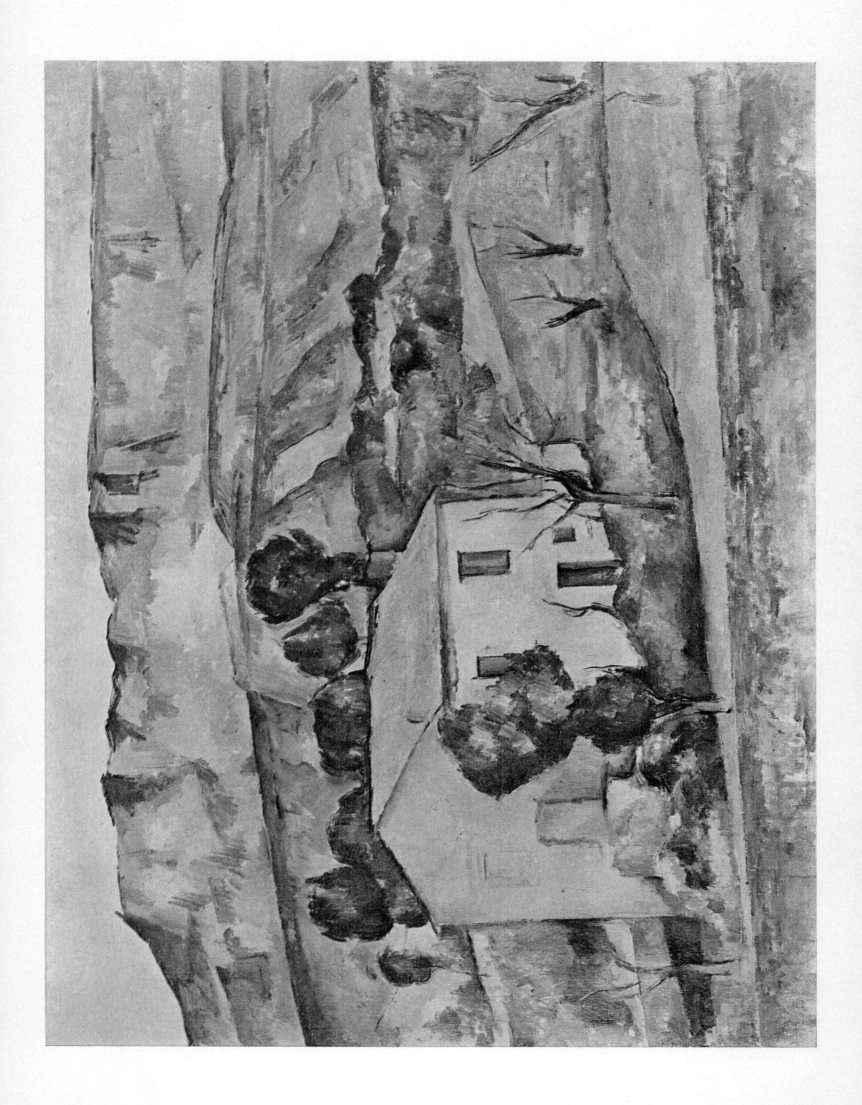

414. GEORGES SEURAT / A Sunday Afternoon on the Grande Jatte / 1884-86. Art Institute of Chicago. Compared to the slow, patient, systematic Seurat, Cézanne looks passionate and impulsive. The entire picture is made up of precise, impersonal dots of color, like a mosaic. Oddly enough, the figures, although completely immobilized, seem relaxed and at ease; each one has a distinctive personality, observed with wit and precision.

415. PAUL CEZANNE / *Mont Sainte-Victoire seen from Bibemus Quarry* / About 1898–1900. Baltimore Museum of Art. (The Cone Collection.) *The pictures of Cézanne's old age have a new energy and strength of feeling. Here the great mountain near Aix-en-Provence looms more majestically than ever above its base of rocks and trees. There is no hint of man's presence— houses and roads, so important in the artist's earlier compositions, would only disturb the lonely grandeur of this view.*

1880 he left Impressionism behind and became the first of the Post-Impressionists. This is not a very telling label for the mature Cézanne, or for those who were in sympathy with his efforts, but at least it suggests that they were not "anti-Impressionists." These men all knew how much they owed to the revolution that Manet had brought on; they were certainly not trying to undo it. On the contrary, they wanted to carry it further, so that Post-Impressionism was actually just a later stage—though a very important one—of the same basic "Manet Revolution."

Let us see now what kind of Post-Impressionism Cézanne had arrived at. His still life, *Fruit Bowl, Glass, and Apples* (figure 412), has the freshness of color and the free brushwork of an Impressionist picture, but after you look at it for a while you will notice all sorts of puzzling things. There are dark outlines drawn around most of the shapes, and the shapes themselves are simpler than they would be in nature; the table top seems to tilt upward, and the foreshortening of the bowl and glass is not "correct." Also, the colors seem to follow a scheme that stresses the contrast of cool and warm tones, and the brush strokes form a sort of pattern that runs over the entire canvas and gives it a shimmering effect. Has Cézanne done all this on purpose, or didn't he know any better? Curiously enough, the longer we study the picture, the more we come to feel that

416. PAUL CEZANNE / *The Card Players* / About 1890–92. Collection Stephen C. Clark, New York. *There is something of the solemn dignity of Le Nain's peasants in this group (compare figure 304), along with a sense of weight and volume, a rocklike firmness of shape that can be matched only by Giotto (see figure 80). Here we find the exact opposite of Caravaggio's* Cardsharps *(figure 250): a slow, serious game played with utmost concentration.*

these things look right in it, although they are wrong according to nature. And that is exactly what Cézanne wanted us to feel. For him, even more than for Manet, a framed canvas was a separate world, with laws of its own that were more important to him than the laws of nature; he could not take something out of nature and put it into a picture without changing it so as to make it fit in. "Bowls, glasses, and fruit," he seems to be telling us, "are not at all remarkable in themselves. They become remarkable only because of what I do with them in my picture. That is my task, my challenge as an artist." But Cézanne did not think of nature simply as his raw material, to be dealt with as he pleased. He had the greatest respect for it and did not change it any more than he felt he had to. In his *Fruit Bowl,* and perhaps even more so in the slightly

later *House in Provence* (figure 413), we can see how delicately he has balanced the claims of art and nature: his forms are arranged in depth, yet they also cling to the surface; they are simpler and clearer than in nature, since the world of painting is a limited and orderly one, made up of color patches rather than of atoms. The forms are carefully related to each other and to the size of the canvas, yet they always remain part of the larger world outside, which does not stop at the frame of the picture.

Cézanne once explained that his aim was "to do Poussin over again, but from nature," which means that he wanted an art as solid and monumental as that of the Old Masters, without giving up what he had learned from Impressionism. The same might be said of Georges Seurat, another great Post-Impressionist. Seurat's career was as brief as those of Masaccio, Giorgione, and Géricault—he died in 1891 at the age of thirty-two—and what he achieved is just as astonishing. His main efforts went into a few very large paintings, on each of which he spent a year's time or more. One reason why he worked so slowly was his belief that art ought to be based on a "system"; like Degas, he had studied with a follower of Ingres, and his interest in theory came from this experience. But as with all artists of genius, Seurat's theories do not explain his pictures; it is the pictures, rather, that explain the theories.

In *A Sunday Afternoon on the Grande Jatte* (figure 414) Seurat has picked a subject popular among the Impressionists—a gay crowd enjoying a summer day on an island near Paris. The colors are of the same rainbow-brightness we saw in Renoir's *Pont Neuf*, but otherwise the picture is the very opposite of a quick "impression." Seurat, even more than Cézanne, sought to regain calmness and monumentality in painting, and he knew that this could be done only by bringing the

417. GEORGES SEURAT / *Drawing for the "Grande Jatte"* / About 1885. Collection César de Hauke, Paris. *Compare figure 414. Seurat's drawings are as impersonal in techniques as his paintings; any trace of "handwriting" has been blotted out by the subtle gradations of tone that define the shapes.*

418. GEORGES SEURAT / *Bathing in the Seine* / 1883–84. Tate Gallery, London. *This is the first of Seurat's large-scale compositions, less complex than the* Grande Jatte, *more broadly painted (the Pointillist dots are not yet in evidence) but just as poised and deliberate. In fact, because of the greater weight of the figures and their unforced, relaxed poses, the picture has a monumentality unequaled by the artist's later works.*

strictest kind of order into the confused, shifting scene, by putting everything in the right place and making it stay there. The *Grand Jatte* is surely one of the most completely "thought-through" pictures of all time, as perfectly controlled as a mural by Piero della Francesca (compare figure 133); in fact, it has a timeless dignity that recalls the art of ancient Egypt. This passion for order can be seen even in the brushwork. Cé-

419. EDOUARD VUILLARD / *Interior at L'Etang-la-Ville* / 1893. Smith College Museum of Art, Northampton, Massachusetts. *Here, under the influence of Seurat and Gauguin, an Impressionist interior has become a scintillating pattern of flat, ornamental surfaces.*

420. VINCENT VAN GOGH / *The Potato Eaters* / 1885. Collection V. W. van Gogh, Laren, Holland. *In this work, the last and most ambitious of his early, pre-Impressionist period, we sense the artist's deep inner sympathy with the poor. The picture has its naïve, clumsy aspects, but they only add to the intensity of expression Van Gogh wanted to achieve. For these simple people, the evening meal has the solemn importance of a ritual.*

421. VINCENT VAN GOGH / *Peasant of the Camargue (pen drawing)* / 1888. Fogg Museum of Art, Harvard University, Cambridge, Massachusetts. *Had none of Van Gogh's paintings survived, his powerful drawings would still be enough to safeguard his place among the great masters of modern times.*

422. VINCENT VAN GOGH / *Sunflowers* / 1888. Tate Gallery, London. *What Van Gogh sees in these flowers is not their ornamental quality but the pathos of all living things. Like miniature suns, they radiate vital energy even as they shed their petals and turn into dry, brown disks.*

zanne's brush strokes, despite their pattern-like quality, still betray a strongly personal touch; with Seurat, every stroke has become a precise little dot of pure color, a tiny, impersonal "building block" in the construction of the picture (this technique is known as Pointillism).

While Cézanne and Seurat were making a more severe, Classical art out of the Impressionist style, Vincent van Gogh led the way in a different direction; he believed that Impressionism did not allow the artist enough freedom to express his inner feelings. Since these were his main concern, he is sometimes called an Expressionist.

423. VINCENT VAN GOGH / *Dr. Gachet* / 1890. Siegfried Kramarsky, New York. *Van Gogh came to Dr. Gachet for treatment in the last months of his life, and found a kindred spirit, almost another self. That is why the anguished face of this portrait so strongly recalls the artist's own.*

Van Gogh, too, wanted to "re-do the Old Masters from nature," but his heroes were Delacroix and Rembrandt rather than Ingres and Poussin. Although he was to become the first great Dutch painter since the seventeenth century, van Gogh did not start out as an artist at all. His early interests were literature and religion; for a while he even worked as a lay preacher among the poor. Only in 1880, at the age of twenty-seven, did he turn to art; and since he died ten years later, his career was even shorter than that of Seurat. Almost all of his important works, in fact, date from the last three years of his life, which he spent mostly in the south of France. Toward the end, he began to suffer from fits of mental illness that made it more and more difficult for him to paint. Despairing of a cure, he finally decided to kill himself, for he felt very deeply that it was only his art that made life worth living for him.

The drawing, *Peasant of the Camargue* (figure 421) is filled with the same sense of pity that had made van Gogh do religious work among the poor. The strongly modeled face stands out with incredible force, since everything else (the background, the hat, the shoulders) has been kept flat, for contrast. In this way the artist compels us to share his own experience, to feel what he felt—the look of inner pain in the eyes, the strange expression of the mouth with its weak, frozen smile. Like Cézanne and Seurat, van Gogh reshapes nature, but for very different reasons. They stress the typical qualities of things; he picks out what is unique. With them, the artist tends to disappear behind his work; with him, every shape reveals his personal feelings. Where they seek balance and stability, he creates movement. Look, for instance, at the dots in the background of our drawing:

425. *Above:* PAUL GAUGUIN / *Bonjour Monsieur Gauguin* / 1889–90. Museum of Modern Art, Prague. 426. *Below:* GUSTAVE COURBET / *Bonjour Monsieur Courbet* / 1854. Musée Fabre, Montpellier, France. *A more telling contrast than this would be hard to imagine. Courbet's picture, painted as a mocking challenge to his critics, shows the supremely self-assured artist being respectfully greeted by a wealthy patron; Gauguin, mocking Courbet, wants to be accepted as a peasant among peasants.*

424. *At left:* VINCENT VAN GOGH / *Self-Portrait* / 1889. Mr. and Mrs. John Hay Whitney, New York. *About a year before his death, Van Gogh began to paint in longer and more undulating strokes which gave his work a new fluid, rhythmic quality (compare figure 430, done only four months earlier). In this picture, the whirling brushwork of the background creates a pool of darkness against which the flame-bright head stands out with incredible force.*

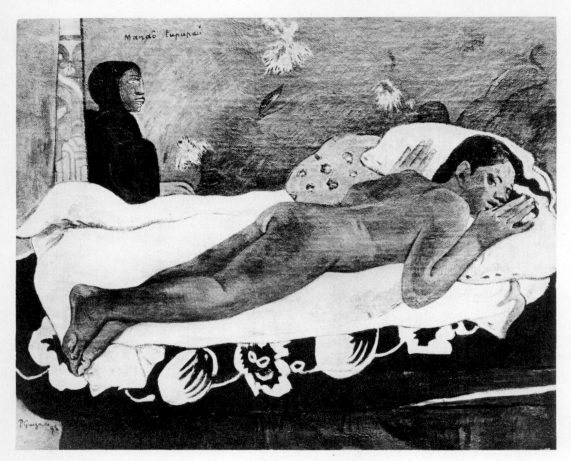

427. *Above:* PAUL GAUGUIN / *The Spirit of the Dead Watching* / 1892. A. Conger Goodyear, New York. 428. *At right:* EDOUARD MANET / *Olympia* / 1863. The Louvre, Paris. *Manet had outraged the "respectable" public because he refused to pretend that his nude model was a reclining Venus. With Gauguin, who echoes Manet's composition, the literary significance returns, but now it is the primitive fear of the supernatural, which he himself had witnessed.*

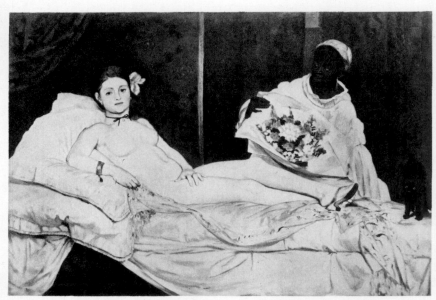

429. PAUL GAUGUIN / *Offerings of Gratitude (woodcut)* / About 1891–93. *In their stark black-and-white patterns and studied simplicity of technique, Gauguin's woodcuts of Tahiti transmit primitiveness more effectively than do his paintings.*

430. VINCENT VAN GOGH / *Road with Cypresses* / 1889. Kröller-Müller State Museum, Otterlo, Holland. *The same southern French countryside where Cézanne had found stability and order, inspired Van Gogh's passionate vision of the oneness and aliveness of all nature, of earth and sky united by the same flow of cosmic energy.*

431. PAUL GAUGUIN / *The Yellow Christ* / 1889. Albright Art Gallery, Buffalo, New York. *Gauguin felt that Impressionism had neglected the role of the imagination. Rather than observe nature precisely, he wanted to "dream in front of it," as he does in this picture, which is meant to evoke the simple and direct faith of peasant folk.*

432. HENRI DE TOULOUSE-LAUTREC / *At the Moulin Rouge* / 1892. Art Institute of Chicago. *Despite its surface gaiety, this is an oddly joyless scene. The stony, masklike faces, the off-key color scheme, the combination of large flat areas and overemphatic perspective, produce a disquieting, nightmarish effect.*

433.   HENRI ROUSSEAU / *The Sleeping Gypsy* / 1897. Museum of Modern Art, New York. (Gift of Mrs. Simon Guggenheim.) *Those qualities which Gauguin was striving to recapture by conscious effort, Rousseau achieved without even being aware of them. He thought of himself as a "realist" (he admired the slick surface finish of Bouguereau; see figure 400) but, fortunately for us, his reality was a romantic dream.*

434. JAMES ENSOR / *Intrigue* / 1890. Royal Museum of Fine Arts, Antwerp. *Like Van Gogh, this great Belgian painter was moved to deep moral anguish by the complacent optimism of his time. He, too, was concerned with expression rather than form. But his is a bitterly mocking art, full of demoniacal laughter. The sinister masked creatures of Ensor's imagination press in upon us as insistently as the nightmarish witches of Goya (compare figure 347).*

they reflect the Pointillism of Seurat, but instead of staying in place they seem to be flowing this way and that, as if they had a will of their own. Elsewhere in the drawing, this same flow of the pen strokes becomes stronger still.

In the *Road with Cypresses* (figure 430) the personal "handwriting" of van Gogh is done with the brush, but every stroke stands out just as boldly, and his passion for movement is almost overpowering. The road streams past us, the trees lick upward like flames, and the sky is filled with the whirling motion of the sun, moon, and stars. This magnificent vision of the unity of all forms of life again expresses van Gogh's religious feeling—a feeling as deep and strong as the faith of the Middle Ages, even though it is based on a belief in the creative force within nature, rather than on the Christianity of the Bible.

Religion also played an important part in the work (if not the life) of Paul Gauguin, who decided to turn artist even later in his career than van Gogh did. Until the age of thirty-five, he was a prosperous businessman who painted and col-

435. ODILON REDON / *Silence* / About 1911. Museum of Modern Art, New York. (Lillie P. Bliss Collection.) *Although linked with the Symbolist movement, Redon was unique as an explorer of dreamlike visions. His* Silence *has a hauntingly poetic air that is not soon forgotten.*

436. EDVARD MUNCH / *Puberty* / 1894–95. National Gallery, Oslo. *Shivering with guilt and fear, this girl has suddenly become conscious of herself as a sexual being. The harsh lighting reveals her nakedness, physically and psychologically, as if she were trapped in the beam of a spotlight.*

lected modern pictures on the side (he once owned Cézanne's *Fruit Bowl, Glass, and Apples*). By 1889, however, he had founded a new movement in art that he called Symbolism. This style, though less intensely personal than van Gogh's, was in some ways an even bolder jump beyond the bounds of Impressionism. Gauguin felt very strongly that Western civilization was "out of joint"; that our industrial society had forced men into an incomplete kind of life devoted to making money, while their emotions lay neglected. In order to rediscover this hidden world of feeling for himself, Gauguin went to live among the peasants of Brittany, in western France. He was

particularly struck by the fact that religion still formed part of the everyday life of these country people, and in his *Yellow Christ* (figure 431) he has tried to express their simple and direct faith. The Christ is of a Late Gothic type, but on the level of folk art, since that is the way the three peasant women in the foreground think of Him. The other forms, too, have been simplified and flattened out, so as to stress that they are imagined, not observed from nature, and the brilliant colors are equally "un-natural." Gauguin's Symbolist style owes a good deal to medieval art (compare figure 79), yet there is one big difference: since he did not share the religious experience of the peasants, Gauguin could only paint pictures *about* faith, rather than *from* faith.

Two years later, Gauguin's search for the unspoiled life led him even farther afield. He went to the South Pacific, as a sort of "missionary in reverse" who wanted to learn from the natives

437. EDVARD MUNCH / *The Scream* / 1893. National Gallery, Oslo. *See comment, opposite page.* "I want to paint pictures," Munch wrote, "that will make people take off their hats in awe, the way they do in church."

instead of teaching them. Gauguin spent almost ten years in this tropical setting, yet none of the pictures he painted there is as daring as the *Yellow Christ*. The most interesting works of this period are his woodcuts; in their frankly "carved" look and bold white-on-black patterns we can feel the influence of the native art of the South Seas. The one called *Offerings of Gratitude* (figure 429) again has religious worship for its theme, but now the image of a local god has taken the place of Christ.

Meanwhile, the ideas of Gauguin were taken up by other artists, among them the important Norwegian painter Edvard Munch. In *The Scream* (figure 437), Munch makes us "see" what it feels like to be afraid. It is a picture of fear, the kind of terrifying fear without reason that grips us after we wake up from a nightmare. The long, wavy lines seem to carry the echo of the scream into every corner of the picture—earth and sky

have become one great sounding board of fear.

There is a curiously haunted feeling about figure 432, too, even though it shows the inside of a well-known Paris nightclub, the Moulin Rouge. Henri de Toulouse-Lautrec, who painted this picture, was a great admirer of Degas, but he also knew van Gogh and Gauguin. *At the Moulin Rouge* still has a good deal in common with Degas' Impressionist *Café Concert* (figure 391); there is the same sudden jump from foreground to background, the same contrasty lighting, the same interest in the gestures and poses of the performers. But Toulouse-Lautrec sees right through the gay surface of the scene. He views it with a cartoonist's sharp eye for character, including his own—he is the tiny, bearded man next to the very tall one in the back of the room. The large patches of flat color, on the other hand, with their dark, curving outlines, remind us of Gauguin. Toulouse-Lautrec was no Symbolist, and

438. HENRI DE TOULOUSE-LAUTREC / *In the Circus Fernando: The Ringmaster* / 1888. Art Institute of Chicago. *This canvas reveals the strong influence of Japanese woodcuts, popular in the West since the 1860's: the flat, bright areas of color; vigorously simplified, dark contours; composition from the edges inward, around an empty center, with every important element cut by the frame; abrupt, overemphatic contrast of near and far.*

439. HENRI DE TOULOUSE-LAUTREC / *Divan Japonais (poster)* Colored Lithograph, 1892. *Here the composition of Degas' Café Concert (compare figure 391) has been filtered through the pattern of a Japanese woodcut, as it were, to yield a strikingly effective poster design.*

yet his picture means more than an Impressionist nightclub scene. Whether he wanted to or not, he makes us feel that this is a place of evil.

In 1886, there appeared in an exhibition of Post-Impressionist works some pictures by a painter nobody had heard of before. His name was Henri Rousseau, and he turned out to be a retired customs official who had just started to paint, without training of any sort, at the age of forty. Rousseau was a folk artist, of the same breed as Edward Hicks, but, strangely enough, he was also a genius. How else could he have painted a picture like *The Sleeping Gypsy* (figure 433)? You will find it difficult to escape the magic spell of this dream in paint. What goes on in this calm desert landscape under the light of the full moon needs no explanation, because none is possible, but perhaps for this very reason the scene becomes unbelievably real to us. Here at last we find that innocence and strength of feeling which Gauguin had thought so necessary for the Modern Age. That is why Rousseau, more than anyone else, may be called the godfather of twentieth-century painting.

440. HENRI ROUSSEAU / *The Dream* / 1910. Museum of Modern Art, New York. (Gift of Nelson A. Rockefeller.) *In a little poem, Rousseau himself described the enchanted world of this canvas: "Yadwigha, peacefully asleep, enjoys a lovely dream: she hears a kind snake charmer playing upon his reed. On stream and foliage glisten the silvery beams of the moon; and savage serpents listen to the gay, entrancing tune."*

Painting in Our Time

IN OUR ACCOUNT of painting since the industrial revolution, we have mentioned quite a number of "isms": Realism, Impressionism (and Post-Impressionism), Pointillism, Expressionism, Symbolism. In the twentieth century we find even more; so many, in fact, that nobody has yet made an exact count. Now, we are apt to find "isms" of any sort confusing, or even frightening. That is why many of us will give up trying to understand modern art before we have really made a start; we don't want to cram our heads full of "isms." Actually, however, this is not necessary at all. We must always keep in mind that an "ism" is just a label to help us put things in their proper places. If it does not do that, we might as well forget about it. A good many "isms" in modern art belong to the latter kind: some of the styles or movements they are meant to label cannot be seen very clearly, while others amount to so little that only the specialist has to bother with them. After all, it is easier to think up a new label than to create something new in art that deserves a name of its own.

Still, we can't do without "isms" altogether, and for good reasons. Let us think back to the Renaissance for a moment: there we came to know many local "schools." Every country, every region, every important city had its own way of doing things, so that we often can tell at a glance where a picture of this period came from. In the Baroque era, we still found such differences, but we also saw more and more international give-and-take. Since then, this trend has grown apace. The Age of Machines has made life pretty much

441. OSKAR KOKOSCHKA / *Self-Portrait* / 1913. Museum of Modern Art, New York. *Like many other Expressionists, Kokoschka here sees himself as a visionary, a witness to the truth and reality of his inner experiences. The hypersensitive look seems to reflect a great ordeal of the imagination.*

the same throughout the Western world; it has also forced the same problems on all of us. Today we are so involved in each other that no man, no nation can remain an island any more. We can see then why local or national "schools" are of little importance in modern art. Their place has been taken by movements, or "isms," that have a way of spreading across all boundaries. Within this bewildering variety, however, we find three main currents, and it is these that we shall keep our eye on. They all had their start among the Post-Impressionists, but in our own century they have been carried a great deal further. One of them, Expressionism, stresses the artist's feel-ings about himself and the world. Another, under the name of Abstraction, is concerned with the order of shapes inside the picture. And the third, which we shall call Fantastic Art, explores the realm of imagination. At this point it is well to remember that feeling, order, and imagination go into *every* work of art: without imagination, it would be deadly dull; if it had no order at all, we should find it horribly messy; and if there were no feeling behind it, it would leave us completely unmoved. But of course an artist may be more interested in one of these than in the others, and that is all we mean when we speak of the three currents.

442. HENRI MATISSE / *Bathers with a Turtle* / 1908. Collection Mr. and Mrs. Joseph Pulitzer, Jr., St. Louis, Missouri. *No longer a violent Fauve, Matisse here aims for "an art of balance, of purity and serenity." And the three nudes, with their background of sand, sea, and sky, do indeed breathe an air of idyllic calm and happiness. This painting hung in the Folkwang Museum, Essen, until Hitler's purge of "degenerate art."*

Expressionism

EXPRESSIONISM is no longer new to us. We have seen it in van Gogh, in Gauguin, and even in Toulouse-Lautrec. These were the artists most admired by a young Spanish painter who arrived in Paris in the year 1900. His name was Pablo Picasso. Later on, he became the most famous, as well as the most fought-over, of all living artists; but during the first few years of his career he was unknown, poor, and lonesome. His state of mind is clearly reflected in *The Old Guitarist* (figure 443), which represents the first of Picasso's many phases. The painting is done almost entirely in blues, the color of gloom; this underlines the hopeless feeling and makes the starved musician look even more pathetic. Picasso must have felt like an outcast himself; that is why his heart went out to those suffering in silence as this beggar does. Yet the picture is not all despair. The way the old man accepts his fate reminds us of a saint. And if we turn back to figure 210 we shall find similar faces and hands among the Apostles of El Greco's *Assumption*. Our guitarist, then, is of a strange breed—part Mannerist, part Gauguin and Toulouse-Lautrec (notice the smoothly curved outlines!), filtered through the personal gloom of a twenty-two-year-old genius.

443. PABLO PICASSO / *The Old Guitarist* / 1903. Art Institute of Chicago. *See comment above. Picasso painted this picture in Barcelona, where he had been forced to return after a miserable winter in Paris. Early in 1904 he went back to Paris, staying in France ever since.*

About this time, a group of young French painters were also turning to Expressionism. These men so outraged the public that they came to be known as the Fauves—that is, Wild Beasts —and they did not resent the name a bit. Their leader was Henri Matisse, another of the "old masters" of modern art (he died in 1954). His fine still life, *Goldfish and Sculpture* (figure 449), is less violent than the earliest pictures of the Fauves; it can still show you, however, why they caused such an uproar. In its extreme simplicity, the picture certainly takes a long step beyond van Gogh and Gauguin, but not in the same direction. Here the quick "handwriting" of the brush betrays no personal anguish; it tells us, rather, that Matisse had strong feelings about one thing only—the act of painting itself. That is

444. HENRI MATISSE / *Carmelina* / 1903. Museum of Fine Arts, Boston. *For strictness of organization this early canvas has few equals in Matisse's work. The solid, clearly defined planes of color and the magnificent matter-of-factness of statement suggest Manet and Cézanne (see figure 411).*

445. MAURICE VLAMINCK / *Houses at Chatou* / 1904. Art Institute of Chicago. *The frenzied movements of the brush, the bold simplification of forms, are characteristic of the Fauve group. Their origin is in the work of Van Gogh, which had a profound impact on these men.*

446. HENRI MATISSE / *The Plumed Hat (pencil drawing)* / 1919. Collection John S. Newberry, Jr., Grosse Pointe Farms, Michigan. *Relaxed and descriptive, some of Matisse's large drawings of 1917–25 recapture the classic precision of Ingres and Degas (compare figures 343, 402, 404).*

447. JAN DAVIDSZ DE HEEM / *The Dessert* / 1640. The Louvre, Paris. *Compare 448. Matisse had copied this picture as a student; twenty years later he did a variant, Cubist in organization and Fauve in color yet with respect for the sensuous reality of the objects.*

448.   HENRI MATISSE / *Variation on a Still Life by De Heem* / 1915-17. From the Collection of Mr. and Mrs. Samuel A. Marx, Chicago. *Compare figure 447. Matisse's accomplishment here is perhaps best summed up in his own words: "What I am after, above all, is expression. . . . (But) . . . expression . . . does not consist of the passion mirrored upon a human face. . . . The whole arrangement of my picture is expressive. The placement of figures or objects, the empty spaces around them, the proportions, everything plays a part."*

449.   HENRI MATISSE / *Still Life: Goldfish and Sculpture* / 1911. Museum of Modern Art, New York.
(Gift of Mr. and Mrs. John Hay Whitney.) *Despite the drastic economy of shape and color, everything
in this still life is clearly recognizable. Matisse always opposed arbitrary distortions or eccentric color.
"The painter," he said, "must always feel that he is copying nature—and even when he consciously
departs from nature, he must do it with the conviction that it is only the better to interpret her."*

450. OSKAR KOKOSCHKA / *Portrait of Dr. Tietze and His Wife* / 1909. Museum of Modern Art, New York. (Mrs. John D. Rockefeller, Jr. Purchase Fund.) *The two figures emerging from the rainbow-colored, mysterious background have the quality of an apparition rather than of material presence.*

451. MAX BECKMANN / *Departure* / 1932-35. Museum of Modern Art, New York. *Compare figure 454.*
Painted shortly before Hitler's campaign against "degenerate art" drove Beckmann into exile abroad,
this triptych shows a solemn image of hope and freedom flanked by scenes of nightmarish torment.

452. GEORGES ROUAULT / *The Old Clown* / 1917. Collection Stavros Niarchos. *The defeated expression of this face recalls Van Gogh's Peasant (figure 421), while the bold black outlines and the translucent quality of the surface evoke memories of Medieval stained glass.*

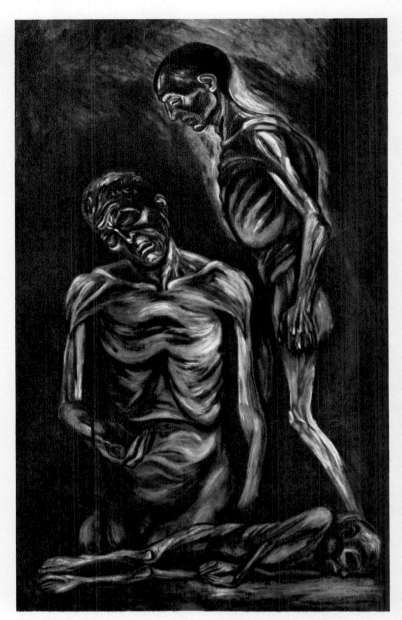

453. JOSE CLEMENTE OROZCO / *Victims (detail of a mural cycle)* / 1936. University of Guadalajara, Mexico. *The Expressionist art of Orozco was shaped by the Mexican Revolution. It springs from a deep humanitarian sympathy with the silent, suffering masses and a contempt for all ideologies.*

why his picture is such a delightful "teaser" for the eye: the bowl, the vase, and the figure are foreshortened, and the lively fish in the clear green water are startlingly "real"; the room, on the other hand, has been flattened out into one solid blue area, the yellow curtain and the view out the window are equally flat, and there is no hint of shading anywhere. It is as if Matisse had said to himself: "Let us see what I have to do to nature in order to change it into a decorative pattern, and yet keep it intact as much as I can." Nobody has ever managed this union of opposites as gracefully as he.

The excitement about the Fauves helped to attract a lot of modern-minded foreign artists to Paris. Among them was Amedeo Modigliani, the talented Italian painter who did the *Girl with Braids* (figure 455). He died young, and his life was far from happy. Perhaps that explains the wistful poetic charm of this picture, which creates a mood not unlike that of Picasso's *Old Guitarist*. The style, however, with its simplified, dark outlines, its blocks of bright color, seems much closer to Matisse, although Modigliani uses subtle bits of shading here and there to lift the head away from its background.

The new style of the Fauves had a particularly strong echo in Germany, where it touched off a

similar movement. *The Dream* (figure 454) is a picture by Max Beckmann, the most powerful and original of these German Expressionists. Beckmann had come to Expressionism as a result of his experiences in World War I, which left him with a deep feeling of despair at the state of our civilization. Like Gauguin, he was an artist with a great deal to say. His problem was how to say it. In order to show what he saw behind the surface of modern life, he could not simply paint the surface itself; he needed symbols, but where was he to find them? All the old ones had long since lost their meaning. So he did what Gauguin had done: he invented his own. But because these are *new* symbols, we must not try to "read" them the way we do those of earlier times. Perhaps Beckmann himself did not know what they stand for, any more than we can ex-

455. AMEDEO MODIGLIANI / *Girl with Braids* / 1917. Collection Dr. and Mrs. Ernest Kahn, Cambridge, Massachusetts. *If this picture recalls Matisse in its bold simplicity of line and color, it also evokes Modigliani's Italian heritage: the sweetness and grace of Botticelli (compare figure 137).*

454. MAX BECKMANN / *The Dream* / 1921. Private collection. *See comment on this page. Some of the elements of this scene, suggesting a grotesque and sinister side show, occur again and again among the imagery of Beckmann's later works (compare the side panels of* Departure, *figure 451).*

456. PABLO PICASSO / *Family of Saltimbanques* / 1905. National Gallery of Art, Washington, D.C. (Chester Dale Collection.) *Here the deep melancholy of Picasso's "blue" period (see figure 443) has begun to lift; he now uses rose and earth colors as well, and instead of beggars and derelicts he paints harlequins, acrobats, and similar circus folk. An aura of wistful, romantic charm clings to these artistes, resigned to their unsteady, wandering life.*

plain the things we see in our own dreams. "These are the creatures that haunt my imagination," he seems to say. "To me they have the power of symbols that sum up our nightmarish present-day world. They show you the true nature of man—how weak we are, how helpless against ourselves, in this proud era of so-called 'progress'." His message may well remind you of Jerome

457. PABLO PICASSO / *Les Demoiselles d'Avignon* / 1907. Museum of Modern Art, New York. (Acquired through the Lillie P. Bliss Bequest.) *This canvas, the opening fanfare of Cubism, sums up the sudden "breakthrough" in Picasso's work since 1905; its distortions are a calculated assault upon sentiment and conventional beauty.*

Bosch (figure 128), and there is indeed something Late Gothic about Beckmann's tilted, zigzag world and its jerky, puppet-like figures. He has painted a modern "ship of fools," as forceful and disquieting as the first.

Only one other painter shows such deep concern with the state of the world: Georges Rouault, who had once exhibited with the Wild Beasts. Rouault, however, has found assurance in his strong Christian faith, and his pictures, such as the *Old Clown* (see figure 452), suggest sympathy and pity rather than despair. His subjects, too, are less violent and of a more familiar kind. The tragic clown, outwardly gay, inwardly sad, is known to most of us, but in Rouault's hands he becomes a symbol for the sufferings of all mankind. We are made to feel this from the way the picture is painted—in a style that owes much to van Gogh and Gauguin but perhaps even more to Gothic stained glass windows. Yet the expressive power of the shapes and colors belongs to Rouault alone.

Lower Manhattan (figure 468), by the American painter John Marin, shows you power of a different sort. If Rouault's picture seems to glow from within, this one fairly explodes with action. What other style could possibly give us as much of the "feel" of the big city with its crowds, its noisy traffic, its restless energy? How relaxed and leisurely the *Pont Neuf* of Renoir is in comparison, even though it was done only half a century earlier. You will hardly find a more striking illustration of the pace of modern life than the contrast between these two pictures, each of them so exactly right for the character of its subject.

458. PABLO PICASSO / *Nude (charcoal drawing)* / 1910. Collection Alfred Stieglitz Estate. *Compare the "skeleton key" at the top of the facing page. The violence of the* Demoiselles d'Avignon *has now given way to a calm and methodical use of the new structural devices.*

459. PABLO PICASSO / *Still Life with Chair Caning* / 1911–12. Collection of the artist. *Here we witness the beginnings of another "breakthrough," which heralds the end of the first, or "facet" phase of Cubism. The canvas has suddenly become a tray on which the still life is "served" to us.*

Abstraction

Bᴜᴛ ᴡᴇ ᴍᴜsᴛ ᴄᴀᴛᴄʜ ᴜᴘ with the second of our three currents, the one we labeled Abstraction. What does the word mean? "To abstract (from something)" means "to draw away from, to separate." If we have ten apples and then separate the ten from the apples, we have an "abstract number," since it no longer refers to ten particular things. Now let us suppose we want to make a picture of our ten apples: we shall find no two of them alike. If we leave out any of these small differences, we are already "abstracting" a part of what we actually see. As a matter of fact, even the most realistic portrait of our ten apples will turn out to be an "abstraction" of sorts, because we cannot do it without leaving out *something*. Abstraction, then, goes into the making of any work of art, whether the artist knows it or not. The ancient Egyptians, for instance, who drew the little "stick men" in figure 9, certainly did not realize they were abstracting, neither did the Greeks who made the geometric vase in figure 24. In the Renaissance, however, artists began to abstract in a conscious and controlled way. They found that the shapes of nature were easier for

460. *Above right:* ᴘᴀʙʟᴏ ᴘɪᴄᴀssᴏ / *Ambroise Vollard* / 1910. Museum of Modern Western Art, Moscow. 461. *Right:* ᴘᴀʙʟᴏ ᴘɪᴄᴀssᴏ / *Ambroise Vollard (pencil drawing)* / 1915. Owner unknown. *These two portraits of the famous art dealer make a fascinating comparison. The Ingres-like drawing shows Picasso rediscovering an interest in exact representation alongside his vigorous pursuit of Cubism; it also helps us to see how strikingly the sitter's features emerge from the facet structure of the painting.*

462. GEORGES BRAQUE / *Le Courrier (collage)* / 1913. Philadelphia Museum of Art. (A. E. Gallatin Collection.) *Such "paste-ups," of which both Braque and Picasso did considerable numbers in 1913–14, demonstrate the importance of the "tray" idea we had first encountered in figure 459.*

463. PABLO PICASSO / *Mother and Child* / 1922. Collection Mr. and Mrs. Alex L. Hillman, New York. *Here Picasso's revived interest in representation, which began with the meticulous pencil drawings of 1914–15, reaches its monumental, "Neo-Classic" climax.*

the eye to grasp if they were analyzed in terms of the simple and regular shapes of geometry (Piero della Francesca did this in figures 133 and 141). Cézanne and Seurat rediscovered this method and explored it further; according to Cézanne, "You must see in nature the cylinder, the sphere, the cone." It was the work of these two men that really started the abstract movement in modern art.

Toward 1906, Picasso turned away from his earlier style and started painting in the manner of Cézanne. He was joined in this by his friend Georges Braque, who had been one of the Fauves until then. These two soon went a long way beyond Cézanne and created an exciting new style called Cubism. We shall understand the reason for the name if we look at Picasso's *Nude* of 1910 (figure 458), full of straight lines and right angles. But where is the nude figure? It is not easy to find at first, so we have tried to disentangle it in a sketch of our own, a sort of "skeleton key" to the picture (you will find it on page 289). At this point, however, you might be even more puzzled than before. Why did the artist insist on hiding a nude among all these shapes? Would not the angles and planes have made a more beautiful design if they did not have to represent anything at all? There were some later artists who believed that, but not Picasso. To him, as to Cézanne, abstraction was "what had to be done to nature so as to make it fit the picture"; it had no meaning by itself. He uses much tighter rules of order here than Cézanne ever did—rules that almost force him to break the human form apart entirely—but he still needs nature to challenge his creative powers. In other words, what counts is neither the nude nor the design but the tension between the two.

464. *At right:* PABLO PICASSO / *First Steps* / 1943. Private collection, New York. *Ever since the mid-1920's, Picasso has been combining the formal discipline of Collage-Cubism with his Neo-Classic representational style in an endless variety of new and exciting creations. Here he makes us relive a basic human experience: what it feels like to stand on one's own legs for the first time—the fright, the tottering unsureness, but also the sense of adventure.*

465. JUAN GRIS / *The Chessboard* / 1917. Museum of Modern Art, New York. *Gris, a few years younger than Braque and Picasso, had become a Cubist in 1912, and soon developed a highly distinguished personal style. The Chessboard has a somber harmony, a tightness of construction unmatched by either Braque or Picasso, yet there is enough tension within its balance to avoid the easy symmetry of the merely ornamental.*

In figure 459, Picasso has applied the same approach to a still life. Everything is broken up into angles and planes except the three letters (whose shapes cannot be made more abstract than they are to begin with). But how can we explain the piece of imitation chair caning pasted into the picture? Why the oval shape, and the rope instead of a frame? Picasso apparently wanted to make the canvas look like a tray on which the still life is "served" to us. It was a rather witty notion of his to put the abstract "shapes of things" on top of the real things (canvas, chair caning, and rope). Picasso probably did not realize it

466. REMBRANDT / *The Carcass of Beef* / 1655. The Louvre, Paris. *This was the model for the picture by Soutine on the facing page. The glowing color and the deeply compassionate spirit of Rembrandt have been a source of inspiration to many Expressionist painters.*

467.   CHAIM SOUTINE / *The Carcass of Beef* / 1926. Collection Mme. Germaine Bignou, Paris. *Compare figure 466. The shape of the carcass has undergone a frightening change: it now suggests a disemboweled human body. Soutine, of Russian-Jewish birth, became a leading Expressionist in Paris.*

468.　JOHN MARIN / *Lower Manhattan (water color)* / 1920. Collection Philip L. Goodwin, New York. *The modern metropolis, and especially New York with its skyscrapers and surging crowds, has challenged the imagination of many painters. This explosive design expresses the city's restless energy and nerve-racking pace.*

469. WASSILY KANDINSKY / *Improvisation No. 30* / 1913. Art Institute of Chicago. *Kandinsky is the father of what in recent years has been called "Abstract Expressionism"; such pictures convey a sensation or a state of mind through freely combined shapes and colors without having to represent anything at all.*

AT LEFT:

470. GEORGES BRAQUE / *Guitar, Fruit and Pitcher* / 1927. Collection Mr. and Mrs. M. Lincoln Schuster, New York. *Among the founders of Cubism, Braque is the most sensitive and poetic, a master of still life in the great tradition of Chardin and Cézanne (compare figures 327, 412). In our example, somber in tone yet wonderfully serene, the strictness of "post-collage" construction is relieved by the fluid and individual brushwork.*

471. PABLO PICASSO / *Three Musicians* / 1921. Museum of Modern Art, New York. (Mrs. Simon Guggenheim Fund.) *Here traditional figures of the comedy stage are put into the idiom of "post-collage" Cubism; their human presence is felt, solemn, even sinister, behind the patchwork of costumes and masks.*

472. PABLO PICASSO / *Still Life on Table* / 1931. Collection of the artist. *The energetic curves and bright colors of this composition create a sense of bursting vitality akin to the Baroque. There is nothing "still" about this still life! The heavy black outlines recall the lead strips of stained glass windows.*

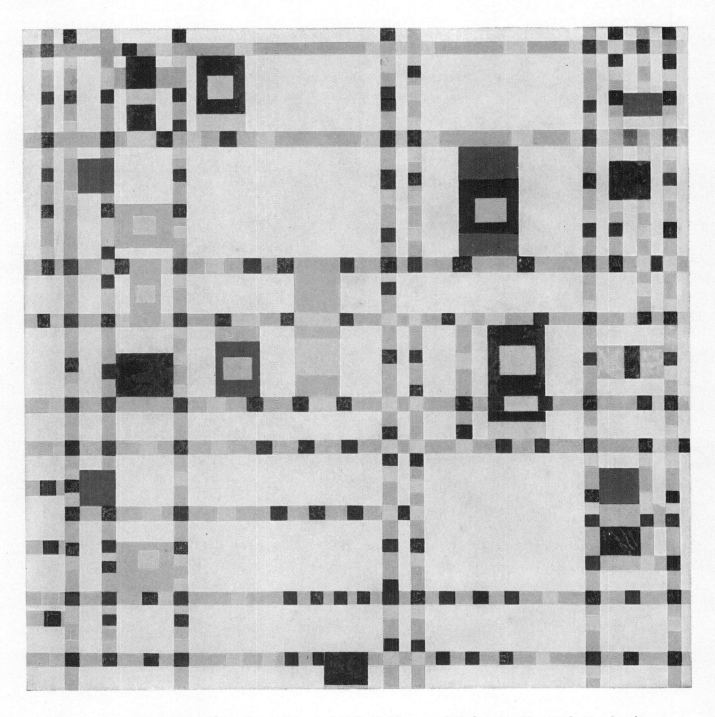

473.   PIET MONDRIAN / *Broadway Boogie-Woogie* / 1941-42. Museum of Modern Art, New York. *Mondrian's picture, too, is full of life and movement, despite its severely restricted vocabulary of shapes and colors. The tingling staccato rhythm of the design captures the very qualities suggested by the musical title.*

474.   MARC CHAGALL / *I and the Village* / 1911. Museum of Modern Art, New York. (Mrs. Simon Guggenheim Fund.) *In pictures such as this, done soon after his arrival in Paris, the young Russian-Jewish artist used the devices of Cubism (compare figure 458) to build a personal world of dream and memory images.*

right then and there, but he had just started to invent a new language of painting. The still life *Le Courrier* by Braque (figure 462) shows us the next step in the growth of this new language. Here the main parts of the design are pasted together out of odd pieces of paper (this is called a collage, the French word for "pasting"), with only a few drawn lines and bits of shading added to make it complete. As a result, the real and the abstract have become so thor-

475. WYNDHAM LEWIS / *T. S. Eliot* / 1938. Harvard University, Cambridge, Massachusetts. *Under the impact of Cubism, Lewis became a pioneer of abstract art in England as early as 1912–14. In this portrait, structural precision is wedded to a keen sense of personality.*

476. FERNAND LEGER / *The City* / 1919. Philadelphia Museum of Art. (A. E. Gallatin Collection.) *Leger's Cubism reflects his love of the clean geometric shapes of modern machinery and engineering. The City is a vivid kaleidoscope of our highly mechanized civilization, full of optimism and pleasurable excitement but also stable and controlled despite the crowding of fragmented shapes.*

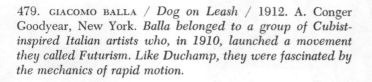

477. MARCEL DUCHAMP / *Nude Descending a Staircase, No. 2*
1912. Philadelphia Museum of Art. (Louise and Walter
Arensberg Collection.) *Here the transparent facets of Cubism
serve to represent motion in terms of successive phases super-
imposed on each other, as in a multiple-exposure photograph.*

479. GIACOMO BALLA / *Dog on Leash* / 1912. A. Conger
Goodyear, New York. *Balla belonged to a group of Cubist-
inspired Italian artists who, in 1910, launched a movement
they called Futurism. Like Duchamp, they were fascinated by
the mechanics of rapid motion.*

478. FRANZ MARC / *Tower of Blue Horses* / 1912–13. Formerly National Gallery, Berlin. *In this picture, the same devices that serve the mock-scientific precision of Duchamp have
become the vehicle of a poetic mysticism. These are celestial
animals, with moons and stars embedded in their bodies.*

oughly interwoven that we can no longer ask: "What is this a picture of?" Even more than before, the white paper acts as a "tray," but does the tray hold the *picture* of a still life, or the still life itself? The meaning, then, is a good deal more complicated here than in Picasso's *Nude*, but the means have become very much simpler, since they can be found in any wastebasket.

Actually, it must have been a great strain on the artist to create balance and harmony from these chance pickings; a fine collage, such as ours, is a rare and beautiful thing. That is why Braque and Picasso did not continue this technique for very long. Soon they took the final step toward the new language: they began to do pictures that looked like collage but were actually painted with the brush. We can see the results in Picasso's *Three Musicians* (figure 471), one of the great masterpieces of modern times. This picture has both the size and the monumental feeling of a mural; its precisely "cut" shapes are fitted together as firmly as building blocks, yet they are not ends in themselves (if they were, the painting would look like a patchwork quilt). Every one of them has a definite meaning, and the image of the three seated, masked figures, translated into this new language, emerges more and more strongly the longer we look at it. There is space here, too, although not the kind we know from the "window pictures" of the Renaissance; instead of looking *through* the canvas into depth, we see space in terms of the overlapping layers of shapes *in front of* the canvas. That is why Picasso can now do without shading entirely, while in the two earlier stages of Cubism he still needed it. At this point let us turn back to another musician, done some fifty years earlier: Manet's *Fife Player* (figure 394). Does he not strike us as the true grandfather of our Picasso? He should, for it was shadow-less paintings such as this one that started off the "revolution of the color patch" which had its final triumph in Collage-Cubism.

For Picasso, however, there could be no stand-

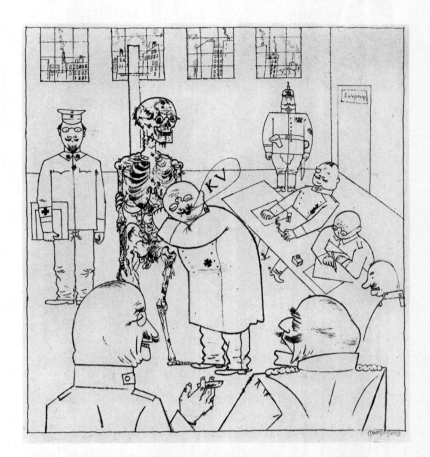

480. GEORGE GROSZ / *"Fit for Active Service"* (*pen drawing*) 1918. Museum of Modern Art, New York. (A. Conger Goodyear Fund.) *Even in this savage satire on the die-hard militarism of the Kaiser's Germany we sense the influence of Cubism (Grosz had been to Paris in 1913).*

ing still. Once Collage-Cubism was fully worked out, he had begun to show greater interest in representation, and by the time he did the *Three Musicians* he also painted "Neo-Classic" pictures such as the *Mother and Child* of figure 463. Here the bodies are as rounded and heavy as carved stone; it is this monumental quality, in fact, that links the two pictures together, different though they seem in so many other ways. Picasso has now returned to the warm, human world of his early works, but with a new strength of form that he owes to his Cubist experience.

Meanwhile, the influence of Cubism had spread far and wide, not only in painting but in sculpture, in the decorative arts, and even into architecture. Many painters felt that Cubism, as an abstract "system" of shapes, had a great deal in common with science and engineering and that, for this reason, it was the only style for putting

his main task in bringing out the hidden force and impressiveness of these industrial shapes. In his canvas, they loom so large that they almost frighten us. However, he also asks a question: "These are the pyramids of modern times; they are our claim to greatness. Will they last as long as the monuments of old?"

Broadway Boogie-Woogie (figure 473), done by the Dutch painter Piet Mondrian shortly before his death in this country, is a more exciting picture in many ways. Mondrian was the strictest and most "architectural" of all abstract painters. His pictures are composed entirely of solid squares or rectangles, and all the lines have to go either straight up-and-down or across. Now one might think that a language with such a small "vocabulary" cannot possibly say a great deal, but our painting proves that this need not be true at all; in fact, it has a spine-tingling liveliness unmatched by any other picture in this book. The entire design moves with the pulse beat of the big city—its flashing neon signs, its stop-and-go

481. JOSEPH STELLA / *American Landscape* / 1929. Formerly Collection Arthur F. Egner, Newark, New Jersey. *The skyscrapers of Manhattan and the tower and cables of the Brooklyn Bridge are here compacted into a rousing vision by an Italian-American who had been linked with Futurism.*

the industrial landscape of·the Age of Machines on canvas. We can judge for ourselves how true this is from *My Egypt* (figure 482). Here the American painter Charles Demuth has done to some factory buildings what Picasso did to his *Nude* in figure 458, but since his "model" was made by man, rather than by nature (and was thus closer to abstraction from the very start) he did not have to change it so much. Demuth saw

482. CHARLES DEMUTH / *My Egypt* / About 1927. Whitney Museum of American Art, New York. *See comment above. Like so many gifted young artists, Demuth had gone to Paris before World War I. His personal response to Cubism, however, did not take shape until some years later.*

483. PIET MONDRIAN / *Flowering Trees* / 1912. Collection Nieuwenhuizen Segaar Art Gallery, The Hague. *There is per-haps no other artist on whom Cubism had as dramatic an impact. Mondrian came to Paris in 1912 at the age of 40, as a painter in the tradition of Van Gogh and the Fauves, but almost at once his work underwent a radical change (Flowering Trees shows the transition) that was to lead him in the end to* Broadway Boogie-Woogie *(figure 473).*

traffic along precisely laid-out patterns. As a pic-ture of the kind of life modern man has created for himself out of his mastery over the forces of nature, *Broadway Boogie-Woogie* makes Ma-rin's *Lower Manhattan,* done only twenty years earlier, look curiously out-of-date.

484. PABLO PICASSO / *The Studio* / 1927–28. Museum of Modern Art, New York. (Gift of Walter P. Chrysler, Jr.) *For Picasso—who here, for once, seems almost as remote from nature as Mondrian—abstraction is not a separate realm of the imagination. We may think of it rather as a state of tension between image and reality.*

Fantasy

OUR THIRD CURRENT, the one we termed Fantasy, follows a less clear-cut course than the other two, since it depends more on a state of mind than on any particular style. The only thing all painters of fantasy have in common is the belief that "seeing with the inner eye" is more important than looking at the world outside; and since every artist has his own private inner world, his way of telling us about it is apt to be just as personal. But why should anybody *want* to tell us about his private world of daydreams and nightmares? And how could it possibly mean anything to us, since our own private world is bound to be different from his? It seems, though,

486. PAUL KLEE / *Conquest of the Mountain* / 1939. Mr. and Mrs. Eero Saarinen, Bloomfield Hills, Michigan. *Despite its playful theme—the toy engine glowing with effort—this picture is severely disciplined in design and purpose; Klee's mountains are a maze that challenges and frustrates conquest by man.*

that we are not as different from each other as all that. Our minds are all built on the same pattern, even if we do not all have equally good ones. And that goes for imagination and memory, too. These belong to the unconscious part of our mind, which we cannot control at will. That is where all our experiences are stored up, whether we want to remember them or not; and at night, or whenever we are "not thinking of anything in particular," they come back to us, and we seem to live through them again. However, the unconscious part of our minds usually does not bring

485. GIORGIO DE CHIRICO / *Melancholy and Mystery of a Street* / 1914. Mr. and Mrs. Stanley R. Resor, New Canaan, Connecticut. *The dream world of De Chirico is truly an "ominous" one; every object here is an omen, a portent of unknown and therefore disquieting significance.*

487. PAUL KLEE / *Twittering Machine (water color and ink drawing)* / 1922. Museum of Modern Art, New York. *Perhaps the laughter here is directed not only against our faith in mechanical invention but also against the sentimental appreciation of bird noises in song and story.*

488. JOAN MIRO / *Landscape with Olive Trees* / 1919. Collection Mr. and Mrs. Leigh B. Block, Chicago. *In this early work, Miró combines Cubist simplification with a very firm grip on observed reality. The wriggling liveliness of the plants makes us think of Harlequin's Carnival (figure 493).*

back our experiences the way they actually happened. It likes to disguise them as "dream images" so that they become less vivid and real to us and we can live with our memories more easily. This digesting of experiences is just as important as the proper digesting of food for our inner well-being.

Now, the way our unconscious mind digests our experiences is pretty much alike in all of us, although it works better with some people than with others. That is why we are always interested in learning about imaginary things, if the person

489. JOAN MIRO / *Composition* / 1933. James Johnson Sweeney, New York. *The artist here contrasts two distinct "personalities" made up of fluid, curving shapes that seem to be full of impulses to expand or contract. This quality, which is not easy to achieve, makes them extraordinarily "lifelike."*

who tells us about them knows how to make them seem real. What happens in a fairy tale, for example, makes no sense at all in the matter-of-fact language of a news report, but when somebody tells it "right" we are thrilled. The same is true in painting. We have already seen one very beautiful and impressive "fairy-tale picture," Rousseau's *Sleeping Gypsy* (figure 433); perhaps we shall like some of the later ones just as well.

Melancholy and Mystery of a Street (figure 485), by the Italian painter Giorgio de Chirico, comes closest to the imaginary reality of the *Sleeping Gypsy*. We cannot explain any of the strange things that happen in it, yet the eerie feeling of the whole tells us that it must be a

490. MAX ERNST / *Collage* / 1920. Collection Jean Arp, Basel. *The mocking bitterness of this Dadaist invention is summed up in the title the artist gave it: "1 copper plate 1 zinc plate 1 rubber towel 2 calipers 1 drainpipe telescope 1 roaring man."*

491. MAX ERNST / *Swamp Angel* / 1940. Collection Kenneth Macpherson, Rome. *Since the early 1920's, Ernst has been the leading spirit of the Surrealist movement. In his pictures a luxuriant, sinister world of plant and animal life seems to grow before our very eyes, born of "natural" chance effects akin to the ink blot landscapes of Alexander Cozens (figure 333) but infinitely more varied and more imaginatively exploited.*

492.   PAUL KLEE / *Park near L(ucerne)* / 1938. Klee Foundation, Bern, Switzerland. *These seemingly simple forms, like simple words used by a great poet, sum up a wealth of experiences and sensations: the innocence and gaiety of young flowering trees along with the clipped orderliness peculiar to captive plant life in a park.*

493.　JOAN MIRO / *The Harlequin's Carnival* / 1924-25. Albright Art Gallery, Buffalo, New York. *Miró here presents a miniature circus where the props are as lively as the performers, and everything is about to turn into something else—a world of self-inflating balloons that bounce, float, wave, wriggle in delightfully unreasoned fashion.*

494.   YVES TANGUY / *The Furniture of Time* / 1939. Collection James Thrall Soby, New Canaan, Connecticut. *Tanguy uses all the devices of realism — precise modeling, cast shadow, atmospheric perspective—in depicting an imaginary world of petrified, jewel-bright shapes against vast desert horizons, disquieting and ironic like the title of this picture.*

495. BEN SHAHN / *Liberation* / 1945. Collection James Thrall Soby, New Canaan, Connecticut. *Deeply convinced that art is a public rather than a private affair, Shahn draws his images from everyday life. Yet to call him a realist hardly does justice to his uncanny eye for the poetic and symbolic qualities of reality, or to the subtle way he combines abstract, imaginative, and representational elements (note the influence of collage in Liberation!).*

dream we are looking at. But de Chirico, who was no folk artist, had a mind much more complicated than Rousseau's. That is why his dream world seems so troubled with hidden fears, as against the wonderful calmness of the earlier picture. Marc Chagall's *I and the Village* (figure 474), in contrast, enchants us by its gaiety. In this "Cubist fairy tale," dreamlike memories of Russian folk stories and of the Russian countryside have been woven together into a glowing vision. Chagall here relives the experiences of his childhood, experiences so important to him that his imagination shaped and reshaped them for years without ever getting rid of their memories.

The "fairy tales" of the Swiss painter Paul Klee are far more purposeful and controlled than those of Chagall, even though at first they may strike

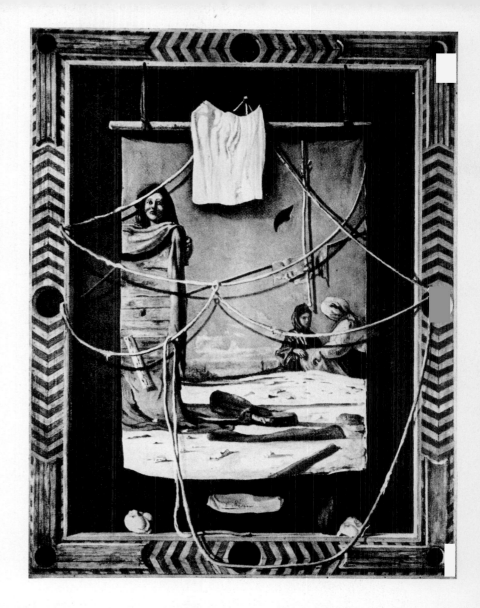

496. EUGENE BERMAN / *Panel for a Mural Decoration* / 1936. Collection Francis S. McIlhenny, Jr., Gaylordsville, Connecticut. *Berman's Neo-Romantic fantasies are filled with a poetic nostalgia based on Baroque themes and techniques (for our panel, compare the "deception" in figure 375).*

497. MATTA / *Deep Stones* / 1941. Museum, Tel Aviv. (Gift of Miss Peggy Guggenheim.) *This Chilean-born painter joined the Surrealists in Paris during the late 1930's. Many of his pictures of those years are the mineral counterpart to the animal and vegetable realm of Max Ernst (compare figure 491)—flaming jewels embedded in vast, mystery-filled caverns. His work is also related to that of Yves Tanguy (compare figure 494).*

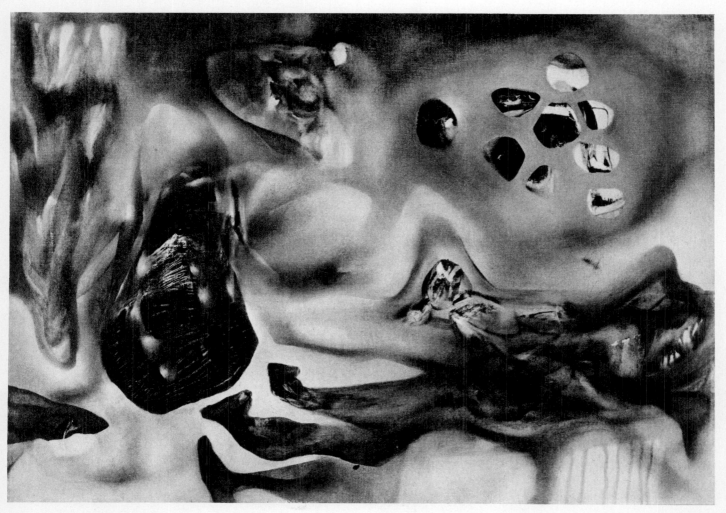

498. ARSHILE GORKY / *The Diary of a Seducer* / 1945. Collection Mr. and Mrs. William A. M. Burden, New York. *The style of this picture, by a gifted Armenian-American who died in 1948, combines Surrealist influences (compare Miró and Matta) with an Abstract Expressionism that stems from Kandinsky.*

499. SALVADOR DALI / *The Persistence of Memory* / 1931. Museum of Modern Art, New York. *Dali's painting technique, dry and mechanically exact, is completely at the service of his subject matter. His pictures are "handmade color photographs" of Surrealist daydreams.*

us as more childlike. Klee, too, had been influenced by Cubism, but he refined and pared it down into a marvelously precise language of his own. His aim was always to create "signs," which means shapes that are images of ideas the way the *shape* "A" is an image of the *sound* "A"; except, of course, that Klee's ideas are very much more intricate than that. One of the simpler ones is his *Twittering Machine* (figure 487), where he mocks the Age of Machines by "inventing" a sort of mechanical ghost that imitates bird noises. *The Conquest of the Mountain* (figure 486), on the other hand, shows a real machine—a locomotive—behaving in human fashion. As it puffs up the mountainside, it glows with effort, just like a climber who gets red in the face from doing the same thing. In this picture, done shortly before his death, Klee's imagination is as fresh, his sense of wonder as strong as ever; at the same time, every shape has a rightness and dignity about it that betray the most serious artistic effort.

The Spaniard Joan Miró will remind you of Klee in some ways. His *Harlequin's Carnival* (figure 493) looks like something one might see under a fairy-tale microscope—a lively and colorful miniature stage where everybody and everything is full of magic tricks. However, Miró also had been a Cubist before he discovered his own world of fantasy, and the effortless gaiety of our picture is actually the result of painstaking care in the design of every detail.

Figure 490 shows us a different kind of fantasy, haunted and disturbing like the dreams of de Chirico. This is a collage by Max Ernst, one of the leaders of the Dada movement at the end of World War I. The Dadaists were so revolted by the cruelty of the war that they declared Western civilization bankrupt from beginning to end. They felt they must start from scratch, respecting only one law, the law of chance, and only one reality, that of their own imaginations. Their main task, they thought, was to shock the public into the same unsettled frame of mind, and they tried to do this by exhibiting their creations, most of which were spur-of-the-moment "gestures" meant to defy all reason. Our collage is more serious than that—in fact, desperately so. It is made up of cuttings from pictures of machinery and other technical equipment, which have been pasted together so as to form two nightmarish "mechanical men." These stare at us blindly through their goggles and demand to know if we recognize them as images of modern man, slave to the machine and thus little more than a machine himself.

Yet the Dada movement was not all negative. It actually helped painters rediscover and make use of chance effects for artistic creation, as a counterweight to the purposeful discipline of Cubism. Those who believed in "taking a chance" and letting their imaginations flow unchecked, founded the Surrealist movement, with Max Ernst as one of its leading spirits. It was he who introduced (or revived, rather) the technique so skillfully employed in the drawing by Salvador Dali (figure 500). The main shapes in this *Landscape with Figures* (the rocks, the beach, and the clouds) are actually ink blots made by chance, just like the one illustrated at the beginning of this book. All Dali had to do was to see a picture "into" the blots and then fill in the missing lines, so that others can see it, too. This does not mean that the drawing is less a work of art because Dali has accepted the "help" of the ink blots. It does show us again, though, that the way our imagination works is still the same as in the days of the cavemen who saw animals in the bumps on the cave walls. Only the things we imagine, and the way we put them into pictures, have changed. These changes are what the history of painting is about.

500. SALVADOR DALI / *Landscape with Figures (ink blots, brush, and pen drawing) / 1936. Schaeffer Galleries, New York. In drawings such as this Dali shows us how his unconscious fastens upon the accidents of technique and transforms them into imaginary reality. They have an appeal that is missing in the paintings, where he has covered his tracks so thoroughly that we can no longer follow the creative act itself.*

Index

All text references are to page number. References
to illustrations are figure numbers, set in *italics*.

Acknowledgments

THE AUTHORS AND PUBLISHER wish to thank the libraries, museums, and private collectors for permitting the reproduction of paintings, prints, and drawings in their collections. Photographs have been supplied by the owners or custodians of the works of art reproduced, except for the following, whose courtesy in furnishing photographs is gratefully acknowledged:

Alinari, Florence (figures 38, 41, 44, 45, 52, 77, 78, 89, 100, 129, 138, 146, 154, 158, 174, 180, 183, 186, 187, 193, 194, 197, 245, 253, 255, 342, 368, and figure 280 through the courtesy of Mr. Leo Collins, New York); **Alinari-Giraudon, Paris** (160); **Anderson, Rome** (39, 51, 56, 76, 88, 91, 148, 175, 182, 196, 198, 240, 301, 345, 367, and figure 42 through the courtesy of Lady M. Gabriel, Mt. Kisco, New York); **Büchergilde Gutenberg, Zurich** (30, 31); **Braun & Cie., Mulhouse** (250, 311, 400); **Brogi, Florence** (28, 36, 37, 49, 64, 87, 142, 149, 150, 153, 177, 181, 184, 185, 188, 228, 237, 254); **Bruckmann K.G., Munich** (203, 236, 283); **Bulloz, Paris** (303, 337, 343, 352, 399, 409); **Clarendon Press, Oxford** (figure 7, from M. Helen Tongue, *Bushman Painting*); **A.C. Cooper, Ltd., London** (320, 363); **Pierre Devinoy, Paris** (71); **Durand-Ruel & Cie., Paris** (404); **Editions "Cahiers d'Art," Paris** (figure 461, from Christian Zervos, *Pablo Picasso*); **Copyright Editions Cercle d'Art, Paris** (460); **Edizione Artistiche Fiorentini, Venice** (200, 201); **Fine Art Engravers, Ltd., London** (392); **Giraudon, Paris** (96, 99, 161, 163, 238, 264, 304, 308, 340, 341, 344, 353, 355, 356, 358, 361, 384, 385, 393, 401, 466); **Hirmer Verlag, Munich** (figure 316, from M.v. Freeden and C. Lamb, *Das Meisterwerk des Giovanni Battista Tiepolo*. Foto Carl Lamb); **Hoffmann SWB, Basel** (226); **Foto Kleinhempel, Hamburg** (92, 374); **M. Knoedler & Co., Inc., New York** (397, 408, 424); **Juan Arauz Lomeli, Guadalajara** (figure 453, through the courtesy of Professor L. Schmeckebier, Syracuse, New York); **Mas, Barcelona** (106, 127, 230, 241, 242, 263, 298, 299, 300, 318, 347, 410); **Pierre Matisse Gallery, New York** (488); **R. Piper Verlag, Munich** (illustration to chapter heading, page 279, from the Collection of Reinhard Piper); **Adolph Studly, Jr., New York** (454); **Time, Inc., New York** (15); **Verlag Herold, Vienna-Munich** (figure 72, from Floridus Röhrig, *Der Verduner Altar*); **Vizzavona, Paris** (425).

Copyright ACL, Brussels (101, 104, 118, 120, 125, 147, 259, 339, 434); **Direktion der Antikensammlungen, Munich** (22, 26, 27); **Archives Photographiques, Paris** (6, 66, 98, 227, 305, 310, 313, 354, 365, 406, 428, and figure 447 through the courtesy of Mr. Alfred H. Barr, Jr., New York); **Bayerische Staatsgemäldesammlungen, Munich** (124, 190, 191, 217, 219, 220, 257, 266, 293); **California Palace of the Legion of Honor, San Francisco** (496); **Foto GFN, Rome** (55, 244); **Hessische Treuhandverwaltung der Früheren Preussischen Kunstgutes, Wiesbaden** (117, 123, 151, 202, 214, 222, 251, 282, 290, 291, 296); **London County Council, Trustees of the Iveagh Bequest, Kenwood, London** (279); **Bildarchiv Foto Marburg, Marburg Kunstinstitut** (315); **Metropolitan Museum of Art, New York** (10, 18, 19, 20, 215, 276, 359, 396); **Museum of Fine Arts, Boston** (218); **Museum of Modern Art, New York** (416, 427, 439, 452, 458, 459, 478, 479, 481, 485, 489, 498); **Board of Trustees for the National Galleries of Scotland, Edinburgh** (312); **Oriental Institute, University of Chicago** (12, and illustration to chapter heading, page 12); **Bildarchiv D. Öst. Nationalbibliothek, Vienna** (58, 75, 121, 212, 216); **Philadelphia Museum of Art** (379); **Pontificia Commissione per Archaeologia Sacra, Rome** (53); **San Francisco Museum of Art** (380); **Copyright of the Trustees of Sir John Soane's Museum, London** (319); **Soprintendenza Alle Antichità Della Campania** (43); **Soprintendenza Alle Antichità, Syracuse, Sicily** (50); **Soprintendenza Alle Gallerie, Florence** (90, 140, 235, 239); **Soprintendenza Antichità, Florence** (46); **Board of Trinity College, Dublin** (59); **Courtesy UNESCO** (8); **Victoria & Albert Museum, London** (294); **The Warburg Institute, London** (143).

Mr. Alfred H. Barr, Jr., New York (243); **Mr. William Chapman, New York** (figure 5, from the color film *Lascaux: Cradle of Man's Art*); **Dr. Herbert Kühn, Mainz** (figure 3, and illustration to chapter heading, page 8); **Archiv Dr. L. Münz, Vienna** (273); **Dr. Lothar Pretzell, Schloss Celle, Germany** (491); **Professor M. Weinberger, New York** (223).

Figures 162, 172, and 173 are reproduced by the gracious permission of Her Majesty Queen Elizabeth II.